Not The Boss of The Year

J. S. Cooper

Copyright © 2024 by J. S. Cooper

All rights reserved.

No part of this book may be reproduced in any form or by any electronic or mechanical means, including information storage and retrieval systems, without written permission from the author, except for the use of brief quotations in a book review.

Blurb

Dear Sir/Madam,

I would like to nominate my jerkface of a boss, Kingston Chase, for the worst boss of the year award. I don't know if that's a category at your esteemed paper as yet, but if not, it should be.

Yours Sincerely,
Skye Redding

Skye,

You do realize you sent this to me, your boss, right?

Not Amused,
Kingston Chase

Kingston,

Maybe if you cracked a smile some days, you wouldn't be the monster that you are.

Skye

P.S. And of course I realized. I was just giving you a heads up before I actually submit something.

Skye,

Just so you know, you never have to let me know before you want to give me ~~head~~...a heads up.

Kingston

This was the email exchange after only a few weeks at my new job. Not even I could have predicted where this was going. I had no idea just how much Kingston Chase would change my life.

Chapter One

Skye

Dear Diary,

This is the year I want to achieve at least one of my dreams. I'm not picky about which one.

1. *Travel to Australia - Need to save $5000. I have $52.*
2. *Have an epic love affair - I have zero prospects.*
3. *Run a marathon- I need to lose 30 lbs and start training. Maybe I'll do a 5K first.*

I need to figure out a way to manifest at least one of these things. Unfortunately, I have to go to work right now and don't have time to plan anything. I'm so fed up with my sucky jobs and horrible bosses. Something has to change or I will jump off of a cliff. Not really, but you know what I mean.

Chat soon,

Skye

"Why don't you just quit?" My best friend, Elisabetta,

stands at the entrance to my bedroom and pouts as I hurriedly brush my hair and attempt to put red lipstick on. "You know you hate that job." Her voice is pained, as if she were the one rushing to get to another dead-end job.

"I can't quit until I find another second job." I stare at my reflection in the mirror. My long red hair is shiny and straight and my green eyes stand out against the gold eyeshadow and black eye liner. I put the hairbrush down and grab the white shirt that is a part of my self-proclaimed uniform. "It's not the job of my dreams, but it's better than nothing."

"Let's agree to disagree." She plops herself down on my queen-size bed and sighs. "I wanted us to go out tonight."

"I can't quit my job just so we can go drinking, Elisa," I shake my head as I gaze back at her. "We don't all have rich dads that are willing to pay all of our bills."

"It just sucks that you have to work Friday nights." She sticks her tongue out at me. "We never hang out anymore. You're always working."

"That's because I have three jobs." I try to stifle a yawn. "I'm Queen Skye of the many jobs. That's what tons of debt and dreams to travel will do to you."

"But you hate all of your jobs," she reminds me, as if I forgot in the last five minutes. "I have no idea how you can work nine to five as a personal assistant at a law firm each week, then two nights a week as a server, and as a dancer some weekends." She waves her finger at me. "How are your student loans not completely paid off yet?"

"Because none of the jobs are paying me Elon Musk's salary." I tap my forehead. "Even though we have the same brain."

"Sure." She giggles as she stares at her nails. "Well, I hope I actually get to spend some time with you soon."

"We will hang out on Sunday when we go on our picnic," I remind her. I pull on my black slacks and stare at myself in the mirror. I don't love the outfit, but Five Star Fresh Fish, the restaurant I work at, demands I wear slacks or a short skirt as a server and I'm not wearing a short skirt. "And maybe tomorrow evening as well, depending on how my blind date goes."

"So that's still on?" Elisabetta brushes her long black hair back and stares at her shiny red nails like she's already ready for another manicure, even though she only got them done two days ago. "Have you decided what you're going to wear yet?"

"No." I purse my lips as I shake my head. "I don't know if I should dress casually or super sexy. Camden says he likes his women in heels, but I don't know if I want him to think he can dictate what I wear." Camden is a guy I've been speaking to on a dating app for the last three weeks. His profile says he's an investment banker looking for a woman to travel the world with. His photos show a cute blond man with baby blue eyes and dimples. The conversation has been mediocre, but I'm hopeful that we will have chemistry in person.

"I think it's weird that a man you've never met before wants you to wear heels." Elisabetta rolls her eyes. "I bet he has a foot fetish and just wants to suck on your toes all night."

"I bet he doesn't." I laugh, though now my mind is filled with images of Camden on his knees begging to suck my toes. "I guess I should get a pedicure tomorrow morning, just in case though."

"You'd let him suck on your toes?"

"When you put it like that, you make me hesitate, but honestly, I wouldn't say no if I liked him." I shrug as she gets up and heads toward me, a concerned look on her face. Elisabetta has been my best friend for ten years. We met on the first day of high school and she allowed me to move in with her after we graduated from college. "Don't judge me," I furrow my eyebrows as she makes a face. "It's not like I'm saying he can lick my ass." I pause and make a wicked face. "The only man I'd make lick and kiss my ass is Kingston Chase, my boss at the law firm. He's such a jerk."

"If he's such a jerk you should quit." She grins as she wrinkles her nose. "Or maybe you want him to kiss your ass...didn't you say he's cute?" She pulls her hair up and wraps it in a loose bun. "What am I supposed to do tonight?"

"No, he's not cute," I lie. "You can see if Carrie is available to hang out." Carrie is another one of our best friends from college. She works as a gopher on a TV show, so is rarely available, but is always fun to hang out with.

"Yeah, I guess I'll text her," Elisabetta says reluctantly. "What good is it that I live with my best friend and yet I never see her?"

"You see me, bitch." I giggle as I grab my handbag and lipgloss. "I just can't hang out all the time."

"I can ask my dad if he's willing to support you as well," she says, only half-joking. "I bet he'd say okay."

"Seeing as I've never met your dad, I'm going to have to say no." I shake my head. "But thanks for the offer." I've often wondered why Elisabetta's dad is never around, but all she says is that he's very busy with his many businesses. Her mom died when she was young and since then, he's thrown himself into his work; which may or may not be above board. She said she thinks he's part of the mafia, but he's never confirmed any of his dealings to her. Her three spinster aunts Lucia, Gabriella, and Evelina raised her with her stepbrother, Romeo, who she keeps saying she wants to hook me up with.

"You will meet him this summer." She grins. "At my princess ball."

"I still can't believe you're going through with that." I shake my head as she twirls around my room, then grabs my hand in an attempt to get me to dance with her. "You're really going to get engaged to some random man?"

"If I like him enough." She nods. "There will be at least fifty men there, all vying for my hand." She spins me around. "You should do it with me. It will be so much fun."

"No one is coming to a princess ball to get engaged to me." I laugh loudly. "I have nothing to offer except a hundred and fifty grand in student loan debt." I groan as I think about the latest statement I'd received. I've been paying on it each month, but the balance never seems to go down. "Speaking of debt, I have to go now or I'll be late for work and then Fabricio will go off on me again and I'll have to throw a jug of water on his pompous head and then I'll end up on the news."

"I'd pay to see that," Elisabetta says as she stops dancing. "He sounds like an asshole."

"That's because he *is* an asshole," I say, thinking of Fabricio, the greasy manager that loves to treat me like I'm his personal servant and not just a server at the restaurant. I can't stand the man, but the tips are pretty good. However, I've been having conflicted feelings about working there since I found out the items listed on the menu are not accurate. "Anyway, we can bitch about him later when I get back from work. Maybe we can watch a movie or something." I lean over and give her a quick hug. "Have a fun evening."

"I'll try." She follows me out of the room and grabs her phone. "Maybe Carrie wants to grab dinner or something."

Her voice trails off in a sad fashion and I watch as she walks across the white oak hardwood floor and drops onto the large white sectional that sits in the middle of our living room.

I love our apartment. It's beautifully furnished and looks like it came out of the pages of a magazine. Elisabetta's dad had given her a credit card with an unlimited credit line to get whatever she wanted and she and I had picked out the best of everything. She grabs the pink silk-covered throw cushion and flings it at me. "I'll miss you, goof."

"Not as much as I'll miss you, Lady Elisabetta." I curtsy and she laughs. "You want to come with me to the center tomorrow?"

"What time again?" She wrinkles her nose and I already know her answer.

"Eight AM." I give her a look. "That's when older people have time."

I grin at her as I explain to her, once again, why I go to the Let's All Read Literacy Center so early on a Saturday morning. My biggest joy in life comes from volunteering to help adults learn to read and write. It helps me to feel like a productive member of society and that I didn't waste $150,000 on student loans for nothing. "I promise you will feel rewarded if you come."

"Maybe..." She makes a face and I would bet my last dollar that she's not going to make it out in the morning. "I'll meet you for brunch afterwards though."

"I'm meeting Camden for brunch," I remind her. "Then we're going to a museum."

"Seems like a lot for a first date," she says nonchalantly. "But I'm sure it will be fun."

"I hope so. I need a good date." I head toward the front door. "What about you? Not calling Bobby back?" Bobby's the man she's been seeing on and off for the last six months. She can't stand him, says he has the personality of a washrag, but supposedly he has a long tongue that knows its way around her body so she sees him every couple of weeks when she's feeling horny.

"I'm not calling him for a week." She winks at me as she holds her phone up. "Bobby has to know that this hot mama is not interested in his games." She leans back onto the couch and shakes her legs back and forth in the air. "He has no idea who he's messing around with. Elisabetta Franco is nobody's plaything."

"You tell 'em." I grin as I open the door. "Have a fun night. Tell Carrie I said hi if you see her. Invite her to Sunday. My law firm friends Lila and Juniper are going to join, as well as Marie, Lila's quasi-sister-in-law."

I head out the door and toward the elevator quickly. I have twenty minutes to get to work or I'm going to be late. And Fabricio hates it when employees are late. I don't have time to take the subway or a bus, so I'll have to grab a cab, which is not ideal. I enter the elevator and check my phone. I have three missed calls from my mom in Florida, who's most probably scared I've been mugged or kidnapped for ransom. I know that I will have to call her as soon as I step out of the elevator.

Chapter Two

Kingston

"I'm sorry, Mom, but I just do not have time to go on a family trip to France. I don't care if Dad can score tickets to the Olympics or not." The silence on the end of the line is deafening. Danica Chase does not like being told no. Not by my dad, not by my brothers, and certainly not by me, the "baby" of the family.

"Go and break my heart, why don't you, Kingston Chase. I only gave birth to you for twenty-five hours. Had the entire hospital thinking a murder was happening because I was screaming so much." She pauses dramatically and I can picture her Skye-blue eyes welling up with tears. "But don't worry about me, sitting here in my living room, struggling to keep my family together."

"Mom, we had family lunch a month ago. With the *entire* family." I stress the word entire because it had been a shit-show, with both sets of grandparents, my parents, four uncles, five aunts—even my uncle Vinny's ex wife showed up just to cause drama—my three brothers, fifteen cousins, two dogs, a crazy cat, and a greedy gerbil. I still have nightmares about the event; though I know Mom had loved every moment. She lives for chaos. I live for peace and quiet, with momentary breaks for a quick prank. Mom calls me her serious son, and when I was a kid, I wondered if I was adopted. Though, I'm pretty sure I just took over the mannerisms from my dad's side of the family, who had hailed from England when he was a boy. My mom was third generation Italian and you'd think her relatives had just got off the boat at Ellis Island.

"When I die, please don't lie and engrave 'beloved mother' on my tombstone..." Her voice trails off and I stand up and grab a beer from the mini fridge in my office. "Kingston, are you there?"

"Yes, Mom."

"Are you listening to me?"

"Yes, Mom. Always, Mom."

"Is that how you speak to the judge?"

"No, I don't call the judge mom." I chuckle and sit back down, swiveling my chair around so I can gaze out of the windows and stare at the New York skyline. I never get tired of staring at the peekaboo-blue sky through the skyscrapers. I look down toward the road and stare at the thousands of yellow cabs and cars making their way through the city. "Did you have anything else you wanted to discuss, Mom? I'm still at work and wanted to finish up what I'm working on before I meet the guys for dinner."

"The guys?"

"My partners, Mom. Remi, Max, and Gabe is back in town."

"That Gabe is such a handsome man. Remi as well. I don't know how you're all single. You work too much, that's what I say."

"Maybe, but you know Max is coupled up now. So that should make you happy."

"I'd be happier if my son were in a relationship and traveling with me to Paris next month."

"I'm not your only son."

"But you're my baby. My favorite."

"Wait until I tell Silvio, Lorenzo, and Adam you said that."

"You will tell them nothing." She laughs slightly and I grin as I lean back in the chair. "I just want you to be happy, Kingston."

"I know, Mom. I am happy. I love you. Tell Dad I love him as well. I'll call you this weekend." I hang up and close my eyes, rubbing my fingers across my forehead as I think about all the work I have ahead of me. I look over at Skye's desk and frown as I see the stack of files in the same place I'd left them this morning. Had she not finished going through them? I head over to the desk and glance down. She's only gone through a few of the files and has already left for the day.

The fiery redhead is far from the best employee I've ever had in my life and I debate calling her back into the office. A part of me is annoyed that I even hired her a month ago.

"It looks serious." One of my law partners, Remington Parker, almost makes me jump as he comes up behind me. "What's going on?"

"Just wondering if I should call in my new assistant to finish her job." I look up at him with a frown. "I told her to go through all of these files today and note down how many of these clients spent over $500 last year on the Glubey Lubey pill for the deposition on Tuesday." I pick up a stack of files and wave them in the air. "She didn't complete the task. I have half a mind to tell her to get her ass back to the office, right now."

"That very pert ass." Remi chortles and whistles and I look over at him in fury. "Am I lying?"

"You shouldn't be checking out her ass."

"Don't worry, bro. I'm not after your assistant, but that doesn't mean I haven't noticed just how cute she is."

"Do not sleep with my assistant."

"As if I would." He smirks like a devious cat, then shrugs because we both know that he very certainly would. Normally, I wouldn't mind that Remi is an outspoken playboy, but right now, I'm not in the mood.

"I'm going to call her." I grab my phone from my pocket and search for her name. I've never called Skye before, only sent her a few texts, and I'm curious to hear her voice on the phone. I have a thing for voices and dulcet tones. Maybe it's the high school poet in me, but I love melodic voices. Not that I think that Skye has one. I find her number and I'm about to press call when Remi gives me a look, raising both eyebrows at me like I'm about to make the biggest mistake in the world.

"What is it?" My finger hovers over the button.

"You sure you want to call her on a Friday night?" He chuckles and a knowing look shines in his dark brown eyes.

"Why wouldn't I?"

"It's a Friday night. She's single. You're single. Max just got together with Lila and I bet everyone in the office is hoping they can catch the rest of us eligible bachelors."

"You think Skye wants me?"

"I don't know about that, but I bet she's open to it. Maybe even hoping for it. And if you call her asking her to 'come into work' on a Friday night, she may think that's code for you want to knock boots."

"But I'm actually calling her to do work."

"Maybe ask her if she wants to grab dinner."

"What? Why?"

"Because if she jumps at the offer of dinner, she's definitely interested. If she says she has plans or something else, then you know she's not trying to have your baby and get on that eighteen year child support plan."

"You watched too much trashy TV when you were younger." I shake my head at Remi. "Are you crazy?"

"I'm just saying, it's better for her to know where she stands before she gets ideas. Especially if you're calling her on a Friday night."

"I don't know that that's a great idea."

"Unless it's not true, of course. Maybe you do want her. You into redheads?"

"I'm not not into redheads." I say. "And I'm not into her like that. She's my assistant. My not very good assistant. I'm not going down the road of romance or sex with her."

"That's what Max said."

"Because Max is an idiot. And he hadn't dated in ages." I smirk. "I don't have that problem."

"Yeah, you're rolling in girlfriends. Got a date tonight?"

"I'm grabbing dinner and drinks with you and Max and Gabe, so no."

"I'm meeting someone for midnight drinks." He grins. "And maybe some dancing."

"The mambo?"

"Something like that." He sits on the edge of the desk and looks me over. "You can join if you want. I can ask Molly if she has a friend she can bring tonight. Maybe two if Gabe wants to join."

"Sure." I say, not because I actually want to go out drinking and dancing. In fact, there's nothing I want less, but I'd rather do that then have him thinking I want Skye. I do not want Skye in any way whatsoever. All I want from her is for her to do her job. "Let's go to the bar and I'll call her from there." I push my phone back into my pocket. "Let me log out of my laptop and then we can head out."

"Sounds good." He grins. "And then you'll tell Skye not to get her hopes up."

"Yeah." I nod. "I don't want her getting any ideas into her head whatsoever. All we have is a boss-employee relationship and she needs to understand that when I say I need her to complete a task by a certain date, she needs to do it."

Chapter Three

Skye

"Skye Blue Redding, are you still alive?"

"That's how I'm able to call you, Mom." I press my lips together to stop from saying something that will get me into trouble. I hate when she uses my full name. It's so cringey.

"Oh, you called me? I thought that maybe it was your AIT."

"My what?"

"Your AIT." She stresses the T like I'm slow.

"Do you mean AI?"

"Yes," she snaps. "That's what I said."

"Mom, I don't have an AI. Or any sort of robot that is able to make phone calls for me. If I did, I'd have them working all these shitty jobs."

She gasps at my use of the word shitty and I try not to roll my eyes.

"How can I help you, Mom? I am on my way to work and I'm already running late. But I saw you called me a million times earlier today so I wanted to make sure I called you back."

"Can a mother not call her only daughter to see how she's doing?" She's affronted and I know my dad will call me sometime this weekend to tell me to be nicer to my mother. I'm already annoyed at the emotional manipulation coming my way.

"Mom, you know I am busy. I'm fine."

"You're always busy, Skye. You're busy in the morning." She pauses dramatically and I once again realize where I get my flair for dramatics.

"Yeah, because I'm on my way to work in the morning when you call."

"You're busy in the middle of the day."

"Because I'm *at work*." I hurry down the road, avoiding trash and people as best as I can. I wish I had a driver that could drop me off everywhere I wanted to go. That's one perk of being rich that I could really get behind.

"You're busy in the evening."

"Because I'm going to my second job."

"You're busy on weekends."

"You know I volunteer and have another job."

"Exactly, you're always busy."

"I know, Mom, but I have a lot of debt. And you know I really want to go to Australia."

"I thought you said you wanted to go to Africa or Asia."

"I guess I want to go to all of the A continents. Africa, Australia, Asia. I want to hit up Europe too. And I wouldn't mind going to South America. You know I've always wanted to go to Peru and climb Machu Picchu and..."

"Yes, dear, but it's not like you're going anytime soon, is it?"

"What's that supposed to mean, Mom?" I snap because I

hate that she never supports my dreams. She thinks I'll get kidnapped or trafficked as soon as I step foot on an international flight.

"I mean, it's like you said, you don't have the money. And you know Dad and I don't have a trust fund for you. We're Reddings, not Kennedys."

"I know that, Mom. That's exactly why I'm working so hard because we come from a long line of 'we work hard, but don't have two brass pennies to rub together' folk and—"

"Money is not everything." Mom sounds offended and I know I need to tread carefully so as not to make her any more upset.

"I'm just working hard right now so that I can save."

"Or you can move back with me and Dad. You won't have to pay any rent. And then, you can—"

"Mom, I'm not moving back to Florida and I don't want to live with you and Dad. I'm twenty-five years old now. I can take care of myself. I *need* to take care of myself. I know what I'm doing." I sound like I did when I was thirteen and begging my mom to let me go to a high school party with my friends. It irritates me knowing I sound like a kid again. Why is it that mothers always make us feel like kids, no matter how old we are?

"Well, you can't say that you don't want to live rent-free, because aren't you living with Elisabetta for free?" Mom knows how to dig in the knife and remind me I'm not as mature and self-sufficient as I'm making out.

"Yes, Mom." I stifle another sigh. I will not pout.

"She's not charging you any rent, is she?" My mom presses on. She knows she's got a winning ticket right now. If she reminds me that she told me that my college boyfriend, James, was a pompous jerk before I realized, I would scream.

"No, but that's because her dad bought the condo for her, so there is no rent."

"Exactly. She's letting her dad pay." My mom's tone is cutting. "So technically, you're not taking care of yourself."

"Yes, Mom, I know that, but I just—"

"You're not sleeping with him, are you?"

"Sleeping with who?" I ask in confusion.

"Oh Lord. Billy, come here," she calls out to my dad loudly. "Billy, you need to talk to your daughter. She's sleeping with her friend's dad to—"

"Mom!" I shout into the phone in shock. "Stop it. I am not sleeping with Elisabetta's dad. Are you crazy?"

"Why then, is he letting you live in his condo for free?"

"Mom. Elisabetta is the one letting me—"

"So, if Dad and I lived in New York, you'd want to live with us? If we moved to New York, you'd move back home?"

"No, Mom." I say quickly. "That's not it. I want my independence." I can hear the panic in my voice. "Please do not move to New York. Look, I love you and I will try and come to Florida for Thanksgiving, but I've really got to go. Okay?"

"Fine," she says after a long silence. I will definitely be getting a call from Dad later to tell me off. "I guess I'll just go and sit next to your dad and watch hockey and crochet."

"Okay, Mom. Enjoy," I say and hang up quickly. I'm not going to let her take me on another guilt trip today. Those seem to be the only trips I'm getting to go on these days. I feel bad about hanging up, but I've already got way too much going on.

I hurry down the street toward the restaurant. I'm running ten minutes late now, and I know if Fabricio catches me walking in late, he's going to write me up. He's already given me a verbal warning. I don't know what it is about the guy, but he makes my skin crawl every time I see him. My phone rings again and I'm about to tell my mom off when I see that it's my main boss, Kingston Chase. He's an attorney at the law firm I work for as an assistant. Even though I find him annoying as well, he doesn't make my skin crawl. My heart races slightly as I debate whether or not to answer. Curiosity gets the better of me and I answer on the fourth ring.

"Hello?" I say breathlessly as I'm practically running down the street now.

"Is that you, Skye?" He sounds confused.

"Who else would it be?"

"I don't know." He pauses. "I didn't catch you doing something reserved for later at night, did I?"

I roll my eyes at his comment.

"No, Kingston. What do you want?"

"I was wondering if we could meet up for dinner?" he asks, and I frown slightly. Why on Earth would my new boss want to meet me for dinner? For a few moments, I think it's because he wants to take me on a date, but then the thought immediately flees my mind. Kingston Chase has not given me any reason to believe that he wants me. In fact, I was shocked that he'd even hired me in the first place. "I need to speak to you about something important."

"Nope," I say, looking at the time on the screen. "And honestly, I have to go. Can this wait until Monday?" My brain is screaming at me because I want to know why he wanted to ask me to dinner and what he wants to talk about. Though I'm not going to let my inner thoughts run away with me like my friend Lila did when she first met her boss, Max.

"No, it can't really wait till Monday," he says, as if I've asked him to wait to eat for seventy-two hours or something. Men can be so dramatic. "I saw the stack of files on your desk this afternoon. And it concerns me that you're not getting through the work as quickly as I think you should be."

"What?" I can hear the irritation in my tone and I don't care if he hears it as well. "What are you talking about?"

"I told you that I needed you to get through all the files by this evening. And it appears to me that you didn't even make a dent."

"You gave me over a hundred files, Kingston," I snap. "I'm not superwoman."

"Obviously," he drawls, and I swear that if I were with him in person, I'd give him a look so fiery that he'd melt into the ground like a snowman when the sun comes out. "In fact, I think you should be in the office right now working, if that's what it takes."

"Really? If a free dinner wasn't possible for me, do you think working was going to be."

"What do you mean it's not possible?"

"Because I have plans this evening and they don't revolve around you. Not having dinner with you and not certainly not working for you."

"Where are you off to?" he asks innocently, but I don't trust him.

"None of your business," I say, and he chuckles slightly. I don't want to tell him about all my jobs because I don't want him to ask why I'm trying to make so much money. I have a feeling he's not going to want to hear that I want to take a year off to travel around the world. Not after I told him in my job interview that the law was my life and that I wanted to be a legal assistant as a precursor to applying to law school. Yes, I lied, but I could hardly tell him that I had no interest in the law and only came to find a job because I'd met a girl on the street on the way to an acting audition. I fully believe that little white lies are okay if they are for the greater good. And the greater good, in this instance, is my bank account.

"Is this your way of trying to make me jealous Skye?" He sounds amused.

"What?" I screech and stop dead in the middle of the street. Is he serious?

"Watch where you're going, lady!" a middle-aged man shouts at me as he nearly bumps into me, then trips. He glares at me and mutters something under his breath, and for a moment, I'm nervous he's going to hit me.

"So sorry," I proclaim, giving him my most apologetic face. I point to the phone and make a face. "My boss is being —" I start but the man sneers, cusses me under his breath, and continues on walking. "How rude." I mumble as I move over to the side of the street and stand outside a closed flower shop. I peer through the windows wistfully. I haven't received flowers since my dad bought me roses on my sixteenth birthday. How have I never received flowers? "Why would I be trying to make you jealous, Kingston?" I ask because I really have nothing else to say.

"I don't know." He pauses. "Who were you saying sorry to, by the way?"

"Not you. There must be a reason why you think I'd be trying to make you jealous. Please explain."

"Maybe because Lila and Max got together and you're now thinking that you might be lucky number two in the office?"

"Lucky number two? What does that mean?" Is there a company lottery system I didn't know about?

"Lucky lady number two. You know, like, I'm the bachelor behind door number two."

"What?" My laughter is instantaneous and loud. I laugh

heartily for what feels like ten minutes. I laugh so hard that I start snorting and my body shakes. I cannot believe what he's just said. He thinks he's some prize behind door number two. What an ego!

I'll give it to Kingston, he's very attractive. And when I say very attractive, I'm understating.

Severely understating.

Kingston Chase is knock-you-off-your-feet sexy.

Like, he could blink at you and your panties would fall to the ground.

And dissolve into a puddle.

He's the sort of tall that makes you have to peer up at him, like he's some sort of Greek god. He has dark hair that looks black indoors and brown in the sun. Hair that is silkier than should be legal. He has big, beautiful blue eyes. And I'm not even a girl that is into blue eyes. In fact, I've hated men with blue eyes ever since Sam Richards, a guy I went on a date with in tenth grade, told me to suck him off for his birthday while we listened to Frank Sinatra in his Chevy pickup truck while referring to himself as "Sexy Blue Eyes." I didn't suck him off and I didn't even think about dating a blue-eyed guy again. Not that I have any intention of dating Kingston.

He's my boss.

Just because he has a chiseled face and the sort of body that bodybuilders would be jealous of means nothing.

I don't want him. He has an attitude that goes on for days. He's the bossiest man I've ever met in my life. And even though he is my boss, I still find it irritating. To be quite frank, I'm not into overly handsome blue-eyed men who think they can boss you around all day and night.

"Are you laughing or crying?" he demands. "Are you upset because I'm not jealous?"

My jaw drops even lower. Is he for real? "You have got an ego the size of the Hoover Dam on you, don't you, Kingston Chase?"

"I don't have an ego. I'm just being matter of fact. It has crossed my mind that you might think that there's a possibility that you and I may end up together."

"Why on Earth would I think that?" I'm being loud now.

"Like I said, you started on the same day as Lila. Now she and Max are together and looking at Brownstones to buy and she barely works."

"That's because she no longer works there full-time."

He clears his throat. "I just wanted to be clear that all we have is a work relationship, Skye."

"Did I say I thought we had more?"

"Just in case you thought that I was interested in going down the same road as Max, I wanted to make it clear that I'm not available."

"Okay." I don't know if I should be offended or not. This conversation is awkward and stupid. I want nothing to do with Kingston Chase. Pompous asshole that he is.

"Is that all you have to say?" He sounds surprised.

"I don't really know what else you expect me to say," I mutter, my anger starting to build. "I don't care if you're available or not. I don't want you. If you were the last man on Earth, I still wouldn't want you. You're not my cup of tea. You're more like kombucha...all sour and weird."

"I'm what?" He coughs and I smile to myself.

"Kombucha, that fermented drink. Kingston, I hate to break it to you, but you're just not my type." That's a bit of a lie, but like I said before, little white lies don't count. "So trust me when I say, if I was seeking a bachelor and chose door number two and saw you standing there, I'd run away so quickly." I snort as I take a runners stance. "Shoot, I'd be running so fast that I might even win a medal at the Olympics." I bounce back and forth on my heels as if I'm ready for the starter's gun. I really do know how to amuse myself.

"Really, Skye?" He doesn't sound so full of himself now. Take that, Mr. Hotshot Attorney. Not feeling so cocky now, are you? I don't know why that makes me feel so satisfied.

"Really, Kingston Not-My-Type Chase. And if you don't mind, I really have to go now."

"Where are you going?" he asks, and his tone doesn't sound so smug now.

"Like I told you before, it's none of your business. You're my boss, and as far as I'm concerned, our interactions end at five o'clock PM on Friday. They won't start again until Monday at nine AM. So, ciao bella." I hang up on him quickly before he can respond, and then because I don't want to be interrupted by any more phone calls, I power my phone off.

"Is he out of his ever-loving mind?" I mumble, as I run down the street. I'm so late that the White Rabbit would be giving me side eye. "Why on Earth would that ass think I want him?" The question makes my head thud. Had I given him some sort of signal that would make him believe I was interested? I think back to our interactions over the last couple of weeks. Nothing I've said or done should have led him to believe that I give two shits about him.

Sue me, yes I think he's hot, but most women in the world would think he's hot. I think George Clooney's hot. I think Brad Pitt's hot. I think Bradley Cooper's hot. I think Boris Kodjoe's hot. Shit, I could probably name ten million men that I think are hot. It doesn't mean I want them.

Had he seen me checking out his arms that one day he came to the office in his gym clothes? Surely not.

I swallow hard as bile rises up my throat in embarrassment. Had he seen me checking out his shorts?

I reach the corner right before the entrance to the restaurant and I know I should go directly inside. Fabricio is going to be pissed at me. I'd have to grovel to keep my job. But instead of hurrying into the restaurant, I power the phone back on.

Because fury has hit me.

Embarrassment has made me angry.

Once the phone powers on, I call Kingston and wait impatiently for him to answer the phone.

"This is Kingston Chase. How may I help you?" he says in clipped tones as he answers the phone.

"It's Skye," I snap. "Which you knew."

"Hello, Skye. How may I help you?" he says politely, as if we hadn't just had an infuriating conversation five minutes ago.

"I just processed what you said to me," I huff out. "And I'm pissed."

"It took you that long to process what I said?" he says slowly. "No wonder you're not getting through those files very quickly." He chuckles like he thinks he's some hotshot lawyer and that makes me even angrier.

"You're just a jackass, a pompous prick, a wannabe, and I think that—"

"May I ask a clarifying question?" he asks matter-of-factly, cutting me off, and I blink. Is he about to fire me for being insubordinate?

"What do you want to know?"

"Well, you just said that I am a wannabe, correct? But I'd like to inquire and find out what sort of wannabe I am."

I just stand there, gripping the phone. "What?"

"You said I'm a wannabe and I want to know, I'm a

wannabe what? A wannabe plumber? A wannabe electrician? A wannabe judge? A wannabe ballet dancer?"

"Oh, you infuriate me. You are driving me crazy, Kingston Chase."

"Doesn't sound so bad to me."

"You are so annoying. I was just calling you to tell you that—"

"That I'm annoying?" he interrupts, again, and I can hear the humor in his tone. "I see."

"No, I'm calling you to let you know that I don't appreciate you calling me to tell me that we're never going to get together."

"Did I hurt your feelings?" he asks softly, like he's nervous he's going to break me. "I didn't mean to do that."

"No, you didn't hurt my feelings. I don't want you."

"You don't sound like someone that doesn't want me."

"What are you talking about? How does someone who doesn't want you sound?"

"They sound like they don't care. You sound like you care a lot."

"I am angry with you," I shout. "And not because I care about you, but because I'm annoyed."

"Because I told you that we're never going to have the relationship that Lila and Max have?"

"I don't want the relationship that Lila and Max have. I am not even looking to settle down right now."

"Oh, in case I wasn't clear, I'm not looking for just a sex thing either," he says, chuckling. "Don't get me wrong, I love sex, I'm good at sex and I have many casual relationships, but I don't think it would really work out between you and me."

"I don't want to sleep with you. Oh, I'm so annoyed."

"Is that all you have to say or are you going to hang up on me again?"

"You wanna know what, Kingston Chase?"

"What, Skye Redding?"

"This." I say, then I hang up. I glare at the phone and stick my tongue out. I'm even angrier than I was before. I put my phone into my handbag and hurry into the restaurant. Of course, Fabricio is standing there, waiting for me. His face looks pinched and thin and I know he's about to let me have it.

"What time do you call this Skye?" he says, staring at his watch and tapping it.

"I don't know." I shrug. "Why don't you tell me? You're the one looking at your watch right now."

His eyes narrow and he shakes his head. "Three strikes Skye."

"Excuse me?"

"You're on strike two. One more strike and you're out."

"What are you talking about? What three strikes?"

"You're late for work again."

"I'm sorry." I press my lips together. "I'm sorry that I'm late," I elaborate through gritted teeth. I hate having to tell this jerk that I'm sorry.

"That's fine," he says, tilting his head to the side and looking me up and down. He takes a step forward and I watch as his nostrils flare. "I thought I told you to wear a skirt."

"That's not the dress code though. The dress code says I can wear a skirt or pants. I chose to wear pants."

He presses his lips together again. "I think you and I should go to the office."

"For what?"

"I think, if you want to keep your job, you're going to have to do a taste test."

"A taste test of what?" I play with my hair. "Am I going to be working in the kitchen?"

"You need to taste a little salami," he says with a straight face.

"What?"

He licks his lips slowly. "Well, to be more accurate, one big salami."

I stare at him for a couple of seconds, my heart racing as he looks me up and down. This can not be happening. Is this the evening of my nightmares? "Are you saying what I think you're saying?" I stare at him.

"Depends on what you think I'm saying." He licks his lips, flashing me his yellow teeth. Gross. "Do you want this job or not?"

I look around the not-so-busy restaurant and then I look back at him. I think about Kingston and his comments. I think about my mom. I think about my student loan debt. I even think about the kangaroos in Australia that I want to pet when I finally travel there.

But none of those things makes me give a shit about sucking up to this creep.

"You know what, Fabricio? Why don't you taste test your own sausage? Because, trust me when I say, I have absolutely no interest."

"Salami," he says, stepping forward, trying to grab my hand. "I want you to taste my salami."

"I don't care if you call it salami. I don't care if you call it sausage. I don't care if you call it a fucking little bitty dick. I want nothing to do with you or this restaurant. I quit. You can't fire me cause I'm already done. And by the way, I will be filing a letter of complaint with HR on Monday." I hold up my phone. "This was recording. So, you're out." White lie, but I hope it scares him.

"Wait, what?" He looks panicked.

He tries to grab my phone, but instead, I knee him in the groin hard and an intense feeling of pleasure fills me as he yells out in pain. I hurry out of the restaurant before he can retaliate and run for about two minutes, just in case he's following me, before I stop next to a light pole and breathe heavily, doubling over to catch my breath.

"What the hell is going on?" I shout loudly, about to lose my shit. "Should I go back to Florida?" I ask the universe because maybe everything is going wrong because I'm not meant to be in New York City.

"Nah, bitch," an old man sitting on the ground rifling through a trash bag shouts back at me. "Florida's for the crazies." He cackles as he grabs a half eaten piece of chicken and takes a bite. "Not for you and me." He looks me over and holds up the leg. "Wanna bite?"

"Uh, thanks." I say, shaking my head weakly. "But no." I run away and I can feel tears trailing down my face as I laugh hysterically. I'm unraveling and I don't know what to do. I'm twenty-five and nothing in my life is going as planned. I've most probably lost both of my jobs, my hot boss that I don't want felt he had to make it clear that he didn't want me, and my mom is probably complaining about me to my dad at this very moment. I have over a hundred thousand dollars in student loan debt, and no boyfriend. Not even a potential boyfriend.

Is this really my life?

I grab my phone again and text Elisabetta. **I just quit my job. Meet me for a drink?**

She responds immediately. **I'll be there in fifteen minutes. You okay?**

Not really. The last place I should be going to is a bar and the last thing I should be doing is spending money, but I don't even care. Right now, I need to get drunk. Right now, I need to forget my absolutely crazy evening. **But I will be after a drink or two. I'm going to invite my work friends as well.**

For a brief moment, I think about calling Kingston again, but I'm not even sure why.

Maybe I just want to let him have it one last time.

Not that this is his fault.

In fact, I was pretty lucky that he hired me.

It isn't his fault that he is the most annoying man on Earth.

I just have to make sure that I don't let him know that.

I didn't want to lose another job.

Chapter Four

Kingston

The shocked look of bemusement on Remi's face irritates me. His dark eyes laugh at me as we wait for a server to come and take our drink order. The bar is still quite empty and I'm glad I'm able to hear myself think as we wait on Max and Gabe. Though, Remi is getting on my nerves. I'm still irked that I let him talk me into calling Skye. The smirk that crosses his face makes me wonder how any women fall for him and his arrogance. I narrow my eyes as he laughs at me.

"It's your turn to call Juniper now and tell her that she shouldn't have her hopes up of getting together with you."

"Are you crazy?" he says, shaking his head. "There's no way I'm going to call Juniper and tell her that."

"What?" I stare at him, fold my arms, and take a deep breath. "It was your idea. You're the one who said we should let our assistants know that there will be no more romantic dalliances between us and them at the office."

He bursts out laughing like I've just told the funniest joke in the world.

"I cannot believe that you just had two conversations with Skye about not wanting to be with her. I can't believe that you actually listened to me and my teasing comments."

"So you're not worried that Juniper is going to think that you and her will become an item?"

"Hell no. She knows that is never going to happen. Neither one of us looks at the other in that way. Juniper is the perfect assistant. For all I know, she's a lesbian. She has no interest in me and I have no interest in her. We have zero sexual chemistry. In fact, if you ask me what color her eyes are, I couldn't even tell you."

"You do realize I just made my assistant extremely mad at me because of what you told me. I don't have time for this, Remi. You know I'm trying to woo the members of the New York Penguins hockey team to the firm. I could have spent my precious time trying to make another meeting for drinks with Whittaker Matlock, the star center of the team. If we sign him, the others will follow suit."

"Well, you're the dumbass that called her and had the conversation," he says, shaking his head. "Plus what do those two obnoxious conversations have to do with signing Whittaker. Why don't you just call him now?"

"That's not the point." I growl.

"I can't believe you asked her to dinner, bro," he says, shaking his head. I want to slap the smirk off of his face. "And to think she turned you down."

"Well, that was the point, right? If she would have said yes, then I would've known she was too interested in me." I don't care that she turned me down. Not like I actually wanted to take her to dinner.

"You really told your assistant not to get any ideas about being in a relationship with you." He bursts out laughing again. "I cannot wait to see you guys interact on Monday."

"If she even shows up on Monday," I say, thinking of Skye's pissed off tone on the phone. I bet her fiery green eyes were blazing with fury. I wouldn't mind seeing what she looks like all worked up.

"At least you know she's not interested. That has to settle your mind and put you at ease. Now you know that she doesn't want to see you naked and sit on your face at any point in her employment."

"You're an idiot, Remi. But you're right, she's not interested whatsoever." The thought doesn't fill me with as much pleasure as it should. "At least that's what she wants me to believe."

"What? Now you're going to say you don't believe her?"

"I just think that it's a little bit weird that she was so vehement about the fact that she wasn't interested, especially considering the fact that she called me back to remind me that she wasn't interested."

"Kingston, dude. She's not interested in you."

"I know that." I snap. "That's good. I don't need any complications at work. Plus, I have plenty of other women," I say as I look across the bar and make eyes with a beautiful lady with long black hair and dark brown eyes. She smiles at me and offers me a small wave and I nod before giving Remi a satisfied look. He's not even paying attention to me, as there's a hot blond making eyes at him and he's making some weird gesture with his hands. I don't even want to know what he's doing.

The hot brunette sips her bright pink drink and pulls out a cherry with her tongue, while still making eye contact with me. "I wonder if I should go and practice my Spanish," I say, nodding toward the seductress giving me fuck me eyes. Remi leans forward and frowns.

"How do you know she speaks Spanish?"

"Because she's got on a top that says '*boricua* forever'." I smirk. "This is why I'm the top partner at the firm. I'm observant. Now, if you don't mind, I think I might go and introduce myself." I'm not sure what my motivation is to talk to her, but what I do know is that I no longer want to talk about my interaction with Skye.

"Okay, if you have something to prove to yourself, then go ahead." He looks toward her. "She is pretty hot, but we're waiting on Gabe and Max, so I don't know that they would be happy to arrive and you're halfway to bedding a hot little mamacita."

"Yeah, well, they're late, so all bets are off." I shrug and stand up. I'm about to head over to the sexy woman when I see Max marching toward us with a beer in his hand. "Saved by the bell." I sit back down, give the seductress an apologetic smile, and look back over at Max as he takes the seat next to me.

"Hey, what's up?" he asks in greeting, putting a hand on my shoulder. His blue eyes are keen as he looks over at the brunette and bursts into a wide grin. "Oh, I see you're making friends."

"Not much. You made it finally." I ignore his latter comment.

"Sorry. Lila was showing me some dresses that she wants to buy and she wanted my opinion on my favorite two." He sips his beer slowly and I can tell by the smug look on his face that he's remembering what he'd seen earlier. "I told her to get all of them. Especially the one with the lace garter."

"Really, Max? Is this evening just going to consist of you talking about Lila's shopping tastes." I think about his blonde former assistant and girlfriend. She's pretty, but she's also extremely dramatic and has a penchant for jumping to conclusions. She's the sort of woman that would drive me crazy, though maybe I'd feel different if I'd been in love with her.

"What can I say?" He shrugs. "I'm pussy whipped."

"I can't believe you're admitting that." I also can't believe how proud he is to make the statement, like it's cool to be under lock and key. I loved Max like a brother. He's been one of my closest friends for years and I always thought we'd both be eligible bachelors for years to come.

I'd been shocked when he'd fallen so quickly for Lila. He'd changed once he fell in love with her. He was no longer the shark he used to be and that annoyed me. It used to be him and me bringing in most of the new clients, wooing them and making plans to get their business. Now it's like he couldn't care less about money or being the top law firm in The City.

Chase, Parker and Spector still means everything to me and I'm still committed to bringing on clients that will show the world who we are. If I can get the top players from the New York Penguins to sign with the firm, I know other sports stars will follow.

"Well, I know if I didn't say it, you would." He grins at me, winks, and then looks over at Remi. "What's good?"

"Not much. You are not going to believe what Kingston just did."

Max's eyes snap back to me and all I can do is glare at both men.

"I don't think we need to discuss that anymore, Remi." Irritation pounds in my temple, coupled with embarrassment. I feel like an idiot, and also offended that Skye decided she needed to call me back to tell me just how disinterested in me she was. As if I hadn't been doing her a favor. I'd rather save her the stress of falling in love with me then realizing it was never going to happen.

Max turns toward me, his right brow arched as he gazes at me. "Whoa, what happened? You look pissed."

"Let's just say that you should never go to Remi for advice about anything." I grab my drink and sip. "Except for maybe the rules of evidence when it comes to—"

"Hold on." Max holds up his hand as he looks at his phone. He's either getting a call or a text message, because his screen has lit up like it's Christmas and he's just turned on all the lights. "I think Gabe just got here."

"Awesome," I say, genuinely excited to see our fourth partner. None of us have seen him in months. I look up and spot him strolling toward us with a cocky grin on his face. Gabe always has a smile on his face and a pep in his step. I notice the hot Latina from the bar staring at him in awe. He notices her and winks and I stifle a groan.

Gabe Lucas is like a candle and the women around him like moths. They cannot keep away from his dazzling flame. He looks like a male model in his dark suit and white shirt; his hair is a little bit longer, but still as dark as I remember; and his dark eyes seem to glow in his tan handsome face. He heads toward us with a leisurely gait to his stride and I shake my head. "Is Gabe still an attorney or did he take up the catwalks of Paris?" I joke as I stand up to greet him.

"Gabe, welcome back." Max steps forward and they hug.

"Hey, bro." He grins and looks over at me. I lean in and give him a hug.

"Looking as handsome as ever," I say, grinning.

"Not as handsome as you, old blue eyes." He grips the back of my neck before turning to Remington. "And you, Remington, brother. How's it going?"

"Not as good as you, I don't think." He grins and they

give each other a hug, then we all just stare at each other. The crew is finally back together. It feels good. I love these men like my brothers. We have a lifelong bond. We're like teammates on a sports team. We all want to be great, so we always come together to ensure we all succeed.

"We're back," Max says what we are all thinking. Even though we're in a packed bar, all time and movement seems to still. I look at each one of them and just take in their spirits and presence. These are good men. These are men I would trust with my life.

"So, Gabe," I say. "We've missed you. Are you here to stay or heading out again soon?" None of us really know where Gabe went and we haven't wanted to push for answers. He likes his privacy, and even though he's confident and charismatic, he can also be very stoic about his feelings and what's going on in his life. I'm much the same way, so I understand the desire to keep things to yourself.

"I'm here," he says, nodding. "I had some things I had to take care of and now I'm ready to get back to work." He smiles nonchalantly, like we aren't all curious about where he was. "How have you bozos been? I hope profits are still up. I've got a new apartment to buy." He grins. "And a new bed to entertain the ladies in."

"Still a ladies man, I see." I point out the obvious and he runs his fingers through his dark hair.

"What can I say? The ladies love my silky hair and dark bedroom eyes."

We all groan at his words and sit down. There's a lightness in my shoulders as I relax back and just take in my environment. Some of my favorite moments in life have been had with these men. We laugh together, we support each other, and we strategize to be the best attorneys in New York. I'd been worried that everything would change when Max got together with Lila. I'd been worried that he would disappear. I'm grateful that he didn't.

"You know profits are still up." Max leans back. "We've been speaking every other week and filling you in on all the work we've been doing."

"I know. So, Max, I hear congratulations are in order." Gabe chuckles. "You and your assistant are doing the dirty, huh? I'm taking it she's not as old as Ethel Wharton?" he teases. Ethel Wharton was the eighty-five year old grandma that had worked for Max for a few months before quitting.

"Well, she's more than my assistant now and she's nothing like Ethel. I can't wait for you to meet Lila. I think you'll really like her."

"Hopefully I don't like her too much. You don't want me to be Mr. Steal Your Girl."

"You won't be stealing Lila from me. Trust me, I have no worries about that. However, maybe you'll steal Skye from Kingston over there. Or maybe he wants you to steal her. I hear that relationship's about to blow up anyway."

"What are you talking about?" I frown as I stare at Max. Had he already heard about the call?

"I'm just saying that Skye doesn't seem to be too happy working for you."

"What? She loves me. We get along great." That's a bit of a lie, but it could be true.

"That's not what she has been telling Lila. In fact..." Max leans forward conspiratorially. "I've heard that the girls have formed a club."

"A club?" I ask. "What sort of club?" Remington holds his hands up like we're in school.

"I bet I know what the club's called."

"Oh, yeah? And what's that?" I say, looking toward him.

"The Bosses I'd Love to Fuck Club," he says, chuckling. I roll my eyes and Max laughs.

"You wish."

"Actually, no. I don't really want to fuck Juniper," he says, laughing. "But, hey. I wouldn't mind fucking Skye. Especially if you don't want her, Max."

"Hands off my assistant. I do not need her life being any more complicated."

"What's the name of the club?" I ask Max.

"I think they call it the Annoying Hot Bosses Club," he says, shaking his head. "And before you ask, yes, Lila is a member."

"No way!" I grin.

"You're taking this much better than I thought you would be," Max says.

"You just said they call us their hot bosses." I grin. "So they think I'm hot."

"Yeah, but there's an annoying part in front of that."

"I don't care about being annoying," I say. "I care that Skye was lying."

"What are you talking about?"

"He told her that he is not interested in her and that she shouldn't get any ideas in her head," Remi answers for me and I glare at him.

"You what?" Max's eyes widen.

"It's all Remington's fault. Look, I basically said just because Lila and Max got together doesn't mean that we're going to get together. So just in case she had any ideas or hopes, to get them out of her head."

"You did not." Max bursts out laughing, as do Gabe and Remi.

"I know. I sounded like a douche. I don't even know if I should call her and apologize or leave it alone."

"I am in shock," Max says. "What on Earth possessed you to do that?"

"Like I said...Remington did. He is the one who got into my head and."

"It's not my fault, bro. If I told you to walk off a cliff, would you?"

"No, Papa," I say. I let out a small sigh of relief when the waitress heads back to us with our shots of whiskey.

"Here you go, sir." She smiles at me as she hands me my drink. "Hi, guys." She looks over at Max and Gabe. "My name is Tropicana. I'll be your waitress, server, hostess with the mostest tonight. Is there anything I can get you guys?"

"I'll have what he's having." Gabe nods towards me.

"Whiskey?" Tropicana asks.

"Sure."

"Me too," Max says. "Make that six more shots of whiskey, please." He hands her his credit card. "And you can put it on this card."

"Oh, yes, sir. Anything else?"

"That's it for now," he says. "Let's sit."

We are all seated around the small table and I look at my partners and best friends for a couple of moments, then smile widely. "This feels good," I say. I look over at Max. "I'm glad you're here. I was a little bit worried you wouldn't make it."

He frowns slightly as he gazes at me.

"Why would I not make it?"

"I mean, now that you're married up and all."

"I'm not married and even when I do get married, it doesn't mean that I'm not going to make time for you guys. We're brothers and we're partners and we run a law firm together. We will have meetings."

"Yeah, but I don't want you to say that all the meetings

suddenly have to be in the office. I like these Friday night get-togethers at the bar."

"Don't get your hopes up. I can't promise every Friday," Max says with a grin. "But Lila's independent. She likes hanging out with her girls just as much as I like hanging out with you guys. Plus, maybe you guys will get into relationships soon and we can go on double dates and stuff."

I shudder.

"No, thank you."

"Yeah, I don't see that happening for me anytime soon," Remington says with a shrug. Gabe holds his hands up.

"I just got back into town. I'm not even thinking about that right now."

"Fine," Max says with a grin. "You three will be bachelors forever and the uncles to my babies."

"You and Lila aren't pregnant, are you?" I lean forward, scowling. "Because—"

"Calm down, Kingston. Don't worry. No, we're not pregnant, but we will one day be pregnant and we will have kids and you will be their uncle, so get ready." I stare at him.

"I'm not ready and I sure as hell hope you're not ready anytime soon either, because..."

"Because what?"

"There are a lot of strip clubs I want to go to and I don't think Lila will like you going to strip clubs."

He shakes his head.

"I think that's going to be the three of you."

"Fine," I say. "Anyways, shall we get down to business?" Gabe pulls out an iPad and white Apple Pencil.

"I'm high-tech now," he says, grinning. "I'm going to take some notes. I guess I should look for an assistant as well. Do any of you have any recommendations?"

"Not me," I say, shaking my head, thinking of Skye. I'm

not the one to be recommending assistants. "I've got one that I'm currently trying to train, but if it doesn't work out, you can have her."

"Yeah, no thanks." Gabe shakes his head and looks over at Remi.

"Juniper is probably the best assistant at the firm and I'm not parting ways with her. I hit gold when I hired her." Remi smirks like he's just won gold at the Olympics. You'd think he was the second coming of Micheal Phelps, the way his smug tone hits us all.

"You only hired her because you weren't attracted to her," I say. "Big deal. You got lucky." He shrugs as he gazes at me.

"Yeah, well, at least I don't have to worry about us accidentally falling into bed and doing the dirty."

"I don't have to worry about that either."

"Only because she doesn't want to."

"I don't want to either."

"Tell me you haven't thought about Skye in that way."

"I have not thought about Skye in that way." My heart thuds.

"Liar."

"I'm not lying." I smirk and look over at Gabe. "Trust me when I say I have not thought about doing the dirty with my assistant."

"He's totally lying. Wait till you see her." Remi smacks his lips together. "She's gorgeous. Long red hair, green eyes. I bet you she is a lioness in bed."

"Um, just in case I haven't been clear, Remington, I don't want *you* doing my assistant either."

"Hey." He holds his hands up. "Would I do that?"

"Yes, I think you would." I'm getting heated so I turn to

Max. "What about you, Max? Do you know anyone that Gabe could hire?"

"In fact, I do," he says, nodding slowly. "I mean, if you don't mind someone a little bit inexperienced." Gabe looks at him with a frown.

"I'm going to be honest here, but I would rather hire someone that has experience because I've been out of the office for a while, but who is it? If you're recommending them you must think they're going to do a good job."

"My sister, Marie, is in need of a job."

"What?" I look at him in surprise. "Marie wants to work at the firm?" His sister has zero legal experience.

"She wants to make some money," he says, nodding slowly and stifling a long sigh. He looks over at Gabe. "You may not know this, but Marie's pregnant."

"No way!" Gabe's eyes widen. We don't know Marie very well, as we've only met her a couple of times, but I know he's as shocked as I was because Marie is only eighteen, about to turn nineteen.

"Yeah." Max sighs. "I don't even want to talk about it."

"Um, I'll think about it," Gabe says with a nod, the expression in his eyes dark. "I would have to interview her and make sure that she's not going to be a liability, but if you think she'll do a good job, I'll consider it."

Max shakes his head and shrugs.

"Honestly, I don't know if she'd do a good job, but I'd be grateful if you at least gave her an interview. She doesn't want to work for me because she thinks it'd look like nepotism."

"But working for me wouldn't?" Gabe asks with an arched brow, and we all just laugh because we all know Marie wouldn't even be a consideration for a job if it wasn't for Max.

Chapter Five

Skye

The Owl and the Pussycat is packed when I arrive all flustered. I walk in, look around the crowd, and debate whether I should find a table for my friends or go straight to the bar for a stiff drink. My bad mood has officially settled in and I'm feeling more emotional than I normally do. I can barely see the other side of the bar through the throngs of people and I decide to head straight to the bar. The girls and I can find a table when they arrive, if they're not here already.

I saunter through throngs of people, trying to ignore the happy and obnoxiously loud couples on either side of me. I am not going to be a hater and give them all death stares, but there's nothing that can make you feel more alone and sorry for yourself than seeing people in love admiring each other.

There's a small space at the bar that is entirely too small for me to fit into, but that doesn't stop me from attempting to squeeze myself into the spot next to a far-too-handsome man. He glances down at me as my thighs brush against him and I take in his beautiful face with a wry smile and wrinkle of the nose. It's a bar. It can't be expecting personal space.

I'm grateful to see that there's a smile on his face as he drinks his beer and continues staring at me with an intrigued look in his eye. Do I somehow look better tonight than I remember for him to be giving me such a thorough look over? I don't think so. I'd done my makeup super quickly and I'm pretty sure my cheeks are blotchy.

"Hey there."

"Hi," I respond back to him, my voice squeaky. "It's busy tonight, isn't it?" I want to groan as I state the obvious. His dark eyes crinkle as he looks around and nods. My heart races as he shifts closer to me and his head comes closer to mine. I'm not really sure what he's doing, but I think he's about to sniff or kiss the top of my head. Is my shampoo that arousing?

I smile weakly as I look into his dark eyes. He's really handsome and I am grateful for the attention, but he's being a bit too familiar for me. I wonder if this is his way of flirting with me.

It's certainly not a style I would recommend to many men. It's this close to being creepy.

Even though all he said is hi, I'm hoping he's not going to test his pickup lines on me. I'm just not interested in that tonight.

"It really is." He takes another sip of his beer. "I've only been here once before and it wasn't this packed. It's a cool bar though."

"Yeah, I've been here a couple of times. My best friend really loves it." Why am I rambling? I lean back against the bar top and fiddle with my handbag, pushing it to the side. I look over my shoulder and see if I can make eye contact with one of the bartenders.

"So do you come here often then?" he asks, then chuckles in a self deprecating way. His eyes narrow and he shakes his head before rolling his eyes. "Wait, I guess you already answered that question before I asked." He grins as he takes another chug. "So, meeting friends?"

"Yeah," I nod. "And no worries, it has been one of those days for me as well."

"I feel that." He smiles and I can feel his eyes on my hair again. This man is really feeling me and it's making me feel a little uncomfortable. He's eyeing me like a piece of meat and I hope one of his heroes isn't Hannibal Lector.

"What do you think of Anthony Hopkins?" I ask him casually, throwing it out there to see if I notice a momentary twitch of excitement or fear that he's been busted.

"Are you a natural redhead or is that dye?" He peers at my scalp and I laugh uncomfortably as he ignores my question.

He wants to eat me. That would be my luck, of course. I get fired at one job, tell off my boss at the other job, and now I'm going to be kidnapped and eaten by a hair-obsessed psychopath. Maybe he needs a redhead to add to his collection.

"I would never dye my hair this color," I say honestly. I love my hair, it's unique and unruly and fits me to a tee, but if I could have chosen any hair color to be born with, this was not it. "It's all natural."

"Pretty." He nods and I swear he raises his hand to touch my hair.

"Thank you." I gulp as I step back. "Excuse me," I say as I turn around quickly and back away. "I need to get a drink and I don't think this is the best spot...they don't seem to be..." My voice trails off as I wave at one of the bartenders that's standing next to the beer fridge and I'm grateful when he heads over to me.

"How can I help you this evening?"

"I was wondering if you had any drink specials."

"Right now, we have well drinks for ten bucks."

"Oh, okay. Can I get a rum and Coke, please?"

"Sure."

I look over at my new friend. "Do you want anything?"

"I'm good. Thanks though." He nods with a knowing look. He's got perfectly even teeth and I notice that his skin is immaculate. Even his eyebrows are perfectly waxed. He's gorgeous. And I hope he's not a wolf looking to gobble me up tonight.

"I try not to mix liquor and beer." He pats his stomach. "Got to stay in shape."

"You look like you're in pretty good shape to me." Am I so desperate for attention that I am flirting with a potential unsub on Criminal Minds?

"Thanks." He laughs. "You never know when you might meet someone."

"Yeah, that's true." My heart races slightly. Now that I'm almost positive he's hitting on me, I feel slightly nervous and desperate, but I am in need of some male attention right now. I don't want him to think that I'm a sure thing. I don't want him to think that I'm going to go home with him. He's handsome, but maybe too much like a pretty boy. I like them a little bit more rough and ready. I'm grateful when I hear Juniper's voice next to me. "Hey there, Skye. You okay?"

"Hey." I reach over and give her a big hug. She looks as dowdy as ever with her big, thick, black owl glasses. Her hair's up in a bun and she's wearing an oversized black cardigan and a long black skirt. She really does need a makeover.

"You want a drink?" I ask her. "I just ordered a rum and Coke."

"Sure. Thanks."

"Excuse me," I call out to the bartender, and he looks up. "Can I get another rum and Coke for my friend, please?"

He nods, then I smile at my potential future stalker. I may need to sign up for a therapist to figure out what I'm still standing here.

"This is my friend Juniper."

"Hey," he says, looking her up and down.

I can tell that he is not impressed, but Juniper doesn't seem to notice.

"So, I was wondering," he says. "Do you go to a stylist?"

"What?" I ask him.

"For your hair. Do you go to a stylist to get a shampoo and conditioner and cut and..."

"Yeah sometimes. I have to admit that I don't go super frequently, but I do go sometimes."

"Oh, great," he says. "Because—"

"Hey there, Skye."

I hear Lila's voice as she heads toward me and spot Marie walking behind her. I'm surprised to see Marie here as she's not yet twenty-one and can't buy alcohol.

"Hey, you made it. So good to see you again, Marie." I look at her in surprise. "They let you in, huh?"

She nods and leans forward to whisper in my ear. "I have a fake ID. I know it's bad, but it's not like I'm going to drink anyway."

"Your secret is safe with me."

"Thanks for inviting me." She grins. "I can't drink, but

it's real nice to get out and my brother would not let me out if I were not with Lila."

"Because he knows I won't let you get into any trouble."

"I think I'm already in trouble," she says, giggling and tapping her stomach.

I don't really know the story as she's only eighteen and doesn't have a boyfriend, but I'm curious who the dad is and what her plan is.

"Shall I go and get a table?" Marie offers, looking around. "It is absolutely packed in here."

"It really is," I say, nodding. "Yeah, why don't you see if you can find a booth or something. Lila, I just got some rum and Cokes. You want one?"

"Sure. Thanks."

I look back over at the bartender. "Excuse me," I call out.

He raises another eyebrow. "Sorry. My other friend just got here. Can I get a third one?"

He nods and I see him reach for the Bacardi bottle again. I can't tell if he seems annoyed or not, but I don't care as it's not my fault my friends keep showing up.

"So, are we all here then?" Lila grins as she looks around. "This place is busy."

"I know," I say, giggling. "But no. My best friend Elisabetta is going to join us. She is so excited to meet you guys."

"I can't wait to meet her. I've heard so much about her," Lila says.

"I know. She is amazing. The most generous and wonderful friend a person can have."

"Are you talking about me?" Elisabetta says, looking stunning as usual.

"Hey, there you are." I give her a quick hug. "You want a drink? I just ordered some rum and Cokes."

"Sounds good to me."

I turn back around and look at the bartender. He's headed toward me with three drinks. He places them down in front of me. "You want to start a tab or?"

"Sure," I say, nodding. "But could I get a fourth one?"

He stares at me for a couple of seconds and lets out a long sigh. He doesn't say anything before he heads back to make another drink. I make a face as I look back at my friends.

"It's his job," Elisabetta says, shaking her head. "Don't feel bad."

"I just think that maybe—"

"Don't worry about it. He's always grumpy," the hot guy from next to me says.

"Oh, okay. I felt like he thought I was messing him around, but it's not my fault my friends just kept arriving."

"Exactly. Just give him a big tip."

"Yeah, I'll do that." I smile at him.

Though I don't know exactly how big of a tip I'm going to give him because I don't have that much money in the bank and I kind of didn't like his attitude, but I know enough about tipping to not make that comment just in case he feels like you should always give 20 to 25% no matter if you think you get bad service. A little voice tells me that I'm the reason why he was in a bad mood. I should have ordered all the drinks at the same time. Maybe I'd give him 30% to make up for having him go back and forth so many times.

"My name's Osprey, by the way," he says, holding out his hand.

"Oh, nice to meet you, Osprey. I'm..." I pause and freeze as he gives me a very thorough once-over. "Sorry. I literally just blanked on my name," I say, staring into his dark eyes. I feel absolutely ridiculous.

"That's okay. Names are hard things to remember, even when they're your own."

"You're really nice. I would say I had a blonde moment, but I'm not even blonde. I'm Skye with an E."

"Nice to meet you Skye with an E. So yeah, about that stylist?"

"Yeah. I can get his information for you if you want."

"Actually, I was hoping that—"

"Hey, Skye, I found a table." Marie tugs on my arm. "Come, let's sit."

"You guys go," I say. "I am just waiting on the last rum and Coke and I have to give this guy my credit card."

"I got it," Elisabetta says, pushing her way next to me and holding out her credit card.

"No," I say. "I am—"

"No, Skye," she insists, glaring at me. "I'll just use Daddy's card. This is nothing. And if you just lost your job, which you have to tell us all about, by the way, I don't think you should be springing for drinks for everyone."

"Oh, Elisabetta, you really don't have to do that. It makes me feel bad."

"Don't feel bad," she says. "Just help me find a hottie tonight."

"I will. At least I'll try."

I look at Osprey and find him staring at his phone. I hope he's not upset by the fact that my friends completely interrupted him.

"So, I think I'm going to go and sit with my friends," I say to him. "But maybe if you want to join us, you can."

"Thanks," he says, nodding. "Appreciate it."

"You're welcome."

I wait to see if he's going to join us or not, but he looks back down at his phone. Maybe I turned him off by having too many friends here. I've always heard that men were intimidated by groups of women together.

The bartender returns with the fourth rum and Coke. "Let me know if you want a fifth one," he says sarcastically, and I give him my best, "I'm sorry and think you're being a good sport" smile, even though I don't think he's being the best sport ever. Though, I'm not sure that I'd behave any differently if I were in his shoes.

Elisabetta hands him the card. "You keep the tab open," she says. "Any of my friends are welcome to order drinks on it."

"Okay," he says, nodding.

"Come on, let's go sit." Elisabetta turns to me, a happy smile on her face. "I'm so glad that we're getting to go out."

"Yeah. I mean, I am glad we're getting to hang out, but I'm not glad that I'm not getting tipped out tonight."

"What happened?"

"What didn't happen?" I say, rolling my eyes as we make our way to the booth.

I slide in next to Marie and Elisabetta sits next to me. Lila is on the other side with Juniper beside her.

"Marie, this is Elisabetta, my best friend. Elisabetta, this is Marie, Lila, and Juniper." I beam at them all. "I'm so happy we are all here."

"So what happened?"

They all lean forward, gawking at me.

"Let's just say that my boss is a jackass."

"Fabricio?" Elisabetta asks.

"Well, him as well, but I'm talking about Kingston Chase."

"Oh shit, what happened?" Lila asks.

"I hate him. He is literally a jackass. You will not believe what he said to me."

"What did he say?" Marie says, sipping on her water bottle.

"He called me and said that he just wanted to let me know that I shouldn't get any ideas about me and him getting together."

"What?" Lila asked in surprise. "Where did that come from?"

"I suppose you and Max. Supposedly, Kingston thinks that all the other assistants at the firm now have designs on their bosses because you and Max got together."

Lila rolls her eyes. "Oh my gosh. He is horrible."

"He really is," Juniper says, nodding. "He and Remington are total fuck boys."

"So is Gabe," Marie says.

We all turn to her.

"Oh?" I ask. "I've never met him."

"Oh, I'm sure you'll meet him soon. Max said that he's back in town. They're actually all meeting tonight," Marie says, rolling her eyes.

"I used to think Gabe was really attractive, but he's just a jackass."

"Oh?" I ask her. "Why is he a jackass?"

"Oh, he's just really full of himself. But I suppose all of them at that firm are."

I look over at Lila, who looks at me with wide eyes. It sounded like there was history there, but I don't want to be nosy.

"Remington's a jackass too," Juniper says. "They're all fuck boys. They basically just have women throwing themselves at them so they never have to settle down." She looks over at Lila. "To be quite honest, all of us are shocked that you and Max got together."

Lila blushes. "I'm pretty shocked myself. I didn't think that he and I would fall for each other like that."

"And so quickly as well," I say, shaking my head. "That must be like a Guinness Book of World Records for the fastest falling in love."

"Not really," Lila says, blushing slightly. "I think it was just a love at first sight thing. It happens."

"I can tell you that I have never fallen in love at first sight," I say. "I mean I've never thought that I have since college anyway. I realize now that I was never in love."

"Really?" Elisabetta asks, and I stare at her.

"Yeah. Why?"

"What about that dude that you met at the animal shelter?"

"What are you talking about?" I ask her.

"What was his name? Andrew?"

I stare at her for a couple of seconds. "Oh, the guy from Iowa?"

"Yeah. Remember how you went to the animal shelter and you came home and you were like, 'I met the man I'm going to marry'?"

"That's because I was young and dumb."

"Girl, that was last year."

"That's because I was young, dumb, and drunk," I said. "I had a hangover from partying with you the night before."

"Okay. I guess that part may have been true." She turns to the other girls. "It was hilarious. She came home and said she met the man she's going to marry, and then they actually went on a date."

"Ooh, what happened?" Juniper asks.

"You don't want to know," I say, frowning slightly at the memory.

"You have to tell us."

"Let's just say we went on a date to the grocery store." I shudder in remembrance.

"A date at the grocery store?"

Everyone looks at me in confusion. Except for Elisabetta, who already knows the story.

"Yeah. He was like, 'Oh, isn't this fun?' And I was like, 'Not really, but it's different.' And he was like, 'Well, you want to have a nice lunch, right?' So my dumb ass thought we were shopping for ingredients from him to cook me lunch."

"Oh my gosh, that sounds so romantic," Marie says.

"That's not what happened," I say, interrupting her. "So anyway, we buy all this stuff. It was like $350 worth of stuff. And he's like, 'Okay, we just have one more stop.' And I was thinking to myself, wow, he's really going all out for this date. Plus, he's spending a lot of money, which kind of made me feel bad because he didn't really dress like he had much money. But I was like, maybe he's trying to impress me. So then we go to this delicatessen. Mind you, we're carrying all these grocery bags down the street and I was super tired."

Elisabetta starts laughing.

"It's not funny, Elisabetta."

"It really isn't," she says. "I just can't believe it."

"Oh my gosh. Tell us," Lila said. "So what happened next?"

"So then we go to this delicatessen and he buys this Spanish chorizo and Manchego cheese, and then we get this French bread from this bakery and a couple of bottles of red wine. And then he's like, 'Oh shit, I forgot the caviar.' And I was like, 'Oh my gosh, you really don't have to get the caviar.' And he was like, 'No, I really do have to get the caviar.' And I was like, 'Okay.' I admit it, I do like caviar. And then he gave me this weird look, which, at the time, I thought he was giving me the look because he thought I had never had caviar before. So I literally spend the next ten minutes telling him about all the different times that I had caviar."

At this point, Elisabetta is laughing so loudly I feel like she's going to have a fit.

"It's not funny," I say, shaking my head.

"Oh my God, it was totally not funny, but I can't stop laughing."

"I mean, it's sounding great so far," Juniper says. "What happened? Did he ask you to pay or something?"

"No." I shake my head. "Anyway, he finally stops me and says that he actually doesn't agree with the consumption of caviar, which I thought was really weird because I'm like, 'Why are you buying caviar for our date if you don't agree with it?' But I was just like, maybe he's doing it because even though he doesn't like it, he still wants to impress me."

I glare at Elisabetta as she starts hiccuping.

"Anyway, he finally pays another $500 and as we leave the store loaded down with even more bags, I turn to him and I'm going, 'Hey, I agreed to this date because I really liked you and it had nothing to do with how much money you have.' And he stares at me blankly and he is like, 'What are you talking about?' I'm like, 'You just spent like, $800 to make a fancy lunch or picnic for us.' And he's like, 'This isn't just for one meal.' And I was like, 'Oh, you're being presumptuous, aren't you?' And he was like, 'What are you talking about?' And I was like, 'You think I'm going to stay with you for the rest of the week?' And he was like, 'Huh?' And I was like, 'Well, you got all this food and it's not going to be for one meal.' And he was like, 'This isn't my food.' And of course, I just stare at him in confusion and I'm like, 'What are you talking about? I thought you were buying this for our date.' He was like, 'We're doing Instacart shopping.'"

"No way!" Lila bursts out laughing. Marie giggles loudly and Juniper snorts like a pig, almost knocking her glasses off.

"No! He did not take you to work with him!" Lila's jaw drops.

"Yep. The date was us shopping and delivering the food." I roll my eyes. "And then after we drop off the food, my stomach is growling and he is like, 'Oh, sounds like you're hungry.' And I was like, 'Yeah, I could definitely eat a bite', thinking he was going to take me out to get something to eat. And he was like, 'Okay, well, I guess you should head home then and make yourself a sandwich because I got some more deliveries to do, but thanks for your help. We should do it again sometime.'"

I shake my head. "And can you believe he actually called me the next week asking if I wanted to meet up again?"

"He did not," Juniper says. "No way."

"He totally did," I say, shaking my head. "Anyway, that's the very last time I believed in love at first sight."

"She totally thought he was so amazing before that," Elisabetta says. "It was so sad. It was so, so sad."

"Yes, it was," I say. "But in other news, I think there is a hottie that wants to talk to me tonight." I nod towards the bar. The women all look at me.

"Oh?"

"Yeah. His name is Osprey and he was hitting on me as soon as I walked in."

"Oh, really?" Lila says. "Oh my gosh, did we cock block you?"

"It's okay," I say, looking toward the bar. He's still standing there looking at his phone.

"He kept asking me about my stylist and then he asked me if I was an actual redhead. And I'm pretty sure he was asking that because he wanted to be me...in a Jeepers Creepers way. Then I subconsciously thought he was like, oh, does the carpet match the drapes?" I moan slightly at the embarrassing memories. "And normally I don't like it when guys ask that question, but he's so handsome that I'm willing to give my thoughts a pass. I know I watch too many horror movies and it's very unlikely that he's Norman Bates."

"He is really good looking," Marie says.

"Yeah, he is. And it's kind of nice that he's so into me, even though I don't know if I really want him. He looks like he's better waxed than I am."

"He sure does look like he manscapes," Lila says with a slight nod.

"Yep," I say. "But maybe I'll flirt with him just a little bit because I've had the day from Hell."

"But at least you're getting to hang out with us," Elisabetta says. "And I'm so glad I got to meet you guys. You're so much fun."

"Thank you," Juniper says and Lila grins.

"Oh, hold up," she says, holding her phone up. "Guess who's calling me?"

"Max," I say, groaning.

She laughs. "Do you mind if I take it?"

"Not at all," I say, shaking my head. "Someone might as well enjoy their love life."

"You'll meet someone soon. And who knows? Maybe Osprey is the one."

"Maybe," I say, nodding, taking a sip of my rum and Coke. "Maybe I also need to get another round of drinks for everyone in a second and chat with him some more." It doesn't really feel like a great idea, but I'm going with it.

"Perfect," Marie says with a nod.

"Hey, honey," Lila says, answering the phone. "Just with the girls at The Owl and the Pussycat."

I stare at her for a couple of seconds, nervous that she's going to invite them to join us. It's not like I don't like Max. I think he's fun, but I don't really want to see Kingston, especially after our conversation. I don't even want to be reminded about work.

I take another sip of my rum and Coke and think about my disastrous love life and my disastrous career.

"I'll be in Australia soon," I mumble to myself.

Soon I'll be traveling the world and maybe I'll meet the love of my life in another country, I think, because he sure as hell didn't seem like he was living in New York City. Unless Osprey is the one. I decide to head to the bar again to get my flirt on one last time. If Osprey is the one, I have to give him an opportunity to let me know.

Chapter Six

Kingston

"How did I let you guys talk me into spending a Friday evening with my assistant?" I say to Max and Remi as we make our way into the bar.

"Well, it's not like she wants to spend an evening with you either," Remington says, laughing.

We look around the room and I can see that the bar is packed. "I'm going to have one beer, then I'm leaving. I have an early morning tomorrow."

"Whatever," Remi says. "Hey, Max. Where's your girl?"

"She's sitting over there in the corner," Max nods towards the back. "Do you want to get some drinks before or...?"

"Yeah, let's do it." I nod in agreement. I don't want to keep going back and forth in this crowd, even though there are a couple of very beautiful women here tonight. I look around the bar, my eyes perusing the single groups of ladies. There's a group directly to the left of us with three tall, beautiful looking stunners. All of them are eyeing me up and down, so I take a step toward them and smile. "Hi. Nice to meet you. My name is Kingston."

"Did we ask you your name?" the lady closest to me with dark, brown eyes says. She has a long gold necklace hanging down the front of her body, falling right between the valley of her beautiful breasts.

"No, but I had a feeling you were going to ask."

"Really?" she says, looking into my eyes.

"Yes really, maybe I wanted to know *your* name, and I figured it would be polite to give you mine first."

"Really, then, Blue Eyes?"

"You can call me that as well. Though, like I said before, my friends call me Kingston."

"Well, I'll have you know that my friends call me India."

"Oh, yeah?" I say, staring at her shimmering darker skin. "And that's because?"

"Because my mother enjoyed visiting India when she was in college," she says. "I really want to go one day."

"I've got friends that went to Goa when I was in college," I say, staring at her beautiful smile. "They said the beach was amazing. So are you having fun tonight?"

"I am," she nods. "Maybe even more so now that you're here. This is my friend, Ashley."

"Hi," Ashley, a cute little blonde says, holding her hand out.

"Nice to meet you, Ashley."

"You too. You're really handsome. Your eyes are so blue."

"Thank you," I nod, and then look at the third girl, who is a petite Asian with very long, black hair.

"Hi. I'm Ariel, like The Little Mermaid, and yes, my mom named me after The Little Mermaid. Please don't say anything."

"I won't," I say. "You guys are really classing up the

place, like we're in Paris or Milan." They all start to giggle. "This is why I love living in the city," I say, nodding. "I get to hang out with supermodels like you three."

"What do you think about the three of us?"

Pausing as my eyes move over to the right, I frown. Is that Skye? I'd recognize her long, red, cascading curls anywhere, but she isn't alone, and she's laughing. I lean forward slightly to see who she's with. A tall, handsome looking man is standing there, looking like Ricky Martin, and a surge of annoyance passes through me. "So what were you about to ask, Blue Eyes?" Ariel says and taps me on the shoulder. I blink because I realize I'm still with the three women.

"Oh, I was just wondering if you wanted a drink." I smile at them, though I'm not feeling happy. I had been about to ask if they wanted to have some fun back at my place, because I'd much rather end the evening having a foursome than hanging out with my employees, but now that I've seen that Skye isn't sitting at the table looking off, but actually having the time of her life, I'm not happy about it.

"Sure. We're drinking cosmos, but we also like dirty martinis," Ariel bites down on her lip, "Because we're dirty girls."

"Oh," I smirk. "Well, that's good to know. I'll go and get the drinks."

"I'll come with you," India says, holding my forearm possessively. "I'll help you bring the drinks back and make sure you don't put anything in them."

"I would never do such a thing," I say.

"I'm sure you wouldn't, but here in New York, girls are born with street smarts and we don't let guys buy us drinks unless we see the drinks being made and handed to us."

"You're very smart," I say. "Well, let's just go and get your drinks. We'll be right back," I say to Ashley and Ariel, who just nod and grin.

"So, you're here by yourself?" India asks, still holding on to me as we make our way to the bar top.

"Yeah," I nod slightly, my eyes not leaving Skye as I watch her run her fingers through her hair and lean over to whisper something into the guy's ear. What the hell? Is this the plan that she had for the evening? Was this why she wasn't able to complete her work, so she could go and flirt with some jackass?

"I think we'll get the cosmos, seeing as that's what we've been drinking all night, and they say you shouldn't mix your liquor, right?" India continues, and I look into her eyes and give her a brief smile.

"Yeah, that's true. So what do you do? I've never seen you around here before."

"I'm an attorney. You?" I ask.

"I'm a DJ. Well, part-time DJ. In the day, I manage a little boutique in the West Village. You may have heard of it. Englewood?"

"Sorry. No," I shake my head.

"You mean you've never bought your girlfriend or your wife any cute bikinis or lingerie? That's what we sell."

"No, I haven't," I say, and she gasps.

"Wait, are you married?"

I blink as I look at her. "No, I'm not married. Sorry, I was just a little distracted. No, I haven't bought my girlfriend or wife any lingerie from your boutique because I don't have a girlfriend or wife." I grin at her. "Does that make you feel better?"

"Yeah, because I don't do married men. I know some women are like, 'Maybe they're in a bad marriage, maybe they're separated. Maybe you'll be the second wife', but I just think it's bad karma."

I nod, my eyes still on Skye. "I mean, if he's going to cheat on his first wife, he's going to cheat on me too, and I don't want to be a second wife. Or rather, I don't mind being the second wife, but I don't want to be the second wife before the third one. You know?" I nod again. "Hey, are you listening to me, Blue Eyes?" We've stopped at the edge of the bar, about two people away from Skye.

"Sorry, I was just thinking about something work related."

"Oh, you must be so busy with work. What, are you like a judge?"

"No, I'm an attorney. Business litigation, some commercial real estate—"

"Oh my gosh, so we just got this new line of bikinis in that I think you would absolutely love," she cuts me off.

"Okay," I say, signaling to the bartender to come over. "Excuse me," I say loudly, and I know that Skye has heard me because I watch her shoulders tense and she turns to look toward me, as if in slow motion. Her eyes widen and she shakes her head.

"Oh, hell no," she says, and I grin as I give her a wave.

"Nice to see you, Skye. Having an enjoyable evening, are we?"

"Yes, I am. Thank you very much," she says, glaring at me now. "What are you doing here?"

"Didn't Lila tell you that she invited Max and us to come join since we were finished at our previous bar?"

"No, she didn't. Oh my gosh. Are you trying to ruin my evening?"

"Are you trying to ruin mine?"

"Yo. I'm standing here, you know." A drunk guy between

us backs away and I push over to the side so that I'm standing next to Skye now, and then I feel India's hand on my arm again as she squeezes. I look back over to her. I had forgotten all about her.

"India, I'd like you to meet my assistant. My not-very-adept assistant. My not-very-hardworking-or-productive assistant."

"Wow. Thank you very much, Kingston. That makes me feel like a really valued employee," Skye says sarcastically, and I laugh.

"This is Skye. Skye, this is India."

"Hi, India," Skye says, giving her a wide smile and reaching over. "Nice to meet you. Are you two dating or...?" Skye's eyes go back and forth between myself and India.

"Not yet," India says in a tone that very clearly says that we will be soon. She gives me a confident smile and I admire her high cheekbones. She was definitely going to make it as a supermodel. "But who knows what could happen if tonight goes well."

Skye nods slightly and looks at me, a smirk on her face that I'm not quite sure about. Her eyes flicker between hurt, consternation, and triumph and when she laughs hoarsely, I wonder if she's losing it?

"What's so funny?" I ask her.

"Just that you're exactly the sort of guy that I thought you were."

"And what's that supposed to mean?"

"I think you know exactly what that means."

"And who's your friend?" I nod toward the Ricky Martin look alike that's standing behind her.

"Hey," the guy says, looking me up and down. "You are extremely good looking." It dawns on me then that this is definitely not Skye's boyfriend.

"Thank you. I'm Kingston, Skye's boss at the law firm."

"Oh, you work at a law firm?" he asks Skye, and I grin. So this dude doesn't even know where she works? They barely know each other.

"I'm his assistant, but I'm also a model and an actress."

"What modeling have you done?" I ask, raising my eyebrow.

"I'll have you know that I was in a Macy's catalog."

"You were in a Macy's catalog. Really?" My mind wonders what she was wearing in the catalog.

"To be clear, Macy's doesn't know I was in a catalog," she admits, laughing. "One summer, my cousin took photographs of us and cut out our faces and pasted them onto models in the Macy's catalog, and then we were able to tell people we were in Macy's catalogs. It was just something for my resumé when I went to look for modeling jobs."

My eyes narrow. "Really? And how many other jobs have you lied about on your resumé?" I ask, thinking about the fact that she has yet to get me her final resumé. I'm pretty sure it's not going to list a long line of attorneys that she had verbally said she'd worked for.

"Like I said, I didn't do it. My cousin did. Everything I do is above board."

"Uh-huh," I say.

"Are you getting those cosmos or what, Blue Eyes?" I feel India's hand on my back, reaching down to squeeze my ass.

"Of course. Anything else?"

"Shots."

I look over at Skye and Ricky Martin. "Would you guys like shots?"

"Yeah. Are you paying?" Ricky Martin says, and I nod.

"No, thank you," Skye says.

"Really, Skye? You don't want a free shot?"

"Fine," she says. "You may buy me a shot."

"I had a feeling you'd say that. Let's see. What should we get?"

"I like buttery nipples," India says.

I look at her and grin. "I think I prefer the whipped cream."

Skye gasps, "Really? This is so inappropriate."

"You're telling me something is inappropriate?" I say looking down into her eyes. "Pot calling kettle?"

"What are you talking about?" she says.

I lean down and whisper in her ear, "If you think you're going home with Ricky Martin there tonight, I think you'll find that you're mistaken."

"You're just jealous," she hisses. "You're just jealous because I told you I didn't want to have dinner with you, and I told you I'm not interested in you and now you're trying to cock-block me with this very handsome man."

"I don't think I'm trying to cock-block you. I think you've cock-blocked yourself."

"How do I cock-block myself?" she demands, glaring at me.

"Maybe because you don't have a cock."

"What? What are you talking about?" She looks confused, and I shake my head.

"Are you ready to order, sir?" the bartender says.

"Yeah. Can I get three cosmopolitans? I will have a Guinness, if you have them, and then we'll get four shots of tequila."

"Tequila?" Skye says. "What? Are you trying to get me fucked up tonight?"

"I don't know. Do you want to get fucked up tonight, or are you just trying to get fucked?"

She gasps again, "Oh my gosh. You did not say that."

"I mean, if you want to get fucked, I would recommend you move on to someone else."

"Excuse me?" she says, blinking at me.

"I really don't think jealousy is a good look on you."

She gives me a smug look. "Just because me and my new man want to—" I tap her on the shoulder to interrupt her. "What?"

"Have a look," I say, nodding behind her.

"What are you talking about?" She turns her head to the right and her jaw drops when she sees Ricky Martin kissing a guy that had just walked up to him, and not as friends. "What?" She looks back at me, and I chuckle slightly.

"Honey, Ricky Martin doesn't bat for our team."

"But I thought he was so into me," she whispers. "He was literally talking to me as soon as I got to the bar, admiring my hair, asking who my stylist was..." She blinks in confusion. "I wasn't even sure if I was into him, but..."

"But, what?" I ask.

"Nothing." She blushes now.

"Hey, guys. I want you to meet my boyfriend. This is Serrano."

"Nice to meet you, Serrano."

"It's a pleasure to meet you too," the skinny man says with a French accent.

"Hi," Skye says. "I'm Skye."

"Ah. You're the one with the beautiful red hair!" He nods. "I heard about you."

"You did?" she asks.

"Yes, I am a stylist. I work for a very famous hairdresser and, well, I wanted to give my card to you so you could give it to your stylist, because we have a new product that we created just for redheads to make the hair shiny, shiny, and silky." He touches her hair. "You have beautiful hair, but it is not at its best. See?" Skye blinks, and I burst out laughing. "I hope you're not offended. I just thought this could be good business for your stylist, and of course, if you buy some products from us, we will give you some free for yourself to take home."

Skye looks to me and shakes her head, "Do not even say a word."

"Okay," I nod.

I look over at India, who's looking bored. "Is there something going on here that I should know about?" India says, pointing between me and Skye. "Does she really work with you, or is this some sort of game, like you guys are fucking and pretending you don't know each other so you can pick each other up in the bar, and then go to the restrooms at the back and fuck?" She rolls her eyes. "Because that's so 2010."

"No. We are definitely not about to go to the back and fuck," I say, though I can feel myself growing hard at the thought.

"I wouldn't touch him with a ten-foot pole." Skye blinks and the bartender arrives with our shots.

"Here you guys go."

"And another one for Serrano here," I say to the bartender, who lets out his sigh.

"What is it with you people?" he mutters under his breath.

I don't even bother to ask him to clarify what he's talking about. He makes another tequila shot, brings it back, and hands it to Serrano. "Cheers, everyone," I say. As I down the smooth liquor, I look into Skye's eyes as she drinks hers and coughs lightly. "You okay? I guess you don't swallow much, huh?"

She stares at me for a couple of seconds, blinking as she

shakes her head. "I'll have you know that you will never know if I swallow or not." She licks her lips, then looks down at my crotch and then back into my eyes. "I know you wish I wanted you, and I know you wish I gave a shit about you being here with a woman, but I don't. I do not care about you whatsoever, Kingston Chase. I don't want you, not even for one night, not even for one second, so get off your high horse and I'll see you on Monday."

Chapter Seven

Skye

"I am so embarrassed!" I wail to Elisabetta as she gets ready for bed. "Scratch that. I'm mortified. Please go and dig a grave for me right now."

"You're so dramatic, Skye." She looks over her shoulder at me as she grabs a makeup remover wipe and starts rubbing it against her skin. "It's fine."

"No, it's not fine. I was freaking acting like a fool and trying to make my boss jealous and telling him he was jealous and the guy was not into me."

"Well, I mean, you thought he was into you."

"Yeah, I thought he was into me, but turns out that I don't have the body parts that he's looking for."

"You could always get some if you want," she says, giggling.

"What's that supposed to mean?"

"You've never heard of strap-ons?" She tilts her head to the side. "Actually, I wonder."

"You wonder what?"

"I wonder if a gay guy would be with a woman if she had a strap-on on."

I stare at her, not blinking.

She looks up and gives me a wry smile. "Sorry. I guess that's not the most helpful right now."

"No, it's not helpful right now. I'm not about to go and buy a strap-on and go back to the bar and ask Osprey if he wants to pretend he's into me and not kiss his boyfriend so that I can tell my jerk face of a boss that he is actually, in fact, jealous of me and my new man." I groan. "Oh, what is going on in my life?"

"I don't know, girl, but I feel like you need to get some dick."

"Excuse me? That's your answer to me?"

"That would solve a lot of problems, right? If you got some dick, then you could legitimately make your boss jealous. And if you got some dick, it would most probably be with someone who wanted to give you the dick and not picture you as a handsome man."

I glare at her some more.

"What? I mean, maybe if you cut your hair, grew out a mustache and a beard, flattened your breasts. Of course, in all reality you'd most probably have to cut them off."

"Don't gay guys like breasts?" I ask her.

"Yeah, but not for fun in the bedroom," she says, giggling. "Sorry. I'll stop."

I sigh. "Oh my gosh. How am I going to go to work on Monday? He probably thinks I'm a fool. And then he was all there with his beautiful model look alike laughing in my face."

"I didn't see him laughing in your face, Skye."

"I'm exaggerating. He wasn't laughing in my face, but he was for sure smirking. Oh, this sucks."

"At least you have your date tomorrow with your blind date."

"Yeah, that's true," I say, starting to feel a little bit better. "And he's obviously interested in women because he was on a dating app looking for a woman."

"I mean, technically."

"Technically? Explain."

"Obviously he's interested in women to some degree, but he could be bi, girl. Or queer."

"Okay, and your point is?"

"My point being that just because he's interested in women doesn't mean he's not interested in anyone else." She shrugs. "I'm just being honest with you so you don't get your hopes up just in case you see him on another date with a guy or something."

"Thanks, Elisabetta. Like, what are you doing to me right now?"

"Sorry. It's the drinks and...I don't know. Maybe I need some dick myself."

"Yeah, I think you do."

"And I don't mean from anyone I already know. I want to be wooed."

"I want to be wooed as well, Elisabetta."

"I know. Should we go speed dating or something?"

"Not again." I shake my head. "The last time we went it was absolutely awful. I mean, at least you've got some options. What options do I have?"

"Well, you have your boss."

"He's not an option."

"But then those other two guys."

"Which other two guys?"

"Gabe and what was the other guy's name?"

"Max? Max is with Lila."

"No, not Max. That Remington guy. The one with the dark eyes and that sexy smile."

"Oh, he's Juniper's boss. He's a jackass as well."

"Oh, yeah. I guess you guys did form the Annoying Hot Bosses Club."

"Well at least the hot bosses part is right. Why do hot men have to be such jerks?" I mumble. "It's just so unfair."

"Life is unfair."

"You sound like my mom."

"Sorry," she says, giggling. "So do you want to do a Korean face mask with me before we go to bed?"

"I might as well." I grab one of the makeup remover wipes and start rubbing it against my skin as well. "Are we going to be single forever?"

I sigh, thinking that this could be our life in thirty years. I love Elisabetta, but I don't want to live with her for the rest of my life. I mean, I wouldn't mind living with her as a Golden Girl after my marriage and my three kids, but I don't just want to live with her straight through.

"No, we're still young. Stop being so overly dramatic, Skye. It's fine. This is why you should not do more than two drinks a night because you always get into your brain and start overthinking things."

"I'm not trying to overthink anything. I'm just..." I wrinkle my nose. "Okay, maybe I'm overthinking it. Maybe it's because I just feel like Kingston thinks I am a big idiot."

"No comment," she says.

"Thank you. That makes me feel great."

"I mean, you have to admit, it's kind of funny. You were going on and on and on about how this guy was into you and how you didn't even know if you wanted him and then it turns out that he's gay and he doesn't want you after all."

"I know. What does that say about me? Does it say that

I'm completely and utterly ridiculous and that I don't have a clue?"

"How were you supposed to know he was gay?"

"Yeah, I'm not a psychic, but him kissing his boyfriend might've been a clue."

"Yeah, but it's not like he was with his boyfriend when you first met."

"True. But also the fact that he was dressed very, very nicely with eyebrows better manicured than my own. And the fact that he kept asking me who my stylist was. I mean, come on."

She grins. "True. True. Anyway, stop thinking about it. You have Camden."

"Uhm you mean I've got a date set with him."

"And we can go out tomorrow night if you want."

"Yeah, I guess."

"Don't sound so excited."

"I am excited, but I don't have money, Elisabetta. I need to find a job. Me losing that job tonight really put a wrench in my plans."

"I know. So what are you going to do?"

"So, actually, I had an idea."

"Oh?" she asks.

"I was thinking I could be a photographer."

"What?" She blinks at me. "You don't even have a camera and you don't really have money to buy a camera either."

"No. Hear me out. So when we were at the bar, you know what I noticed?"

"No." She shakes her head. "What?"

"I was noticing that everyone was trying to take selfies."

"Okay." She nods. "That is true. I mean, we took a couple of selfies ourselves."

"And half the time the selfies end up looking like shit, right?"

"If you don't know your angles and you don't have good light, then they don't always look great."

"Elisabetta."

"Sorry." She holds her hands up. "But that's normally the reason why."

"Anyway. Wouldn't most people kill to have someone take their photo when they're out at the bar and having fun and make them look really good?"

"I don't know that they would kill for that. No," she says, shaking her head. "But," she says quickly. "I think they would love it."

"Exactly. So I was thinking, what if I am an unofficial photographer at bars like that?"

"What? You're going to go and ask managers if they'll hire you?"

"No," I say, shaking my head grinning. "That's why it's unofficially."

"I don't get you."

"I mean, I'm just going to be at the bar hanging out, hopefully with you."

"Okay, so you do want to go out tomorrow night?"

"Yeah, but I'll also be working."

"What? You got a job?"

"No. As the unofficial photographer."

"Girl, you're confusing me. I don't understand what you're saying. How are you going to be an unofficial photographer with no camera and the people don't even know that you're working there as a photographer?"

"Because I don't need a camera. Their phones will be my camera. Their phone will be my lens through which I capture the world."

Elisabetta just blinks at me. "Sorry. You're going to have to break this down a little bit better."

"Look, when I see people taking selfies, I'm going to go up to them and I'm going to be like, 'Hi, I'm Skye, unofficial photographer of the evening.'" I grin at her. "And then I'll show them my pearly white teeth."

"They're not that pearly."

"You know what I mean."

"Sorry," she laughs. "So you're going to see people taking selfies..." She laughs slightly. "And you're going to go up to them and ask them if they want you to take the photo?" She's almost in tears by now, she's laughing so hard.

"What is so funny?"

"Honestly, I don't get it," she says. "That's what we do normally to help people out anyway."

"I know, but I do that just as a regular good person. I'll start doing it tomorrow night as an officially unofficial photographer. It's not like you have to have a degree in photography to be a good photographer. Plus, I can't take an actual camera with me like a DSLR or anything because the clubs would probably get upset and then probably want me as their official photographer."

"So then why don't you become an official photographer?"

"Because they'd probably want a cut of the money."

"So wait, you're going to charge people to take these photos?"

"Yeah, that's the whole point. That's how I'm going to make extra money. I figure maybe $20 a photo."

"I know you're drunk, but this is not a good idea, Skye!" She laughs so loud that she starts slamming her hand into the countertop. "Oh my gosh." She hiccups as she giggles. "No way. You're going to take a photo with someone's phone camera and charge them $20. Are you out of your mind, Skye?"

"Obviously, it's going to be more than one photo and I'm going to take some props with me so that they're cool, of course."

"Some props?" She looks at me and raises an eyebrow. "What props?"

"You'll see tomorrow night," I say, slightly miffed that she's not taking me seriously. "I think it's a good idea to make some money on the side."

"I mean, it's an idea all right," she says. "I don't know how good it is. I'm sorry. Please don't be mad at me. I just don't know that I would be happy if I was trying to take a selfie and someone came up to me and was like, 'Hey, you want me to help with that?' And I said, yeah. And then they said, 'Oh, and that's $20.'"

"But they won't have the props that I'm going to have tomorrow."

"Okay," she says, making a face. "If you think this sounds like a sound business plan, Skye."

I stare at her for a couple of seconds. "Look, do I think it's going to net me millions? No. But what if it becomes a thing? What if people want to franchise the unofficial photographer gig?"

"Girl, who's going to franchise that? They can go into any bar or restaurant and be an unofficial photographer without having a franchise from you. You won't even know."

I laugh slightly. "Okay, you make a point there. Maybe it's not going to become franchises, but maybe if I patent it."

"Girl, really?"

"Okay," I say, laughing. "Maybe I won't patent it, but it's worth a try, right? Especially if we go to some really bougie places and I have some really rich people pay me."

"Can I make a suggestion?"

I nod slowly as she reaches for the Korean mask packs.

"Why don't you make it tip based?"

"Tip based? You think so?" I ask, frowning as I think about asking for tips. It wasn't what I'd had in mind. "It's not like I'm getting an hourly wage. Are you saying that I should ask the clubs to give me an hourly wage?"

"No, that's not what I'm saying," she says, laughing. "What I'm saying is what if you do what you were thinking. You go up to these people and maybe you have a sign around you that says 'unofficial photographer of the evening', which sounds kind of cheesy, but I think we'll make it look a bit more legit."

"I like that," I say, nodding. "I can probably get something made."

"And then after you take the photos, have a jar, and on the jar just say 'unofficial photographer for tips' or something. That way they don't feel pressured into giving you $20, especially if you don't necessarily get a great photo."

"What do you mean if I don't necessarily get a great photo?"

"Girl, I know you are an unofficial photographer, and I know that you're using their phones and that it's all for fun, but I've had you take official photographs of me and they turn out looking like shit."

"No, they didn't. I take realistic photographs. If that's how you look, that's how you look."

"People don't want to look at themselves in a photo and see how they really look, girl. No one wants to see their extra twenty pounds or their double chin or their fat belly."

I stare at her and blink.

"I'm just saying you're going to have to learn the angles a

bit better and capture the lighting a bit better and maybe figure out some filters."

"So you want me to make them look fake?"

"I want you to make them look good, at least if you want those big tips."

I nod slowly. "I guess so. Maybe you're right."

"Trust me, girl, I'm right. I cannot believe that I'm even giving you tips for this job because..."

"Because what?" I say, staring her.

"Nothing. I promised you before that I'm going to be supportive of your endeavors. And I am. But do you really need all these multiple jobs, girl? You have a good day job."

I stare at her. "The day job is fine and it pays well, that is true. But one: I don't know how long I'm going to be able to work there without either quitting or being fired. And two: it doesn't pay me enough to pay off all my debts and save a lot of money for my trip."

"Okay," she says. "I get it."

"And you know how important it is for me to take this around-the-world trip. I've dreamed about it all my life. I want to see different cultures and experience different things and..."

"And guess what?" she says. "You can make it a working vacation."

"Huh?" I say, staring at her.

"I mean, you could be an unofficial photographer anywhere in the world."

I look at her for a couple of seconds and think for a few seconds. My heart is racing as I process her words. "Really?"

"I'm just saying," she says. "In case you run out of money. Here." She hands me the face mask and we both start laughing.

"I have no clue what I'm doing."

Chapter Eight

Kingston

I wake up hard and horny, and I picture Skye's face in my mind. I groan as I rub my forehead and roll out of bed.

"You're the last person I want to be thinking about," I mutter under my breath as I head to the bathroom to splash my face with water.

I stretch my arms and look at my reflection in the mirror and shake my head yet again. I'm still tired. I drank way too much the night before, and all I can think about is how I wondered how Skye could not possibly have known that the dude she was flirting with was gay.

Get a clue, girl. I think to myself as I smile.

I head back to the bedroom and grab my phone and I see that Remington has messaged me. I call him.

"Yo, what's up dude?" he says, answering within a couple of rings.

"Not much. Why are you blowing up my phone on a Saturday morning?"

"I wanted to know if you wanted to hit the gym, do some bench presses, and—"

"Uh, not at five o'clock in the morning, and I was out last night."

"I was out last night too, but I woke up early."

"Okay, good for you."

"So how are you feeling today?" he asks, his tone slightly amused.

"'How am I feeling today? Is that a loaded question?'"

"Well, you kind of had an interesting night."

"You know what, Remington? If you are trying to discuss how I embarrassed myself by calling my assistant, then you're out of luck because I am not going to be discussing that anymore."

"You want to bang the living daylights out of her, don't you?"

"No, I do not, and as far as I'm concerned, that's the end of that discussion as well."

"Uh-huh." He chuckles. "Why don't we bet on that?"

"Actually, Remington, I have a date tonight with a woman who doesn't work for me and I need to make a reservation for dinner, so unless you have something mightily important to discuss with me right now, I've got to go."

"Oh, you have a date tonight? With who?"

"You don't know her."

"Uh-huh. Her name's not Skye, is it?"

"No. Maybe her name's Juniper."

"Juniper?" He bursts out laughing. "Oh, you think that would upset me if you wanted to date my assistant?"

"Yeah, I have a feeling it would."

"For real, dude, she probably needs to get some. She looks like she spends every Saturday night with her books, cuddled on a couch with her cats."

"She has cats?"

"I mean, I don't know, but she reminds me of a cat lady."

"What's a cat lady, Remi?"

"I don't know. Someone that's librarian-like? The truth of the matter is that maybe she has a man, I don't know. She and I have never discussed it. We don't discuss those sorts of things."

"Well, good for you." I say. "Anyway, I've got to go, okay?"

"Okay, have fun on your date tonight."

"I will." I say, hanging up on him.

I don't actually have a date tonight, but it sounded like a good excuse. I do need to get my mind off of Skye, and there's nothing better to get your mind off of one woman than another woman.

I think for a few moments, debating which woman I'm going to call and ask out. There's Olivia, but she loves to hear herself talk, and I have a feeling if I invite her out for dinner, she'll already be planning an engagement. Then there's Popsella. Popsella is a stage five clinger, though, and I don't need that in my life. I rack my brain and come up with Angelica; beautiful, blonde Angelica. She's a model from Lithuania and always a good time. She isn't looking for anything serious, and that's what I need right now.

I scroll through my contacts and press dial once I get to her name. It rings five times before she answers.

"Why, hello there. Is this the handsome Kingston Chase calling me?" she says in her Eastern European accent.

"Hey, darling, how are you?"

"I'm very good. I'm quite surprised to hear from you."

"Why is that?"

"It's been a while," she says.

"I wasn't sure if you were in New York or not. I know your career's been blowing up."

She pushes her shoulders back and tilts her head higher. It's clear she's happy at the compliment. She waves her well manicured fingers in the air, flashing a large diamond ring and tosses back her hair. "Well, that's true. I did just get back from Croatia. I'm in a small movie that was filming there."

"Oh, congrats."

"Thank you. Now, to what do I owe the pleasure, Kingston?"

"I was wondering if you'd like to grab dinner next week."

"Oh, really?" She pauses.

"Yeah, that's kind of why I called. Are you free, or...?"

"Yes, I can be free. Where are we going?"

"Well, I was going to let you have your pick."

"What about dinner at your place?" she says. "I think I'd quite like to become familiar with your new bedroom set."

I freeze for a moment, wondering what she's talking about, and then I remember the last time we went out. We had both been anxious to have sex, but then she wanted to come back to my place so she could wake up to me making her breakfast in bed. I told her that I didn't have a bedroom set and a new one was being delivered, and we'd gone to a hotel instead. I'd almost forgotten about that.

"Yeah. Well, I mean, I don't want you to think that I'm only interested in your body, Angelica. I would love to take you to a nice meal first," I say, not really wanting to make her dinner and have her stay the night.

When women stay the night, it makes me uncomfortable. I hate waking up to them staring at me, to them touching me. It isn't that I don't enjoy their company, I just like being by myself that much more, especially in my own bed.

"Oh, so I take it you still have those same issues, Kingston," she says, with a small sigh.

"I'm not sure what you're talking about, Angelica."

"Your fear of commitment."

"I don't know that I have a fear of commitment."

"Then why, in all the years that I've known you, have you never told me you have a girlfriend?"

"Because I feel like it'd be unfair to all the women in the world."

"What would be unfair, Kingston?"

"To lock me up. I mean, shouldn't everyone have a chance with me?"

"Oh, Kingston," she titters. "You are very American."

"I don't know what that means."

"It means that you're arrogant, that you're pompous, but I let you get away with it because you're very rich, you're very handsome, and you have a big cock."

I chuckle then. "Well, I'm glad that you enjoy your time with me."

"I do, and I'm very much looking forward to meeting Mr. Big Cock again tonight." She whispers in a sultry tone. "Will we be getting another hotel room, or...?"

"Sure," I say.

Part of the reason I like Angelica is that she's so straightforward. It's been over two years since we've seen each other, and yet she still wants me.

"So, I'll make a reservation and I can have a car pick you up?"

"It's fine. I'll probably be getting drinks with my friends before dinner, so send me the address and I'll meet you there."

"Perfect. See you next weekend."

"Bye-bye, Kingston. See you soon. I guess I will go and

get waxed on Wednesday." She squeals like a strangled cat and hangs up.

I stare down at the phone and shake my head.

"Well, she's certainly not leaving much to the imagination, is she?" I mutter to myself as I grin.

I head toward the kitchen and turn on my espresso machine so I can make a coffee.

"Okay, where shall we go to dinner?" I ask myself as I reach for a bag of bread to make some toast.

I have no idea where I'm going to take her. All I know is that it's going to be a good night, and I will the fuck living daylights out of Angelica and completely forget about Skye and her red hair and her fiery green eyes and the way she scowls when she sees me.

My heart thuds for a second as I think of her. She is definitely something, and I don't know what I'm going to do with her. I wonder if she's going to be angry at me forever for the comments I made, even though I was only trying to avoid any potential heartbreak. And if I'm honest with myself, it isn't that I don't want to bang her, it's just that I know the consequences of banging her would be horrible for both of us.

I think about calling her for a moment to explain my thought process in regards to the call the previous day, but I know that would be a mistake. I just need to let it go. I just need to forget that Skye is anything more than my assistant because I need to enforce and remember that I am the boss and she is the employee, and if there is one thing I've learned from experience, it's that you should never sleep with the people that work with you.

That never ends well.

My phone beeps and I pick up when I realize it's Max.

"Yo, what's going on? I'm about to head out."

"Whittaker Matlock is going to be at The Z Club with two of his teammates tonight. I suggest you get your ass down there with some paperwork and try and woo us some new clients."

"I have plans tonight and no paperwork."

"Tell your damn assistant to write some shit up and meet you there." He growls. "This is big money, Kingston. We're talking well over seven figures." His comment makes me freeze. There's nothing I love more than money.

"Fine. I'll see what I can do." I hang up and call Skye, ignoring the slight thrill of excitement I feel as I listen to her phone ringing.

"Yes?" she snaps and I grin into the phone.

"You sound happy to hear from me."

"I'm a better actress than I thought then."

"I need you to go to the office, print off some new client documents, and meet me at Club Z."

"What? Is this a joke?"

"Do I sound like I'm joking?"

"But I have plans tonight."

"Cancel them. You have a job to do."

"But..."

"Do you want this job? This is important Skye."

"I'm so annoyed right now." She sounds pissed. "I have really important plans."

"Change them. I had a hot date tonight and I will have to change it as well. This is life when you work in—."

"Save me the lecture. It's not like we're Superheroes saving the world." She mumbles. "But fine, I will see if I can change my plans."

"Good. Wear something slinky as well. I need you to dress to impress."

"Really?"

"Really. I'll send a car to your place and it will bring you to Club Z. Be ready in an hour."

"Yes boss, no boss, anything you say boss."

"That's what I like to hear."

"You would." She sounds annoyed but I just laugh.

"If we sign Whittaker, I'll give you a fifty-thousand-dollar bonus, how does that sound?"

"Doesn't sound like enough, but I guess I'll accept." The giddiness in her voice belies the fact that she doesn't think it sounds like enough and I know I've got her.

"I'll see you later." I say and hang up. I need to stop teasing Skye and get my mind out of the gutter. Whittaker Matlock is a huge star. If I can sign him to the firm, I know more sports stars will follow. And with them, unimaginable riches. And I'm ready to take my net worth to the next level.

* * *

I look at my watch and tap my foot impatiently against the ground. Skye should have been here ten minutes ago. I'm starting to feel increasingly frustrated that she's late, and anxious about trying to sign Whittaker Matlock. He is the biggest star in the NHL, and I know that I have my work cut out for me.

I let out a small sigh of relief when I see the car pull up and stop outside the club. The driver jumps out, nods at me, and opens the back door. I step forward so that I can greet Skye.

The first thing I see is a long slender leg with a bright red fuck-me heel attached to it. My eyes travel up her beautiful legs and I watch as she gets out. She's wearing a short, tight, black dress, and her hair cascades down her back in ringlets. She's got more makeup on than I've ever seen before, and she looks absolutely stunning. I lick my dry lips as I swallow hard. My eyes are then immediately drawn to her breasts that are almost busting out of the very loose-fitting top.

"Hi," she says. "I have the paperwork." She holds up the folders in her hand. "Do you want it?"

"Sure." I say, taking it from her.

For a few moments, I'm almost speechless. I don't know what to say. I'm taken aback by how beautiful she looks, and my loins stir as I stare at her.

"Here you go, Kingston," she says, waving it in front of my face.

"I got it," I say, snatching it from her. "So you took your time."

"What do you mean I took my time? I had to log in and print the paperwork, and of course we were out of toner, and I had to..." She pauses. "Well, you don't want the full breakdown, I'm sure, but I'm here now."

"I'm glad," I say roughly. "Thanks, McCartney," I say to the driver. "I won't be needing you for the rest of the evening."

"You're welcome, Mr. Chase. Have a good evening. You too, Miss Skye."

"Thanks, McCartney." She beams at him.

He gets into the driver's seat and takes off and we just stare at each other.

"I could kind of get used to having a private driver." She gives me an impish smile. "And yes, that is a hint."

"Hint heard, but not received," I say, grinning at her. "You ready to make our entrance into the club?"

"I mean, I guess," she says. "That's why I'm here, right?"

She tilts her head to the side and I watch as one long curl bounces against the valley between her breasts.

"Sorry, what did you say?" I blink, distracted again.

"I said that I'm here for a particular reason, and I'm not even really sure why, other than to bring you this paperwork, which you probably could have gone to the office and printed yourself."

"You're here because Whittaker Matlock likes beautiful women, and I don't want to approach him by myself and obviously be seeking his business."

"So what, you want to pimp me out to him?"

"No." I chuckle. "We're here on a quasi-date."

"A date?" she practically shrieks. "Oops, sorry." She places her hand in front of her lips. "Is this your way of trying to—"

"It's not a real date, obviously." I cut her off. "It's just for appearances' sake."

"Okay, so we're going on a fake date because...?"

"Because I want Whittaker to think that we just happened to be there, and you just happen to be a huge fan of his, and we just happened to get into a conversation, and I just happened to sign him." I grin. "Comprendo?"

"I guess so, but you are forgetting one thing."

"And what's that?"

"I'm not a fan of his. I don't like ice hockey, I couldn't tell you anything about it."

"And you're an actress, right?" I stare at her.

She presses her lips together. "Yes, I'm an actress, but—"

"Are you a shitty actress or a good actress?"

"Well, what sort of question is that? Who's going to say they're a shitty actress?"

"Exactly, so you're a fairly good actress."

"Hey, that's mean. What do you mean by fairly good?"

"I mean you still work for me full time and you haven't

won an Oscar yet, so I wouldn't say you're exactly up there with the Meryl Streeps and Sandra Bullocks of the world."

"Has Sandra Bullock won an Oscar?" she asks.

"I don't know." I shrug. "But..."

"But what?" she says.

"Fine, you're not a Viola Davis."

"Fine, I'm not Viola Davis," she admits. "But I could be one day if I get some really juicy and meaty roles." She bursts out laughing. "Okay, let's be real. I'm probably never going to be a Meryl Streep or a Viola Davis, but I'm not absolutely shit."

"So then you can work this role tonight?" I ask her hopefully.

"I'll try my best," she says, nodding. "Fine."

"Thank you."

I grab her hand and she looks at me in surprise.

"What's going on?"

"I wanted to show you Whittaker's photo and bio before we go into the bar, so you aren't completely out of your element if we see him."

"Ok." She nods as I show her my phone. "Ooh, he's cute." She squeals and I glare at her.

"You seen enough?"

"Not really. Any shirtless pics?"

"No." I growl. "Come on. I think we should walk into the club holding hands, so when people see us they'll immediately think we have a close connection."

"Fine," she says, holding my hand.

"Also, I wanted to say thank you for coming."

"What?"

"I know you had plans tonight and I'm sorry. Genuinely, I'm sorry that you had to cancel."

"Oh. Well, thank you."

"I hope the person you were meeting wasn't too upset..."

I know I'm prying, but I am curious who she'd been intending to meet.

"They were not happy," she says. "But we were able to reschedule." She nods. "So we'll see."

"So are you going to tell me more about..." I pause as she shakes her head.

"No, I'm not." She smiles sweetly at me. "Shall we make our way inside so that we can get to work?"

"Okay," I say, nodding. "Let's do it."

We head toward the front and a burly security guard looks me over.

"Can I help you?" he asks.

"Yeah, we're here to get some drinks and maybe some appetizers."

"Are you on the list?"

"Sorry, what?" I stare at him.

"The list. This is an exclusive invite-only bar. You can't just get in."

"Oh, what?" Skye says, looking at him with pouted lips. "But he's been promising me all night that he was going to bring me here." She looks up at me. "If we don't get to go into Club Z, we're not going to make love tonight," she says.

I stare down at her and then look over at the security guard.

"Is there nothing that we can do to get me in? Perhaps I'm on the guest list, I'm not sure."

He looks at me for a couple of seconds, and then at Skye. He stares down at my $500 Italian leather shoes, at my $10,000 Rolex, my $20,000 suit, and he nods slightly.

"What do you do?"

"I'm an attorney, a partner at a law firm here in the city."

"Okay. I mean, I can see if we're allowing any guests for the evening." He stares at me. "For a price."

I nod. I pull out my leather wallet from the back of my pocket and take out five crisp $100 bills and slip them into the palm of his hand.

"I would appreciate that very much."

He stares at me and I stare at him. He looks down at his palm and gives me a small little nod and smile.

"I think that there may be one guest spot available." He opens the door. "Have a good evening."

"Thank you."

I usher Skye inside before me and she looks up at me with wide eyes.

"How much money did you just give him?"

"$500." I say.

"Wow, that's a lot of money."

"I would've given him $10,000." I grin at her. "But he doesn't know that."

"You would've given him $10,000 just to get in here tonight?"

"I mean, I do want to sleep with you after all," I say, and she bursts out laughing.

"Very funny."

"What? Maybe it's the truth."

"You just want to speak to Whittaker Matlock so you can get his business."

"That is true, but there may be other perks to the evening."

"Really, Kingston?"

"What? I'm just being honest."

"Come on. Where do we go from here?" she asks as we look down the dark corridor.

"I think that we continue down this path and see where we end up."

"I hope this club isn't creepy," she says, looking up at me nervously.

"What do you mean?"

"I hope there aren't naked women dancing around."

I'm about to make a joke, but I can tell by the concern in her eyes that she's serious.

"Hey, if anything about this makes you uncomfortable, we'll leave."

"What?" She sounds surprised again.

"If anything—"

"No, I heard you," she says, cutting me off. "But really? You would leave?"

"Yes, of course I want to make a connection with Whittaker, and of course he's a very important potential client for the company. However, I do care about your safety and how you feel, and if you're not comfortable, we will leave."

"Oh, wow. Thank you. I didn't expect that you would say that."

"I'm not a jerk all of the time."

"Just some of the time, huh?" she says with a laugh, and I chuckle.

I grab her hand again and we continue walking down the corridor.

The door opens as if by magic and a pretty woman in a purple dress smiles at me. She has white-blonde hair and the most sparkling blue eyes I've ever seen in my life.

"Welcome to Club Z," she says in a Russian accent. "This is your first time?"

"Yes, it is. Both of our first times." I nod over to Skye.

The blonde looks at her and then back at me.

"Welcome. My name is Anastasia. I will be your hostess for the evening."

"Oh, okay." I frown. "Do we not get to seat ourselves?"

I look around to see if I can spot Whittaker anywhere.

"We have very different areas for very different members. You are not a member," she says. "You're just a guest tonight."

"Yeah, I'm a guest, but I'm very interested in becoming a member." I say.

"Well, we shall see. Follow me."

She guides us to the side of the room to a small table.

"You can sit here. This is the Peacock Room." She ushers us to a booth. "You press this button and someone will come out and take your drink order."

"Is this the only bar in Club Z or—"

"No," she says. "But for now, you start here. Understand?"

I nod. "Perfectly. Thank you."

"Very welcome," she says. She touches my upper arm and runs her fingers down the side of my jacket. "Armani, no?" She looks my suit up and down. "Very nice."

"Custom-made," I say. "By the man himself."

"I can tell." She smiles and looks over at Skye. "Have a good evening, madame."

"You too, thanks," Skye says before we sit down. "I think she thinks I'm a prostitute," Skye says out of nowhere, and I burst out laughing.

"Why do you say that?"

"Because you're obviously very well-to-do in your fancy suit with your expensive watch and shoes, and here I am in my knock-off Valentino dress."

"Your what?" I ask.

"It's a knock-off Valentino dress." She grins. "I got it

made in Chinatown, and I just feel like she knew that it wasn't real, and I suddenly feel like Julia Roberts in *Pretty Woman*."

"You shouldn't. You're not a prostitute."

"I know I'm not a prostitute, I just feel like she thinks I was." She sighs. "Anyway, let's get a drink. I really need a drink."

"Sure. What would you like?"

"Maybe a Cosmopolitan."

"Sounds good. I'll get us two."

"You drink cocktails?" she asks in surprise.

"Not generally, but when we're in a place like this, I feel like we should class it up a little bit."

I press the button that Anastasia had pointed out to me earlier and another cute blonde comes rushing up to the table.

"Good evening. What would you like to drink tonight?" she asks in a deep voice and accent I can't place.

"We'd like two Cosmopolitans, please. Unless there is a house special that you recommend?"

"We do have the Club Z, but it is very potent," she says, glancing at me and Skye. "Would you like to try it?"

"Sure." I say. "What about you, Skye?"

"Sure. When in Rome, right?" She grins.

"Of course. So I will get two Club Z specials. Just so you know, they are $1,000 each."

Skye gasps, but I just shrug.

"Sounds fine."

The waitress hurries off and Skye looks at me with wide eyes. "$1,000 drinks, are you crazy?"

"It's the cost of doing business here," I say, shrugging. "Don't worry about it."

"You've already spent like $1,500."

"$2,500, two drinks plus the $500."

"Oh, yeah." She moans. "I'm not that good at math."

"It's a good thing you're not a math teacher then, isn't it?"

"Ha ha," she says, rolling her eyes. She leans back and looks around, then she gasps. "Oh my gosh, that's him."

"Who?" I say, my shoulders stiffening.

"Whittaker Matlock, of course." She nods toward the other side of the room. "He's there with two other guys that look like they might be athletes as well."

I stare in the direction she's nodding in and my eyes narrow. That is, indeed, Whittaker Matlock, but I don't recognize the two men that he's with.

I look at her. "Okay, that is him, good job."

"You're welcome," she says. "So what do we do now?"

"I'm not sure," I say, frowning. "We're seated too far away from him to make casual talk."

"I have an idea," she says.

"What's your idea?"

"Just wait and see."

She jumps up, and before I know what she's doing, she's hurrying to the other side of the room. I watch as she walks past the table, and then doubles back, fawning and gushing over Whittaker.

"What are you doing, Skye?" I mutter under my breath, as I sit here watching her.

She's laughing and playing with her hair, and I can see that she has all of the men's attention. For a few seconds, I'm slightly jealous. For a few seconds, I feel guilty. Am I pimping out my assistant for a client? But no, I hadn't told her to do that. And then, before I know what's happening, Whittaker is shifting on the seat and she's sitting down next to him.

"What did you say to him, Skye?" I mutter under my breath.

I'm about to up and go and approach the table when the waitress comes back with two crystal flutes filled with a bright purple liquid.

"Here are the two Club Zs," she says, placing them on the table. "Just press the button if you need anything else."

"Thank you, I will."

"You're welcome," she says as she backs away.

I take a sip of the drink and I cough immediately. I don't recognize the alcohol that's in the glass, but it tastes disgusting. *What a waste of $1,000*, I think to myself.

My eyes traverse back over to Skye, and now I see she's sitting in Whittaker's lap. I feel myself growing annoyed and angry. She's definitely playing her role a little bit too well. I take another gulp of the drink, because even though I don't like it, $1,000 is a lot of money to spend on something just to not drink it, then I grab Skye's glass and head over to the other side of the room.

"Darling," I say, as I stop next to the table, staring down at a laughing Skye.

I see Whittaker's arms wrapped around her waist and it takes everything in me to not grab her out of his lap.

"I have your drink."

"Oh, thank you," she says. "Whittaker, this is my part-time boyfriend. Honey, this is Whittaker Matlock. He's my favorite NHL player ever."

"Oh." I stare at him.

The man looks up at me with amused eyes. I can tell he thinks that I'm an idiot for leaving my woman alone for a second.

"Nice to meet you, Whittaker. I've followed your career for a number of years. My name's Kingston. I'm a—"

"Hey," he says, nodding, touching Skye on the side of the face as he cuts me off. "Did I tell you yet just how sexy you are, Skye?"

"Yes." She smiles awkwardly and I stiffen as I realize how uncomfortable she seems to be. "But don't say it in front of my part-time boyfriend. I don't want him to be jealous."

"I mean, if he's only part-time, I'm sure he wouldn't mind." Whittaker looks up at me again, his eyes assessing me. "Do you?"

"I'm going to say this nicely, but I kind of do mind that your hands are all over my girlfriend," I say, giving him a toothless grin. "But I know how sexy she is and I know how hard it must be for you to resist. But I'm going to have to ask you to desist." There's an edge to my voice and I know that I will knock him to the ground if he steps out of line anymore than he already has.

This was a stupid idea.

I keep having stupid ideas.

I am too old and too professional for this crap.

And Skye is too special to me to use her like this. The thought makes my heart race for a few seconds.

Why am I feeling this way?

"Sorry, what?" He blinks at me.

Skye's jaw drops as I grab her hand.

"What are you doing?"

"I think that he's getting a little bit too handsy," I grate out.

I'd noticed that Whittaker's right hand was moving up her thigh, and his left hand was moving closer to her breast. There was no way in Hell I was going to let this man feel up Skye.

"It's fine," she says, whispering in my ear. "It's just a game."

"It's not fine," I say. "I'm not going to let this man touch you just so I can sign him as a client."

She blinks slowly and nods. "I mean, it's not like I was going to let him finger me or anything." I glare at her. "Or play with my nipples. Sure, he was trying to grab my breast, but I wouldn't let him slip his hand in."

"We will talk later," I say.

I stare at Whittaker, who is now glaring at me. "You got a problem, man?" he says.

"Yes, I do. My girl is a fan of yours and she wanted to get your autograph, which I'm okay with. I'm even okay with you flirting with her. But I'm not okay with you touching her when you barely know her. That's not acceptable."

He blinks for a few seconds then jumps up, and I'm scared that he's going to deck me. I'm not scared because I think he's going to hurt me, I'm scared because I know if he does punch me, I will fight him back and have him on the ground within minutes, and the last thing I need is to be in the newspaper for beating up Whittaker Matlock. He definitely would not become my client then. He stares at me for a couple of seconds and I wait for the first blow to come, but he bursts out laughing instead. I feel him squeeze my shoulder.

"You're all right, man."

"What?" I say in surprise.

"I like it when a man speaks up for his woman. Yeah, she's cute, and yeah, I would've loved to have had her tonight, but I respect the fact that you spoke up to me."

"Okay." I say, wondering what the hell is going on.

"Most men don't say shit because I'm Whittaker Matlock and I make $50 million a year, sometimes more."

"Okay."

"Men are intimidated by me. I've got it all. The looks,

the money, the cock." He grins as he looks over at Skye. "Honey, you're missing out on a pretty thick hard cock."

Skye blushes and looks down.

"Dude," I say.

"Sorry." He grins. "I was just letting her know. I mean, you guys open to it?"

"Open to what?" I snap.

"Me fucking her."

I take a deep breath and count to five.

"Excuse me?"

"Look, I'm just saying that there are plenty of men that let me their fuck women and like to watch. I don't know if you're one of those dudes."

"I'm not."

He grins. "Okay. Well, if you want my autograph, where's the paper or something?" he asks her.

"I guess I can get one," she says, looking over at me.

I can tell she's uncomfortable, and I feel really bad putting her in this position.

"Hey, dude, my name is Kingston Chase. I'm an attorney for a law firm here in The City, and I know that you're looking for new representation. I'm interested in signing you as a client.

"Oh." He frowns. "Is that what this was about?"

I'm surprised that he doesn't sound angry or pissed off.

"I mean, kind of." I nod.

"Okay. I'm not going to sign any paperwork with you right now, but I guess we can have a meeting next week or something."

I stare at him in surprise. "Really?"

"Really. This is not the weirdest way I've been approached to do business." He laughs. "I like working with people that will act like desperados to work with me. It shows me that you'll do anything that I ask."

"I mean, within the law, of course."

He chuckles. "Of course." He looks back over at Skye. "You're a pretty thing, aren't you?" She blushes again and he chuckles. I feel him wrap his arm around my shoulder and squeeze. "You're lucky to have a pretty one like this." He grins. "But get out of my space. Me and my boys here are talking about something that I don't think you're going to want to hear if you're about to become my attorney."

"As your attorney, it would be better that I know everything about—"

"I don't think you're going to want to hear this," he says. "Plausible deniability. That's the term, right?"

"It is a term," I say, nodding my head.

"Great." He sniffs and I can see that he's studying me. "If I were you, I would go back to wherever you were sitting, because I'm pretty sure that Anastasia will be over here in a couple of minutes and kick you out if you don't leave me alone."

"Okay." I slip him my business card. "Looking forward to hearing from you next week."

"You will," he says.

I grab Skye by the hand and guide her back to the table. I can feel her heart racing as we make our way. We sit back down and she stares at me.

"Whoa, what just happened?"

"I'm actually feeling the same way that you are right now." I shake my head in disbelief. "Did I really just get Whittaker Matlock to agree to come into the office?"

"You did," she says. "After you defended me." Her voice sounds wispy. "You didn't have to do that, you know."

"I did. I put you in this position and I feel bad. You're

not just an object. You're not just a hot, sexy woman that can be talked to any old way." She stares at me, not speaking. "What are you thinking?" I ask her.

"I was just thinking that sometimes you talk to me any old way, like I'm nothing."

I realize that her words are true, and I feel slightly guilty.

"I know, and I—"

"It's okay," she says quickly, her eyes darting away from me. "I kind of like going back and forth with you. I kind of like crossing those lines with you. Maybe because I feel comfortable." She presses her lips together. "You know what I mean?"

I nod slowly, because I do know what she means, and I also don't know how to voice it.

"Shall we finish these drinks and leave?" I say.

"Yeah. I guess we do have paperwork to do."

"Yeah." I stare at her and smile then reach over and grab her hands. "Thank you for being here with me tonight. I'm sorry that I made you cancel your plans. I'm sorry that...you know. Things are weird between us."

"You have nothing to apologize about. It comes with being your assistant." She smiles. "Plus, if you sign Whittaker next week, I'm going to get a huge bonus, and you know what that means?"

"No, what does that mean?" I ask, as my lips twitch.

"That means I am going on an around-the-world trip." She bursts out laughing at the expression on my face. "Don't worry, I'll give you my two weeks notice before I go."

"You better," I say, smiling.

For some reason, I feel comfortable and happy with her. For some reason, I feel more alive than I've felt in a long time, and it has nothing to do with potentially signing Whittaker Matlock.

Chapter Nine

Skye

"I'm so lucky that Camden agreed to push our date back by a week," I remind myself as I apply mascara to my lashes. "If a date had asked me to postpone mere hours before the date, I'm not sure what I would have said."

"You would have been understanding." Elisabetta pops a piece of gum into her mouth. "It's not your fault you had to work."

"I know. I guess that's what happens when you plan dates with law firm closers." I giggle as I remember how impressed Kingston had been when I'd convinced Whittaker to sign with the firm. "I just hope that he thinks I'm worth the wait. How do I look?"

"You look absolutely stunning." Elisabetta gazes at me as I twirl in my white dress. "Beautiful Skye."

"Thank you," I say, as I run my fingers through my silky straight hair. "And thank you for helping me flat iron this. I can't believe how straight we got it."

"You look amazing. I have a feeling tonight is going to be your night. I'm so glad that you made it a dinner date."

"And he's taking me to a top-notch restaurant."

She grins at me. "Camden and Skye sitting in the tree, K-I-S-S-I-N-G."

I groan as she sings.

"First comes love. Second comes marriage. Third comes the baby in the old tin carriage."

"Elisabetta, oh my gosh. This is our first date."

"Yeah, but he's taking you to a really fancy restaurant. I mean, that is a great sign."

"I guess. I just hope that he likes me and he's cute and we get along and he thinks I'm pretty."

"Girl, he's going to think you're beautiful because you are." She smiles at me. "I have a really, really good feeling about tonight. I have a feeling that Camden is going to become your new man."

"You think so?" I ask her, and she nods.

"Yeah, I do. And ask him if he's got any hottie friends for me because I'm looking."

"But what about the ball that your dad is planning for you?"

"Yeah, yeah. When that happens, I'll worry about it then, but I need to get laid. Your girl's got needs."

"Don't we all," I say, giggling. "Okay. I better go. I don't want to be late."

She steps forward and gives me a big hug and a kiss on the cheek.

"You look stunning, Skye, and you know I don't just say that. Have an amazing night. Okay?"

"Thank you," I say, grinning at her. "I am so excited." I grab my handbag and hurry to the front door. "Bye." I give her a quick wave and head out of the building.

"Camden is going to be the one," I mumble under my breath as I make my way down the street. He has to be the one. I mean, I am in need of a one.

I sigh. I feel a little bit desperate as I make my way to the restaurant and I don't really like that feeling. I don't want to be with him just because I want to be with someone. I want to be with him because he is special. I want to be with him because he makes my heart flutter. Kind of like Kingston Chase does.

Don't even think about that man.

I groan as Kingston's face pops into my mind. I can't lie, he's sexy. Really, really sexy. His blue eyes make my heart flutter and his dark hair looks so silky that I just want to run my fingers through it. I want to press his lips against mine and against my skin and in places that he would probably blush if he knew I was thinking about him kissing and touching me there. *I want to do so many dirty things to you, Kingston Chase, but only because you're hot,* I think to myself. *Your personality sucks.*

I think back to the previous evening and I feel mortified yet again. I do not like the person I am when I'm around him. I always become flustered and stupid and angry and nervous and all sorts of things that make me question if I'm absolutely losing my mind.

Focus, Skye, I lecture myself. *Stop thinking about Kingston Chase. He's your boss. Nothing more, nothing less. Tonight is about Camden. Camden Camden Camden. He could be your future husband.*

"Imagine if he's your future husband," I mumble to myself. "And you're thinking about your boss. How embarrassing would that be in twenty years if you had to say, 'hey honey, you know I love you, but that first night we met, I was kind of having dirty thoughts about my boss. But I'm so glad I met you.' That's not going to fly Skye," I lecture myself.

I take a deep breath and try to picture Camden's photos from the dating app. He looks like he's going to be gorgeous. Really, really gorgeous. I'm excited. Maybe one of my dreams is going to come true, or maybe all of them will. Maybe Camden and I will take a trip together. Maybe he'll be interested in traveling across the world. That would be cool and then I'd write a book about our adventures. Maybe *Eat, Pray, Love* number two, but a happy one. One where the relationship works out. One where love conquers all. "Women want to see that," I say to myself. I can just picture a movie being made. *Who would play me?* I think to myself. I try to think of red-headed actresses and my mind goes blank. Julia Roberts is too old. I guess, Emma Stone? I smile to myself. Emma Stone can play me in the movie that's made from the book I write about my adventures with Camden.

Maybe Elisabetta is right. Maybe everything really is falling into place and I don't have to worry about dealing with Kingston on Monday morning. Maybe Camden and I will hit it off and he'll turn out to be a secret billionaire and he'll offer to take me on an all-expenses-paid trip around the world and pay my rent while I'm gone. *That would be amazing*, I think to myself. Though, highly unlikely. Get a grip.

I take a breath. My phone rings and I look down. I'm about to press end to send it to voicemail when I see it's Zara.

"Hey, Zara," I say. "How's it going?"
"Good. Just checking to see how you're doing."
"I'm good. What's going on?"

"I have Lila on the other line. I'm going to connect her. Okay?"

"Okay." I nod. I continue walking as I wait, then I hear a click.

"Hey, are we all connected?" Zara says.

"Hi, I'm here," Lila says.

"Hey, girls. What's going on?"

"We were just calling to see how you're doing," Zara says, and Lila starts giggling.

"What's so funny?"

"What happened with you and Kingston the other night?" she asks. "I heard through the grapevine that—"

"Uh-huh. Through the grapevine," I say. "Like your man is now the grapevine?"

She shrugs and winks, her eyes laughing. "You got me. Well, anyway, I heard that the other night was interesting."

"Interesting? What else did Max tell you?"

"Well, he said that you and Kingston had a little bit of back and forth at the bar and you were trying to pretend that you were not interested by hooking up with some gay guy or something."

"That is not exactly what happened. I was chatting with this guy at the bar who I thought was interested. Remember? I told you about him."

"Vaguely," Zara says. "The guy you told me about that you thought really wanted you, but actually wasn't?"

"Yeah, let's just say he was not interested in me in that way and it all came out in the open when that douche bag Kingston was there, and of course he thought it was hilarious while he was there with his supermodel date or whoever she was."

"He's not dating anyone," Lila says. "And from what

Max says, he's as single as can be. He does not do relationships."

"That does not surprise me," I say. "Because who would really want to be in a relationship with that douche bag?"

"Oh no, you can't stand him, huh?" Lila says as she gives me a knowing look that makes me think she's reading my mind.

"More than that. Anyway, I'm about to get to the restaurant where I'm meeting my date, Camden. Can I talk to you girls later?"

"Oh, yeah. I forgot that was tonight," Lila says. "Have fun."

"Have so much fun," Zara says. "I hope it works out."

"Thanks girls."

I hang up and smooth down my hair. I'm pissed all over again. What the hell is Kingston telling people about me and him and our relationship and everything that went down? I don't want people thinking that I'm into his sorry ass and that I'm doing stuff because I'm being reactionary to him saying he isn't interested in me.

I stop outside the restaurant and take a deep breath, lick my lips, and step inside.

"Stop thinking about that jackass," I mumble to myself.

"Holy shit, Batman. Is that you, Skye?"

I blink and look to my right. There's a very tall, very skinny guy with a lot of acne and a huge Adam's apple staring at me.

I look around and shrug slightly. Is this Camden?

"Hi. Are you Camden?" I say softly, as I take a step closer to him and narrow my eyes. This guy does not look anything like the photos.

"Hey. Yeah, it's me. Nice to meet you, Skye." He looks

me up and down and whistles. "I like that dress. Though, it's a bit presumptuous, don't you think?"

"Sorry, what are you talking about?" I ask him, slightly confused.

"White? Are you trying to make me think of you in a wedding dress? This is our first date, girl. I'm not about to propose just yet." He throws his head back and starts laughing like he told the most funny joke in the world.

"Oh, funny. No, it's just a dress that I like." I look him up and down. He's wearing black jeans and a white shirt. "So you look a little bit different," I say, staring into his eyes.

I try to ignore the big pimple on the end of his nose. What the fuck is going on here? He does not look anything like the Camden in the photos.

"Hey, you need to stop checking me out. You look like you just want to get me into your bed," he says, grinning as he steps forward to give me a hug. "I mean, I'm down for that, but I'm more than just a piece of meat." He chuckles and blows into my ear.

I want to recoil, but I don't. "I was just thinking you look very different from your photos."

"Better, huh?" He grins. "I've heard that."

"You just looked kind of different." I don't want to say he looked more handsome, more built. That he didn't have acne.

"Yeah, I used those AI filters." He shrugs. "I wanted people to see me from all different perspectives."

"Huh?" I say, gazing at him in confusion.

"I mean, don't they say show your ugliest pictures online so when people meet you they're impressed?" He grins and I try to ignore his yellow teeth.

"Yeah, I guess, but don't AI pictures generally make you look better? Kind of like filters?"

His eyes narrow as he looks me up and down. "I was about to say, I was wondering if you had a filter in your photos. Don't get me wrong, I love big boobs and a big ass, but I thought you were going to be a little bit slimmer."

My jaw drops as I stare at him. There was no way in hell he was saying this to me. "Well, I actually thought that you were—"

"Is that you Skye?" A familiar deep voice sounds from behind me and I freeze.

"Oh my gosh," I mumble under my breath as I turn around.

There is Kingston, standing there with a beautiful blonde bombshell. His eyes from me over to Camden and back. He's grinning.

"Wow. Don't you clean up nicely."

"Thank you," I say.

"Who's this?"

Kingston takes a step toward us. I notice that the blonde is clinging to his arm and she's not looking particularly happy to see me.

"This is my date, Camden," I say, trying not to groan.

"Yo, what's up dude?" Camden says. "Whoa, you are *hot*." He looks at the blonde. "Yeah, girl, I like what you're working with." He stares at her cleavage, which is practically busting out of her dress. We can all see her nipples poking through as well. "I definitely appreciate when my girl wears no bra," Camden says as he looks back at me in my dress.

I definitely have a bra on me and I'm glad that I do at this point. Kingston's eyes narrow and he frowns slightly.

"Are you guys dating? Like boyfriend-girlfriend or..."

"Nah, this is our first date," Camden says with a chuckle. "To be honest, I'm only on the app to hit it and quit it, but..."

He grins. "You never know what could happen, right, Skyeus?"

I press my lips together. I have no idea why he's calling me Skyeus and I vow to tell him to shut the fuck up, but I don't want to let Kingston know how pissed off I am.

"Oh, I see." Kingston stares at Camden and then at me. "So this is date number one?"

"It's our first date," I mumble, trying not to flinch. "We were just about to go in for dinner."

"I see," Kingston says, looking at his date, then looking at me, then looking at Camden.

Camden slips his arms around my waist and I feel his hand reaching down to my ass and he squeezes. "Hey, plumpity plump plump." He grins. "You want to know something, Skyeus?"

"No," I say, as I take a step forward.

"I like big butts and I cannot lie." He grins and I stifle a groan. "I know you didn't ask me this, but I figured we'd talk about it tonight, but I like to hit it from behind. That's my favorite position."

Kingston's eyes widen and I see him staring at me before he looks back at Camden, narrowing them.

"You think that's really appropriate for a first date?" he asks Camden in a gruff voice and I shiver at his tone. He reminds me of a lion right before he roars.

"What? I believe in honesty."

"Do you though?" I ask him. "That's why you used AI photos on your profile?"

"What are you trying to say? You've brought that up several times." He looks annoyed. "Wait. Are you trying to say I don't look as good as my photos or something? I mean, I wasn't going to say that you looked like you were 110 pounds in your photos and in person you're looking like you're 200."

"Excuse me?" My jaw drops. "I am not 200 pounds, thank you very much."

"Okay, I'm just saying. With that badonkadonk on you."

This man is going to see my right hook in T minus five seconds. If he says one more word, I will show him that Mike Tyson has a redheaded daughter that doesn't play.

"Shall we share a table?" Kingston asks me as if he's unsure as to my answer. I'm surprised to hear something other than confidence in his tone.

I stare at him for a couple of seconds, blinking. Is he crazy? Does he really think I want to stay? "I think that I'm just going to go home," I say, shaking my head. "I don't know that this is going to work for me, Camden."

He holds his hands up in the air. "Hey, man. I'm sorry. I'm sorry. I was just nervous because I saw you in that white dress and you had me thinking that you were thinking we're going to get married when all I'm thinking about is getting some. But I'm not trying to be rude or crude or make you feel uncomfortable and please, let me buy you dinner. I mean, we had such great conversation and—"

"Come on Skye," Kingston says. "Why don't you let the nice man buy you dinner?" His lips twitch and I can tell he's deliberately being a jerk. We both know there is nothing nice about this twat.

I stare at him through narrowed eyes. "Because."

"Because what? You got better plans tonight? I think it will be quite enjoyable for the four of us. Don't you think so, Angelica?"

She frowns slightly, her very red lips pouting. "But I thought tonight was going to be about us getting reacquainted, my darling Kingston. It's been so long."

"And we will get reacquainted," he says with a slight nod. Then he looks back at me with an S.O.S. in his eyes. "I think a double date would be quite fun."

"Okay," I say, nodding slightly.

Maybe Kingston isn't doing this just to help me. Maybe he wants me to help him as well.

"Shall we go and check the tables?" Kingston offers, grabbing my arm. "Angelica, why don't you and Camden stay here for a few moments and Skye and I will check the reservation."

"Okay," she says, looking annoyed.

Kingston guides me towards the maître d'.

"So you and Camden, huh?"

"You and Angelica, huh?"

"At least she didn't lie about her appearance."

"Yeah." I make a face. "Can you believe that jackass said I was 200 pounds?"

"Nope, you don't look an ounce over 100."

I giggle slightly as I shake my head. "That's not true. I'm definitely not 100 pounds, but I'm not 200. I'm like, 150. Okay, maybe 160." Why am I talking about my weight? I've seriously lost the plot.

"Nothing wrong with that," he says with a smile. "You also didn't have to tell me, but just in case you were interested, I lift 350 pounds so I got you, anytime you need me to get you."

"Uhm, thanks. I'm just offended, and my ass is not even that big."

He looks me up and down in the dress. "I mean you don't have a flat ass," he smirks. "Which is good."

"Thanks, I guess."

"You look very beautiful, Skye," he says softly, almost like he's dumbfounded. "And your hair, it looks different."

"I straightened it out for the day. I cannot believe I wasted my time doing that." I don't know why I feel so self-conscious about my hair. Or why my heart is racing like I'm about to be crowned Ms. America.

"I like it curly, but it looks really nice straight." He stares into my eyes and the intensity of his gaze warms my insides. "Chin up. It's not like you were going to marry the man," he says, chuckling slightly.

"That's not even funny. He's such a douchebag. Why do I always meet douchebags?"

"I don't know." He shrugs. "Maybe because you haven't met a man like me yet."

I raise a single eyebrow. "No comment. Anyway," I say. "Why do you want to have a double date when you're with someone like Angelica?"

"To be honest? she is a lot more needy than I remember. Besides, I just wanted to have a fun thing and she's already talking about diamond rings from Tiffany's."

"What?" I say, grinning. "She's your girlfriend or...?"

"No." He shakes his head. "She's someone I went on a couple of getaways with a couple of years ago and I just gave her a call to see if she wanted to hang out."

"I see." My mind is wondering when he says a couple of dates a couple of years ago, did they just go to dinner, or did they do more? I bite down on my lip.

"What is it?" he asks.

"Nothing," I say, shaking my head quickly. "I just..."

"You just what?"

"I was just wondering something."

"Wondering what?"

"You know, if you guys..." I open my eyes wide and he bursts out laughing.

"Oh, Skye, you know I'm a man, right?"

I feel jealousy surge through me. So he and Angelica have slept together and now they're on another date. Were they going to sleep together tonight? I try not to think about it. I don't want to think about it. I don't want to picture him with another woman, which is crazy because he's my boss and it's not like he's my man.

"I mean, good for you. She's very beautiful." I nod.

"I don't think I'm going to go down that road with her again though," he says, smirking. "Not that that's any of your business."

"Not that I wanted to know anyway," I say.

"Sure you didn't," he says. "So, we combining the reservations?"

I stare at him for a couple of seconds before I nod slightly.

He grins. "So we have a little bit of a truce?"

"For tonight," I say. "I'm still mad at you."

"As you should be." He grins. "But I am sure you are quite happy that I was here to save you from your horrible date tonight."

"I didn't need saving. I was about to leave, but I am hungry, so I'll take a free meal and some drinks and enjoy the night as best as I can."

"So is that all this night is about for you then? A free meal and free drinks?"

"I mean, obviously that's not what I was hoping for when the night started, but..." I sigh. "It is what it is. I guess Elisabetta was wrong once again."

"Oh? Why? What did she say?"

"She said she had a feeling that tonight was going to be my night and that he was going to be the one." I roll my eyes. "He's definitely not the one."

"So you're looking for the one, huh?" Kingston says

softly, looking me up and down. "You're looking for your mister forever?"

"I don't know about that," I say, shrugging, looking away from him. I don't want to confess everything about my life to this man who is still quite an asshole. Just because he's being nice to me today doesn't mean much.

"Fine," he says, holding up his hands. "You don't have to tell me. But if you are looking for the one, then I suggest you don't set up dates with people like Camden."

"I didn't know he was going to be that much of a douche bag. I didn't know he lied about his photos and I did not know that—" I sigh. "Why does it matter? I just don't have good luck with guys."

"Well, maybe your luck will change."

"Maybe," I say, shrugging. "Anyway. Let's get some drinks and let's get this party started because tonight, all I want to do is get fucked up."

I'll start my unofficial photography business on another night.

Chapter Ten

Kingston

Skye is pretending to laugh at something Angelica is saying, but I can tell that she's uncomfortable. Her date, Camden is an even bigger douche than he'd initially appeared and I feel guilty for convincing her to stay. I'm not even sure why I did. Okay, maybe that's a lie.

She'd taken my breath away when I'd seen her standing there in her white dress. I've never seen her looking quite like that. She's beautiful no matter what she does with her hair or what she wears, but she's absolutely stunning tonight. And it's clearly wasted on Camden.

"So I said to Nick, 'you can't hog all the coke, you're not the only one that wants to get high.'" Camden slams his fist on the table as he chuckles at his overly long story. "So he turns to me and says, in his best Tony Montana voice." He pauses and looks over at Skye. "He's from Scarface."

"I know who Tony Montana is," she says through gritted teeth.

"He was played by Al Pacino." Camden presses his

fingers to his thumb and moves his hand up and down. "He—"

"So, Angelica, how was Europe?" I cut Camden off as I talk to my date. "Tell us about your latest trip."

"I had so much fun in Prague." She leans forward and plays with her long hair. "I met two men from Denmark and they showed me what it means to be a Viking." She presses her hand to her lips. "Oops, didn't mean to make you jealous." She winks. "Or did I?"

"So then the tall, sporty football player." Angelica pauses and licks her lips. "He tells me to get on all fours." She pauses slightly, as she arches her back. "Sorry. I'm not making you uncomfortable, am I Kingston?" She gives him fuck me eyes and I want to tell her that we can all tell exactly what she's trying to do, but I keep my mouth shut.

I look at her and don't say anything. I can see that Camden's eyes are glued to her and that he's absolutely loving the conversation. I don't want to be rude and tell Angelica that I couldn't care less how many men she did in Prague. I can tell from Skye's look that she's in shock and not sure what to think of the situation.

"Oh my gosh. Then what happened?" Camden says, almost gawking. "Did you have a threesome?"

"Well, women don't tell their secrets," she says, playing with her blonde hair and winking at him.

"Holy shit, Batman," he says. "I'd love to have a threesome. I mean, especially with someone as gorgeous as you."

Angelica giggles slightly. "Well, I'm sure your friend here would be more than willing." She looks over at Skye. "I do believe the homely women are much more likely to—"

"She's not homely," I interrupt Angelica, and she frowns at me.

"Excuse me?"

"She's not homely." I look over at Skye. "She's a beautiful woman."

"If you like the sort that looks like they came in on the last train." She looks Skye up and down in disdain. "Where did you get your dress?"

"Does it matter?" Skye asks.

"I'm just curious." Angelica sniffs. "It's weird that you're at a nice restaurant in New York City with a very handsome man and you chose to wear that? It looks like it came from Goodwill. Or are you from Idaho? Is it a potato sack?"

"Even if it did come from Goodwill, I see nothing wrong with that, but I got it on Amazon."

"Amazon?" Angelica titters. "Like the website online? You bought a dress on Amazon?"

"Yeah. Do you have a problem with that?" Skye says, starting to sound incensed.

"I mean, who buys their dresses on an online website? What did that cost you, like five dollars?"

Skye presses her lips together and looks over at me as if to say, "I hate you."

"That's enough, Angelica," I say, staring at my date. "That's uncalled for."

"What? I'm just saying maybe you should pay her a bit more if she can only afford to wear dresses like that."

"I kinda agree. I wasn't going to say anything," Camden says. "But I was thinking you'd..." He pauses and sips some of his beer.

"You were thinking what?" Skye says, standing up. "You know what? Why don't the three of you enjoy your dinner and have a threesome or do whatever you want to do because I'm out of here." She looks down at me. "And do not call me. Do not text me. I will see you on Monday morning."

She leaves the table and I stare at Angelica and then at

Camden. "Excuse me a second." I jump up and follow behind Skye. I grab her by the wrist and pull her to me.

"What are you doing?" she says, glaring at me, her eyes flashing.

"You're mad at me?" I realize I'm still holding her wrist. "Sorry, I didn't mean to grab you like that."

"Yeah, I'm mad at you. I should have just left as soon as I realized Camden was a dick. But no, you convinced me to stay and now your stupid girlfriend has been insulting me the entire evening and—"

"She's not my girlfriend," I interrupt her.

"Well, you slept with her."

I stare at her for a couple of seconds. "Years ago."

"Yeah, and you're not going to bang her again tonight?"

I look down at her and shake my head. "She's not the one I'm interested in banging," I say softly.

Her eyes widen slightly and she gasps. "I know you're not trying to imply what I think you're trying to imply," she says, her face going a delightful color of red.

"What do you think I'm trying to imply?"

"You're not trying to say that you want to bang me, are you? Especially not after the conversation that we had just yesterday when you told me that—"

"Do you ever shut up Skye?" I say, leaning toward her, my lips so close to hers. I want to kiss her. I want to taste her.

"You can't talk to me like that."

"But I just did," I say softly.

"You're my boss. You can't…"

"I can't what? You can't tell me that you haven't thought about me kissing you at least once."

"Kingston Chase, are you crazy? Literally just yesterday—"

"Literally just yesterday I said something that I shouldn't have said, and tonight I'm saying something else that I also probably shouldn't say. But if you're upset because you think I'm going to take Angelica to my home and bang the living daylights out of her, that's not going to happen. She's an old friend that I may or may not have hooked up with in the past, but she's not the one that I've been staring at all evening wondering what she tastes like."

Skye licks her lips nervously. "Super unprofessional."

"I know, and that's why I'm not going to do anything about it. But you've had a shitty evening and I figured why not make you feel better about your night?"

Her jaw drops. "What? You think you telling me that you want to bang me is going to make me feel better about my disastrous date?" Her lips twist. "You are so full of yourself."

"But there's a little smile on your face," I say. My finger runs up her wrist and I can feel her heart racing. "It's okay to be attracted to me."

"I'm not attracted to you." She blinks.

"You know that's a telltale sign."

"What are you talking about? What's a telltale sign?"

"Every time you lie, you blink and look away and your nose twitches every so slightly."

"My nose does not twitch."

"It does. Just like a little bunny rabbit," I say. "I've noticed it."

"You have?"

"Yeah. I am pretty observant. Just like I've noticed you checking me out."

"I'm not checking you out, Kingston. I..." She presses her lips together and her nose twitches slightly. She glares at me. "Fine. I have perhaps admired the clothes that you wear. The *clothes*, not you in particular. It could be any man in the clothes that you wear. I just think that you have a nice sense of fashion." She licks her lips again. "Sue me."

"I don't think it would be worth suing you seeing as you don't have much money." I grin.

"Really?"

"Sorry. Too soon?"

"Yes." She takes a deep breath. "I'm not going back to that table, by the way. I'm leaving."

"But aren't you hungry?"

"Yeah. I'm going to grab a slice of pizza and go home and hang out with my roommate."

I stare at her for a couple of seconds before looking back at the table. Angelica and Camden seem to be flirting. "Let's go then."

"What?" Skye looks at me in shock. "What do you mean let's go? Your date is waiting on you."

"And maybe I am over the date."

"You're not going to tell her?"

I stare down at her, my eyes light with glee. "I can, or I can let them enjoy a date together." I shrug because I don't really care.

Skye's eyes widen. "You would just leave your date like that?"

"She was rude to you. I don't like people being rude to those I..." I pause.

"To those you what?"

"To those who work for me," I say quickly. "You're my assistant, and as such, you deserve respect and no woman that I take on a dinner date is going to disrespect my assistant."

"Yeah. Okay," she says. "Just you, huh?"

"I mean, I don't find that I disrespect you. I try to be honest with you."

"I guess." She shrugs and makes a little face and a feeling of shame washes through me.

"If I have disrespected you and hurt your feelings, I'm sorry. I know I'm not perfect—."

"You can say that again."

"I'm trying to be a better man." I'm not going to say *for you*. I'm not going to be some Hallmark Channel sap, but the sentiment is the same. I feel like I've let my macho chauvinistic humor allow me to treat her like a piece of meat and I don't want to be that man anymore. I want to show her that, while I find her sexy as hell, I still want to be the sort of man that sees her mind first.

"You're not the worst man ever." She grins. "You're not the best, but you're definitely not the worst."

"Come on." I grab her by the arm and we leave the restaurant. We step outside and she bursts out laughing.

"I cannot believe we just left them."

"Why not? They deserve each other."

"I guess so. So you really didn't have any plans to sleep with her tonight?" she asks me, and I just stare into Skye's green eyes.

The fact of the matter is, when I'd contacted Angelica, I hadn't really had any plans. If sex had happened, I wouldn't have been upset, but it wasn't like that was something I'd been looking for. For some reason though, I don't want to tell Skye that. I don't want to tell Skye that the only reason I invited Angelica out was to get Skye out of my mind. But as soon as I'd seen her in her white dress and her slinky heels, all thoughts of Angelica had vanished.

"I don't know what you want me to say," I say. "Had you thought about hooking up with Camden tonight?"

"I never hook up on a first date," she says, shaking her head. "Never."

"Second date?" I ask curiously.

"Nope."

"Third date?" I ask in surprise.

"Nope."

"So what are we talking here? Three months, four months?"

"Nope." She gives me a coy little smile. "And it's none of your business anyway."

"I'm curious though. Are you a—"

"I'm not a virgin," she says, glaring at me. "Why? Do I look like a virgin?"

"I don't know what a virgin looks like." I shrug. "I just didn't think you were old-fashioned."

"I like a man to woo me," she says. "I like to know that when I give myself to a man, it's because he respects me for my mind, my body, and my soul. I like to know that—"

"That sounds kind of unrealistic," I say, laughing.

"Well, that's kinda rude. Are you calling me unrealistic for wanting a man to respect and love me?"

I frown at the hostility in her tone. "No, sorry, that came out incorrectly. I just meant to say that most men aren't thinking of your mind and soul when they want to bang. I'm not saying that's right." I frown. "Maybe I'm just saying that many of us men are douches." I run my fingers through my hair as my head pounds. Have I been one of those douches my whole life? I suddenly feel extremely uncomfortable at the reality of my own thought processes when it comes to love and sex. "I want you to find what you want. I'm just saying there are a lot of men who will not offer that."

"So you're saying that wanting the entire package is asking too much?"

"No, I'm just saying that sometimes you meet someone and the chemistry is right and the passion is there and all you want to do is rip off their clothes. You're not thinking about anything else. You know?"

"No," she says, shaking her head, but I can see her staring at my lips.

"You want to go and grab that pizza now?" I ask her.

"I mean, sure." She blinks. "So, have you had a lot of one-night stands?"

"One-night stands?" I asked her. "Where did that come from?"

"Well, if you just follow your passion and want to rip people's clothes off right away and you don't really do relationships, I'm figuring you have a lot of one-night stands."

I stare at her for a couple of seconds. "I can't say that I've had a lot." I reach over and touch the side of her face. "But I can't say that I've had none. You're telling me you've never had a one-night stand?"

"Not because I couldn't if I wanted to," she says, blinking. "I just don't have any interest in that." She bites down on her lip. "So, you going to buy me some pizza now or what?"

"Sure. Pizza and shots?"

"You just want to get me drunk," she says, giggling slightly.

"I just want to make you forget your horrible date with Camden."

"Well then you need to get me a lot of shots because it's going to be a long time before I forget that jackass."

"Yay," I say, raising my hands in the air.

"What are you doing?" she asks me suspiciously.

"I'm just happy to hear you call someone a jackass that isn't me."

"Oh." She wrinkles her cute little nose and I can tell she thinks I'm funny because her eyes light up in that way that tells me she's laughing inside. "You're stupid. You know that, right?"

"Is that any way to speak to your boss?" I wink at her. "You do know I got a perfect 180 on the LSAT."

"Maybe not, but right now I'm not thinking of you as my boss." She sticks her tongue out at me. "And just because you have book smarts, it doesn't mean you have street smarts."

"What are you thinking of me as?" I lean forward and catch her eye. I want to stroke her face, but I don't want to be creepy. I can't tell her that my love language is touch. Not that it matters. Because we are most certainly not in love.

"I don't know." She shrugs. "My friend for the evening who's going to buy me pizza and copious amounts of alcohol."

"You know that could lead to trouble, right?" I ask her, a glint in my eyes.

"I think that I'll be okay. I can resist your advances."

"Really? Who said there were going to be any advances?"

"Well, it seems to me that you want me," she says.

"Oh, okay. It seems to me that *you* want *me,* but don't worry, I can resist your advances as well."

"Really? You can resist my advances? Not that I'm going to make any, but..."

"But what? You don't think I could?"

"I bet you if I told you I wanted you tonight, I could have you."

"Really? You think you could have me tonight if you really wanted?"

"Yeah, I do," she says, nodding. "I don't want you, so I'm not even going to try, but if I did want you, I could have you."

"I don't think so," I say, shaking my head. "Remember, you're my assistant."

"Yeah, and?"

"And I like to keep things professional. I've already told you that. I mean, I'm honest that I find you sexy and attractive and if you weren't my assistant, I'd fuck the living daylights out of you, but I'm not going to cross that line with you, no matter how much you beg me."

"I'm not going to beg you. I wouldn't need to beg you."

"Well, it's a good thing you're not even going to try because I wouldn't want to upset you."

"How would you upset me?"

"By telling you no." I lick my lips.

"You wouldn't tell me no if I really wanted you," she says, her green eyes staring into mine. "I feel like if I really wanted you, I could have you."

"I guess we'll never know," I say. "It's a good thing that you don't really want me."

She presses her lips together. "You really think you're something, don't you, Kingston Chase?"

"No," I say. "Now, come on. Let's go and get that pizza and let me get to learn more about you, Skye. I have a feeling that we're going to become much better friends."

Chapter Eleven

Skye

"This pizza is delicious." I'm almost singing as I stuff my face with pepperoni and mushroom pizza. I lick my lips and look over at Kingston, who is staring at me with a bemused expression on his face. His blue eyes are dazzling and I try not to shiver at the glance that he's giving me. I feel really comfortable in his company and I'm putting it down to the three glasses of wine that I've already had and the fact that he was super nice to leave the restaurant with me.

"It is pretty good pizza. I'm glad you're enjoying it." He nods as he reaches for another slice. "Do you still want to order those breadsticks that you were talking about?"

"Is that an actual question?" I ask him, groaning.

"Yeah, it is. You said you wanted breadsticks as well as pizza."

"I didn't realize this pizza was going to be so huge." I lick my lips. "I mean, I'm hungry, but I don't know that I can eat breadsticks as well, even though they look absolutely delicious. That marinara dipping sauce?" I nod over to another table. "Well, I can smell it from here. It feels like I'm in Italy."

"Oh, you've been to Italy?" he asks.

"No," I say reluctantly, taking another bite of my pizza. "But not because I don't want to. It's definitely on my list of places to go."

"Oh? Anywhere in particular?"

"Well, I want to go to Roma and Sicily and Milan and Florence and Tuscany and..." I pause. "Well, almost everywhere in Italy, and then France and Greece and Spain and Portugal. Oh, and the UK, of course, and then Denmark, Sweden, Norway."

"Oh, so you want to go all over Europe." He looks impressed as he grabs another slice of pizza. "You're a Europhile?"

"I'm just a travelphile. I want to go all over Europe and then I want to go to Africa, North Africa, and mainland Africa. I have heard that the safari in Kenya and Uganda is amazing. And then I want to go gorilla trekking and maybe down to South Africa to see penguins. Even though I do want to go to Antarctica as well to see penguins, but that's so expensive and I don't know that..." I pause and sigh apologetically. "Sorry, I'm just rambling now."

"Not at all." He looks at me keenly. "So you are a travel bug, huh?"

"Not really, though I want to be." I sigh a long, deep sigh. "It's always been my dream to travel the world, but I haven't really been anywhere yet." I wrinkle my nose. "It's on my list, but..."

"Your list?" he asks, an eyebrow arched. "Sorry, I know you mentioned it before, but I didn't process what you were saying before."

"Yeah, my dream goal list. I want to"—I hold up my fingers—"one, travel all around the world. Maybe take a year off and just see everywhere I can see. And then I would love to meet the man of my dreams and fall in love and have a fairy tale romance. And three, write a book about my travels and my love and have it become a bestseller and then a movie and..." I giggle again. "Well, you know. They say that you should dream big."

"Yeah." He nods. "So when are you going on this big adventure?"

"I don't know yet." I grab my wine and take another sip. "That's why I've been working so much. I'm trying to save money. The signing bonus from Whittaker will certainly help."

"Oh, the truth comes out." he says with a mocking smile. "And that's why you work for me, then you work on the weekend, and what else?"

"I had a weekend job that I would start on Fridays," I finally admit to him. "So no, I wasn't going on a hot date."

"Oh I see. Well good for you."

"You know I lost that job." I scowl at him.

"Yes, I do. But at least you still work for me."

"I'm going to get another job. I had this idea where I'm going to be a photographer."

"Oh? Of babies? Weddings?" he questions.

"No, a professional selfie taker. Argh, that's not the right name, but—"

"Sorry, what?" He blinks at me. "A professional selfie taker? Maybe I'm not understanding what you mean by that."

"Let me try and explain. You know when you go out and you see people taking selfies?"

"Yeah?"

"And you know how hard it is to get the right angles and the right light?"

"Not really." He shakes his head.

"Well, trust me, it's really hard, especially for a woman. Women know you hold the camera up and you look down. That way, you look slimmer. But a lot of men, they don't get it. And even friends who are haters don't get it. But as a professional selfie taker, I know the right angles to hold the camera."

"Okay, so you're going to take selfies with people?"

"No. Basically, people who are taking selfies, I will take the photo for them instead."

He looks confused, "So then it's not a selfie."

"Well, no, it's not a selfie because I'm not going to be in it, but I'm going to replace the selfie with my photography skills."

"Okay, cool. And what sort of camera are you using?"

"I'm not going to be using any professional camera. I'll be using their phones, but maybe I'll get one of those Polaroid cameras? But then you can't really do much with them and you can't really post those images online, which is primarily what a lot of people are taking selfies for, to post and show their friends and family. Look at the life I'm living. I'm living my best life. Be jealous." I bite down into my pizza again and lick my lips. "You know what I mean?"

"Not really. I don't take many selfies and I certainly don't post them on social media to say, 'Look at me. I'm living my best life.'"

"That's because you don't want all your women knowing that you're with another woman," I say, smirking as I sip my wine again. I watch as he picks up the wine bottle and empties the last of the Pinot Noir into my glass.

"Do you want another?"

"I shouldn't," I say as I nod.

"Is that a yes or a no?"

"I shouldn't." I nod again.

"You shouldn't, but you're nodding."

"I'm saying I shouldn't, but get another bottle, Goofy," I say with a grin and he bursts out laughing.

"You're different when you're drunk."

"I'm not drunk," I counter. "I am just tipsy."

"Well, you're different when you're tipsy."

"Don't think that means you're going to have your wicked way with me."

"I think we've already decided that neither one of us is going to have our wicked way with the other."

"I could totally have my wicked way with you if I wanted to," I say, leaning forward and reaching over. I press my finger against his lips and rub my thumb against his lower lip.

He stares at me, his blue eyes hardening. "What are you doing?"

"Just feeling your lips to see if they're as soft as they look."

"And are they?" he asks in a gruff voice.

"They feel soft, but I don't know if they would be soft to kiss," I lick my lips and swallow. My throat is dry.

"And is that something you want to find out?" His voice is soft, low and breathy.

"Maybe, maybe not. Maybe I'll find someone else to kiss tonight." I look around the restaurant. "There are a lot of cuties here."

"There are," he says, though he doesn't look around.

"Are you hoping to kiss a hot woman tonight?"

He shakes his head.

"There are plenty of good-looking women here," I say,

staring toward the bar. There's a group of three women that keep looking at Kingston and they're kind of getting on my nerves.

"I'm sure there are," he says. Still, he doesn't look around."

"You're not even looking."

"I don't need to look," he says. "I'm here with you and we're enjoying pizza and wine and that's all that matters.

"Really? If I told you there was a hot brunette staring at you, looking like she wanted to eat you, you wouldn't want to know what she looked like?"

"Nope," he says, grinning. "Why? Are you telling me you want me to look? Are you telling me you want me to—"

"I'm not telling you anything," I say. "I'm just saying..." I grin. "You're kind of cute when you're not being all bossy and annoying."

"Bossy and annoying, huh?" He smirks. "When am I bossy and annoying?"

"When we're in the office and you're telling me what to do."

"Oh, you mean when I am acting like your boss?"

"Yeah. You're bossy when you act like my boss and you can be grumpy. Shit, I didn't know men could be as grumpy as you."

"I don't think I'm grumpy. I just think—"

"You're grumpy. Trust me." I laugh. "You know, this is really nice," I say sitting back, all of a sudden feeling nostalgic.

"What's really nice?"

"Just being here, eating pizza, drinking wine, hanging out. The evening started out kind of shit with Camden and if I'm honest, it didn't improve when I saw you."

"'Thank you." He gives me a hurt look.

"Oh, come on now. After the conversation we had the other day?"

"I get it. You were like, 'Oh no. There's my jerk face of a boss.'"

"Exactly." I laugh. "But you were kind of cool telling off Camden and leaving Angelica in the restaurant." I give him a small smile. "And this place is cool and it's just nice chatting and...you know."

"And not trying to seduce each other," he says with a wink.

"And not trying to seduce each other," I agree, laughing. "You going to get that additional bottle of wine or what?"

"I've already nodded at the waiter and he's bringing one," he says with a smirk. "You just didn't notice."

"Oh, well, thank you."

"You're welcome. So you want to travel the world?"

"Yeah, I do. What about you? What are your dreams and goals?"

"My dreams and goals? Well, I want to have the most successful law firm in The City."

"You guys are practically there already," I say.

"We are." He nods. "We're not number one yet, but if things keep going as they are, we will be."

"Is that really your only dream now?" I push, surprised. "To be successful at work?"

He stares at me for a couple of seconds. "Not really. When I was younger, I used to want to be in a rock band."

"Oh, really?"

"Yeah. To be clear this was when I was like fourteen years old and I thought I had an inkling of talent."

"You're telling me you're not talented?" She feigns shock. "I thought you were the second coming of Mick Jagger."

"I'm telling you that I don't think I would've been the front man for a successful rock band."

"You're good looking enough to be the lead singer of a rock band," I say, checking out his handsome face. "Though, I guess you're more suited to being the lead in a film."

"You think I'm good looking?"

"You're all right," I say. "I mean, you have got the most mesmerizing blue eyes." I stare at him for a few seconds. "Like when people say they could swim in someone's eyes, I never really got it, but as I stare into your eyes, whoa. I feel like I'm in the Maldives or something just staring into the blue water."

"Really?" he says. "Thank you. I never expected such a compliment from you."

"Don't get used to it or anything. I'm just saying that you got nice eyes."

"Thank you," he says. "And you do as well."

"Thanks." I blink and then I blush, biting down on my pizza again. "I wonder if the chef is from Italy," I ponder, changing the subject because I'm feeling slightly uncomfortable.

The mood has shifted slightly. Staring into his eyes has made my heart start racing and my stomach is churning with butterflies and my skin feels hot. I don't want my skin to feel hot. My finger is still burning from when I touched his lips and I wanted to kiss him. I wanted to feel his body pressed against mine. I wanted to smell him. I wanted to run my fingers through his hair. I wanted to feel him pressed against me.

I'm on fire and suddenly, I understand what he'd meant earlier. Suddenly, I understand what it is to have chemistry, to have passion with someone, to just want to feel their naked skin against yours without thinking about anything else.

I don't care about his intentions for our future. I don't care about whether he sees me as a woman he could marry or have a long-term relationship with. I just want to extinguish this fire. I just want to touch and taste and be consumed by him, and it's something I've never felt before. I can feel my face going red as I stare down at his strong hands; hands I can feel pressed against my skin, massaging me, touching me, teasing me, taunting me, making me feel things that I haven't felt in a really long time.

"What are you thinking about, Skye?" he whispers in a low voice and I blink as I gaze up at him.

"You really want to know what I'm thinking about? What if it's something you don't want to know about?"

"Well, you've just been staring at me and your face is getting redder and redder and I was just wondering what you were thinking about."

"It must be the wine," I say quickly. "Wine always makes my face go red, you know?"

"Oh," he says. "It's not something that's on your mind?"

"What could possibly be on my mind that would make my face go red?"

"I don't know. I mean, maybe you're thinking about—"

"I'm certainly not thinking about your hands or your lips on me. I'm certainly not thinking about how..." I pause, realizing that I've said way too much.

He's smirking now. "Where would you like my hands to be on you?"

"I don't want your hands on me anywhere," I say. "Sure, if you were to offer to give me a massage, I may say yes, but only because I've been so stressed out and you look like you have strong hands and oh my gosh, I need a massage so badly. I'm definitely carrying tension in my shoulders and my neck and—"

"You want me to give you a massage?" he asks softly.

I blink at him, "What? You'd give me a massage? Really?"

"If you really desperately need one from me."

"I do," I say, not sure where the words are coming from. I do not desperately need a massage from this man. Definitely not. Definitely, definitely not. "I mean, if you think you give good massages," I say quickly.

"I've been told I give the best massages," he says softly as he licks his lips. "However, you would not be allowed to have clothes on."

"What?" I blink at him. "No clothes? Like naked naked?" My heart races at the thought of his strong warm hands on my bare skin. Naughty thoughts crash through my mind and I want to slap myself. I should not be enjoying thinking about being naked around my boss right now.

"The best massage is when you're naked. Just so you know, you'd be face down though, and we'd wrap a towel over your ass, so I'd only really be seeing your back..." He smiles, "And then I would put some essential oils on you and...well, I don't want to tell you everything I do. I don't want to ruin the surprise."

"The surprise?" I ask him.

"Yeah. That's if you want a Kingston special, that is."

"A Kingston special." I take a sip of water. I know I'm playing with fire, but I can't help myself. "What's a Kingston special?"

"Let's just say it's the best massage you'll ever receive in your life."

"Really? You think you would give me the best massage I've ever received in my life?"

"I do think so, as a matter of fact, but it doesn't look like you really want one."

"Oh, I do," I say. "I really want one. But you don't think it would be kind of unprofessional for my boss to give me a massage?"

"I don't think it's unprofessional. Do you?"

I stare at him for a couple of seconds and every brain cell in my body is screaming at me, saying that getting a massage from this man would be the worst mistake of my life. "I don't think it would be a mistake, but I can't really have you come back to my place. Elisabetta would be like, 'What's going on?' and I don't really want to—"

"You could come to my place," he says with a small smile. "I have a king-size bed. I can give you a massage there and then you can take a taxi home."

I blink at him. "Are you sure?"

"I mean, I feel partly responsible for all the stress that you're feeling right now." He gives me a warm smile. "I guess I should help get rid of it."

"It *is* partly your fault for being such a jackass to me and getting me so upset that I ended up losing my job and now..." I stare at him. "Si I guess if you think that you can give me a great massage, I'm not going to say no."

"Perfect," he says. "We'll take the wine with us to go."

Chapter Twelve

Kingston

"Damn, this is big," Skye says with a slight grin as we enter my apartment.

I watch as she slips off her heels and gives a huge sigh of relief.

"Oh my gosh, those were killing me." She turns to me with a big smile. "Your place is amazing," she says, as she runs her fingers along the countertop in the kitchen. "Is this marble?"

I nod.

"Wow, you are rich." She looks me up and down. "You are very rich."

"I mean, I *am* a partner at a top law firm," I say, watching her as she walks into the living room, runs her fingers across the lever couch, then heads over to the floor-to-ceiling windows that run across the entire length of the living room and provide a beautiful view of Manhattan.

"Look at this view," she says. "Oh my gosh, I feel like I'm in a movie, or maybe in Heaven." She grins and starts doing pirouettes around the room. "I'm in Heaven," she sings, laughing. "And I feel like I'm on top of the world," she continues, chuckling. "Oh my gosh, I'm so drunk." She hiccups as she looks over at me. "Mr. Kingston Chase, you didn't tell me that you lived in a dope ass apartment like this."

"The conversation never came up," I say, as I place my keys on the counter and head toward her. I watch her dancing in her white dress, her red hair spinning across her shoulders, and for a couple of moments, I wonder what I'm doing with this beautiful woman in my apartment at one o'clock in the morning.

"You must get laid all the time," she says as she heads over to me, poking me in the chest. She looks up at me with a girlish smile and bats her eyelashes at me. "Is this your lair?"

"I wouldn't call it my lair, no," I say, shaking my head as I grab her finger and her hand and pull her into me. "Though maybe I should call it that."

I glance down at her, at her parted lips, and for a few moments I think about kissing her. I can tell that she wants that as her eyelashes slowly lower and she tilts her chin up toward me and waits. I think about it for two seconds before I let go of her hand and take a step back.

"Would you like some water?" I ask.

Her eyelashes flutter open and she stares at me in dismay, but then she starts dancing again.

"I would like some water, kind sir. And maybe some more wine or champagne and caviar and strawberries with chocolate dip," she sings, laughing.

"You didn't tell me you were a singer. Are you the second coming of Taylor Swift?"

"Ha ha. Very funny," she says, rolling her eyes. "I cannot carry a tune to save my life."

She's correct about that. She would never be able to make it as a pop star, but she does have a nice, sweet lilt to her voice that is quite attractive.

"So you would like champagne or wine?" I say, as I head to the fridge. "The champagne's not cold, but—"

"Oh, whatever you have. What are you going to have?" she asks. "Mr. Kingston Chase."

"You don't have to keep saying my name. I do know who I am."

"I know you know who you are," she says loudly. "Oops." She presses her hand toward her lips. "I'm being loud. I think I'm drunk."

"I think you are," I say. I wonder for a few moments if it's a mistake having her here.

"You're handsome," she says. "In a way too handsome for your own good way."

"What does that mean?" I ask as I open the fridge. "Okay, I have a bottle of Riesling, some cider, some beer. I can also make you a rum and Coke or a Sprite and vodka."

"What ciders do you have?" she asks, heading toward me and the fridge. "This fridge is really nice. What is it? Samsung?"

"It's Bosch," I say, smiling down at her. "I'm quite unused to all these compliments."

"Yeah, well, don't get too used to it. I'm only trying to butter you up so you give me an amazing massage."

"I will," I say, nodding slowly. Though, if I were being smart, I would send her packing. I don't know that this is the best idea I've ever had, offering to give her a massage in my apartment, in my bedroom, naked, while she's all geeky and flirty like this.

"Do you ever grow a mustache or a beard or a goatee?" she asks, reaching up and touching the side of my face before running her fingers to my chin. "I think you'd look quite handsome with a goatee."

"You don't think I look handsome now?" I ask, a single eyebrow raised.

"You'll do," she says, giggling. And before I know what's happening, she leans up on her tippy-toes and gives me a quick peck on the lips.

"Oops," she said. "I wasn't supposed to do that."

"But you did." I know now is the time I should call the Uber.

"So am I getting that cider or not?" she says, running away from me and back into the living room.

I watch as she plops down onto my oversized sofa. "This is so comfortable. I can tell this costs a lot of money."

"You are quite preoccupied by money, aren't you?"

"I suppose it's because I don't have any," she says, laughing. "I mean, if I did, I'd most likely be in Europe right now, or Australia, or maybe even South America."

"So when are you planning on going on this trip?" I ask her, feeling a little bit sad at the thought of her traveling around the world and gone from my life. But I try to reason with myself. It's only because she's my assistant and I don't want to have to find another one. I'm starting to feel like a record on repeat.

"When I have enough money, I suppose." She blinks at me. "Don't suppose you want to give me a raise."

"You don't suppose right," I say, smiling. "So, cider?"

"Yes, please." She nods. "I might have to give up my weekend job as well."

"Oh? The one where you work as a stripper?"

"I'm not a stripper," she says. "We don't take off our clothes. Yes, we dance around in bikinis and skirts for bachelors, but nothing untoward happens. I mean, it's not like

I've ever fucked any of them and it's not like they've touched me or anything. Though, can you keep a secret?"

"Yeah. What?"

"There's one girl, and let's just say she lets guys give her hundreds."

"Sorry. What? What do you mean she lets guys give her hundreds?"

"Well, right at the end of the day."

"Yeah?"

"Men put hundreds in their lips."

"Okay." I head toward the couch and hand her a cider, then sit next to her.

She takes a sip and lets out a moan. "This is amazing," she says.

The sound makes me hard and I shiver slightly. "So explain to me how they put hundreds in their mouths?" I ask. "I'm confused."

"Well, she can take all the hundreds she wants, but guess how she gets them?"

I stare at her and take a sip of my own cider. "No idea."

"What? You can't guess?" She takes another sip of her cider. "It's kind of crazy. I know I could do it as well. Some of the guys have asked me, but I said no. I am not going to do that no matter how much money I think I could make."

"You have me confused, Skye. What are you talking about?"

"You seriously don't know?"

"No. Are you going to tell me?"

"See if you can guess."

"I'm not sure. She takes the hundreds out of the guys' mouths?"

"Yeah, she takes them out of their mouths all right." She makes an o shape with her mouth and takes another swig of cider. I watch her staring at my lips and I want to kiss her. Hard. "I can show you if you want."

"Show me what?" I shift slightly. She's going to be the death of me. My cock is straining against my pants and I know it wants to bust out like a prisoner in jail.

"How she takes the hundreds out of their lips. but you've got to put a bill in there."

"I'm not putting cash in my mouth."

"Fine," she says. "You probably don't have a hundred dollars anyway."

"I do have a hundred. I have multiple hundreds, but I'm not going to put it in my mouth. I mean, does it have to be in my mouth for you to show me?"

"No, but fine," she says, pushing me back.

"What are you doing?" I ask her.

She giggles slightly. "You got to be lying on the ground. That's what the guys are doing when she picks up the hundreds."

"So you want me to get on the ground or...?"

"No. You can stay on the couch. I'd put that cider down though."

She grabs it from my hand and puts it on the coffee table and sets hers beside it. "Okay. This is what she does," she begins, giggling. "I don't do this though. Only one of the girls. Well, maybe two."

"Okay," I say in a bemused tone, looking at her. "And just exactly what do they do?"

She shifts onto my stomach and I stare up at her.

"What's going on, Skye?"

"I'm going to show you how they get the hundreds," she says, throwing her hair back.

She stares down at me and all I can see is her heaving

bosom. She shifts back slightly against my crotch and I hold in an involuntary sigh. Is she trying to tease me or...?

"Okay, I'm not going to actually do it, do it, but I'll show you. Kind of."

"What are you talking about?" I ask, confused.

She shifts up my body. "I mean, they don't have their panties on when they do it."

"They don't?" I stare at her for a couple of seconds until it suddenly dawns on me exactly what she's talking about.

I know I should tell her to stop, but I can't. She shifts up and before I know what's happening, her panties are over my face and she's crouching on it. I can smell her sweet wetness as her panties brush my nose and my lips. She presses down into me for a couple of seconds and I swear I can feel the wetness. Fuck, she smells good.

She starts laughing as she quickly moves off of my face and looks down at me. "They pick up the hundreds with their pussy lips," she says, giggling. "Can you believe it?"

"No," I say, shaking my head.

Fuck. I want her. I should send her packing. This was a bad idea. I should not have invited her to my place. I can feel her body still on top of mine, warm and soft in all the right places. I reach up and grab a tendril of her hair and play with it, my hands moving to her back. I grab her around the waist and shift her down.

"Oops, sorry. Did I smother you?"

"No," I say through gritted teeth. I am not really sure how to tell her what I'm feeling right now.

"I was just trying to show you what some of the girls do. I don't do that. Not at all, and I guess that's why I'm not making enough money, you know? They make thousands, but I guess guys like that. You know what one of them told me?"

"One of who?" I ask, narrowing my eyes. "One of the guys?"

"No, one of the girls. She told me, well, it's kind of crazy."

"Crazy?" I raise an eyebrow.

"Yeah." She leans forward and presses herself against me. "I'll whisper it into your ear," she says.

Her lips move to my ear and I can feel her hair across my face. She shifts slightly so that she's grinding against my cock and my hands reach up and squeeze her ass.

"Ooh, Mr. Chase," she says, laughing. "Naughty, naughty."

"My bad," I say, grunting.

She shifts her face slightly so that her eyes are next to mine. "So do you want to know?"

"Yeah," I say, my voice hoarse. "Tell me."

"Well, my friend, her name's..." She pauses. "Well, maybe I shouldn't tell you her name."

"No, tell me," I say, not really giving a shit about her friend's name, but loving the way her body feels against mine.

"Her name's Beth Leana."

"Okay."

"Well, Beth Leana told me that sometimes when she sits on their faces..."

"Uh-huh," I say.

"They slip their tongues inside of her." I can feel her chest shaking against me as she tries to contain her laughter. "Can you believe that?"

I stare at her for a couple of seconds, not knowing what she wants me to say. Of course, I can believe that a man at a bachelor party who's lying on the ground with a $100 bill in his mouth waiting for some stripper to lower her naked pussy onto his face would stick his tongue inside of her. Probably wanted to stick a whole lot more than that, but I don't want to be crude.

"I guess I can," I finally say.

"It's crazy. I totally wouldn't do that. The only men that are going to stick their tongue inside of me are men that I'm dating."

"Oh, yeah?" I say. "Only men that you're dating?"

"Yes." She nods as if that's a given. "I mean, sure, it would be fun to have some hot dude make me cum as I grind on his face and get money. But I'm just not that sort of girl."

"Of course you're not," I say, wondering what she'd do if I grabbed her hips and pulled her up onto my face again.

"It would be totally inappropriate for me to do something like that."

"Totally," I say.

"Absolutely, one hundred percent. I'd feel like a prostitute, you know? Doing that for money."

"Of course, but, you know, I don't have any money in my mouth right now." I look over at her with an innocent expression.

"What?" She blinks at me.

"I'm just saying if you want to see what it feels like." I grin at her. "You can."

"I can?" she asks, blushing furiously. "You want me to—."

"I mean..." I grab her around the waist and I slide her up again. "Why don't you show me what they do again?"

"You want me to show you?"

"I kind of didn't really know what you were talking about at first. Show me again what they do." My heart is racing and I'm rock hard. This conversation is the best foreplay I've ever had. Well, maybe not the best, but definitely up there.

She looks down at me and runs her fingers through her hair. I know that she knows what I'm saying and it has nothing to do with the parties that she works.

"If you really want me to show you, I can real quick."

"Of course. Real quick," I say, hardening as she slowly lifts her body.

It's only a few more seconds before she lowers her panty-clad pussy onto my face, but it feels like an eternity. This time, I'm not caught unawares. This time, I'm not in shock. I nuzzle my nose into her pussy and reach my lips up and suck.

She gasps as I feel her clit through her panties and suck on it. She grinds against my face for a couple of seconds before I reach up and squeeze her ass and push her against my face some more, pulling a quiet groan from her throat. I run my tongue against her panties and quickly reach up and slip the material to the side so that I can feel her clit against my naked tongue. She gasps as I eagerly lick her, then she rubs against me two more times and I'm about to slip my tongue inside of her when she shifts off me.

"Well, that was very good," she mumbles, blinking at me. She quickly jumps off of the couch and I groan. "Can I use your restroom?" She looks over at me. Her face is red.

I sit up slightly and nod. "Sure. Just down the hallway to the right."

"Okay," she says, swallowing hard.

I watch as she pulls her dress back down and groan as she makes her way toward the bathroom. I'm not really sure that I should have done that, but I couldn't resist. She was the one that was playing with fire, but I was definitely the one willing to get burned.

I tell myself that I'm going to send her home as soon as she comes back out of the bathroom. Giving her a massage will definitely be a bad idea. A very bad idea. But as I lick my lips, I can still taste her and I know that I don't care what sort of trouble I get myself into this evening. If she's willing, so am I.

Chapter Thirteen

Skye

I make my way to the bathroom and turn on the light. I close the door behind me and laugh to myself quietly as I walk to the mirror and stare at my reflection.

"What am I doing?" I mumble. I can't stop myself from smiling. I'm drunker than I've been in a long time, but I feel high. I feel like I am on top of the world.

I open my handbag and pull out my phone and see that I have a missed call from Elisabetta. I call her back.

"Hey, where are you?" she answers, and for a few seconds I'm not sure if I want to tell her the truth.

"Be quiet," I whisper, nervous I will be heard.

"What's going on? Are you okay?"

"I'm fine. You'll never believe where I am," I whisper into the phone.

"I can barely hear you, Skye. What are you saying?"

"I can't speak loudly. I'm in the restroom right now."

"You're still out on your date with Camden?" Elisabetta sounds shocked. "Wow. Congratulations."

"No, I'm not with Camden." I giggle, though I'm not sure why. "He was a dickhead."

"What? Where are you?"

"I'm at Kingston's place."

"Kingston? Wait, you mean your boss, Kingston?"

"Yeah. You will not believe what happened."

"What happened?"

"I sat on his face." I burst out laughing. "Oh my gosh. I need to pee. Hold on."

"Skye, what is going on? I'm dying here…you really sat on his face? What did he do then? And why are you on the phone with me now? What is going on here?"

"Hold on a second." I pull down my moist panties and take a seat on the toilet and pee. "Sorry about that. I really had to go."

"Skye, you need to explain to me what is going on. Why do you sound like that? Are you drunk?"

"Just a little bit. We drank two bottles of wine." I pause as that sinks in and I remember what a great time I've been having with Kingston.

"You and Camden?"

"No, silly. Me and Kingston."

"But what happened to Camden?"

"Oh my gosh. He was such a jerk face. Anyway, Kingston was there at the restaurant with a blonde bimbo who thought she was like frigging Kate Moss or something. So, Kingston and I left and we went and got pizza and had wine and now I'm back at his place because he's going to give me a massage. I was trying to show him how Beth collects hundred dollar bills after a bachelor party and I kind of danced on his face, but not really. But then he slipped my panties to the side and oh my gosh, his tongue."

"Whoa." Elisabetta sounds shocked. "He went down on you?"

"No. Yes. No, kind of but not really." I giggle. "Let's just say his tongue did touch me in my most intimate places, but I got a little bit nervous and I hurried to the bathroom and that's where I am right now."

"Skye, are you crazy? You let your boss go down on you? The same jackass that told you that he wasn't interested in a relationship with you?"

"No, I didn't let him go down on me. We were on the couch talking about something I can't even remember. Maybe about me wanting to travel and me talking about how I make money. Well, anyway, we started talking about the bachelor parties that I've worked at and I was just telling him nothing bad goes on. It's not like I'm having sex for money. And then somehow I brought up Beth. Remember I told you about Beth and how she loves to make extra? She's the one that gives blowjobs for money, right? Yeah. And she'll pick up hundred dollar bills from men's lips with her own lips, if you know what I mean."

"I'm taking it you don't mean the lips on her face."

"Exactly. So, he was kind of lying back on the couch. Well, he was sitting on the couch and I kind of pushed him back and I wiggled across him and just sat on his face for like two seconds just to show him."

"Oh my gosh. Skye, are you out of your mind?"

"Not every day. Was I out of my mind, maybe? It wasn't crazy crazy. I had my panties on." I laugh. "Oh my gosh. What did I do? Am I crazy? I'm crazy. I should leave right now. What is he thinking?" All of a sudden I feel slightly sober. "I sat on my boss's face. Whoa. How am I going to look him in the face on Monday?"

"I don't know. But how are you going to look *you* in the face when you walk out of the bathroom in five minutes?"

"I don't know. I guess I should come home, huh?"

"Well, you can, but I'm about to head out."

"You're heading out? Now? Isn't it like one o'clock in the morning?"

"I got me a Tinder date."

"You did? With who? How? Where are you going?"

"I figured you were out having fun and I was bored and I figured I'd meet up with some dude that's been messaging me on Tinder."

"No way. But this late? That's like a hookup."

"I mean maybe, maybe not." She sounds defensive. " Maybe I'll sit on a face tonight as well."

"Oh my gosh, Elisabetta." I am protective of my best friend. "It's okay to be alone, you know."

"I'm just joking. We're going to meet at a bar for a drink and then I'll come home. Are you coming back tonight or?"

"Yes. He's just going to give me a massage to destress me and then I'll be back home."

"Skye, listen to yourself. Your boss, whose face you just sat on, is not going to give you an innocent massage."

"I know it will be innocent. I'm going to tell him don't try any funny business mister."

"Okay. You think that's going to work?"

"Honestly, Elisabetta, I don't even care right now. When I felt his nose pressed up against me, I almost came. Do you know how long it's been since I had an orgasm? Do you know how long it's been since a man has touched me? If he wants to feel up my ass and feel up my boobs while he's massaging me, then let him go ahead. Shit, I don't care."

"Skye, I believe that is the wine talking and not your common sense."

"Then let the wine talk. Tonight I just want to have fun. Tonight I just want to be a young woman in New York City making crazy mistakes."

"Do you really want to be making crazy mistakes?"

"I mean, it can't be any worse than the mistakes I've already made in my life. Remember Freddy?"

"Oh, gosh. Don't remind me of Freddy," she says. "He was bad news."

"He was more than bad news. Remember how he attempted to pull off my bra in the movie theater?" I groan.

"Girl, He didn't attempt anything. He did remove your bra."

"I know, but I didn't expect what happened next."

"It was crazy that he kneeled on the floor in front of everyone and pulled up your shirt and started sucking on your boob."

"Yes. And then we got chucked out of the movie theater."

"I know," Elisabetta groans. "Trust me. Remember, I had to come to the police station?"

"It wasn't a police station. It was just the back office at the movie theater."

"I know." She chuckles. "But you almost got sent to the police station."

"Oh, that was just awful. Do you know the telling off I got for him slobbering all over my boobs?"

"Girl, you should not have let that man do that."

"I didn't know he was going to do it. It all happened so quickly. But anyway, my point being that that was a mistake that I regret to this day. Am I going to regret my boss giving me a massage?"

"Okay, Skye. What if the massage ends up with him fingering you?'.

"How many fingers?" I say and burst out laughing. "Okay. I mean he's not going to do that. He's a gentleman."

"Girl, didn't you just say he slipped your panties to the side and his tongue was all up inside of you?"

"His tongue was not all up inside of me. It flicked my clit and maybe I wet his face a little bit. I don't know."

She sighs. "Skye, enjoy your evening. I have a feeling that we're going to have a whole lot to talk about tomorrow."

"I'm going to be a good girl," I say. "I promise."

"Uh-huh. Just don't do anything I wouldn't do."

"What wouldn't you do, Elisabetta?"

"I don't know," she says. "But I guess I'm about to find out. I'll see you later tonight or possibly tomorrow morning."

"Okay," I say. "Also, send me the information of the Tinder guy that you're meeting just in case I have to call the cops in the morning."

"Oh, I am. I'm texting you right now."

Two seconds later, a photograph appears and my jaw drops. "Whoa. That guy is absolutely gorgeous."

"Yep. His name is Brad and he's in finance and he loves to work out." Elisabetta purrs. "So let's see if he works out as much as I think and hope he does."

"Elisabetta, are you trying to have a one-night stand?"

"I don't know about that. I am just trying to have some fun."

"I feel you. Be safe."

"You too, girl. Okay?"

"Okay. Bye. Love you."

I hang up, wipe myself quickly, flush the toilet, then wash my hands. I splash some cold water on my face and take a deep breath as I straighten my dress down.

"What am I doing?" I whisper as I stare at my reflection. "You should go home," I lecture myself. "You should really go home." I point at myself in the mirror. "Don't be a bad girl that could be on *Girls Gone Wild*. You've gone all this way in life without doing anything crazy. Just go home. Go home." I stare at my reflection and burst out laughing because...

Chapter Fourteen

Kingston

"I thought you went swimming," I say to Skye as she comes back into the living room. Her hair is wavy now, and her white dress is flowing against her long legs.

"I got lost," she says, then giggles. "Okay. I didn't get lost. That was a lie."

"I had a feeling it was a lie. My home is not that big."

"Yeah, I guess that's what all the women say to you, huh?" she sways as she winks flirtatiously and I just shake my head. I've never seen her like this before.

"I think you know that women never say that to me."

"If that's what you want to think, Kingston," she says.

"So what were you doing in there so long? Or do I not want to know?"

"That's really inappropriate of you to ask me why I was in your restroom so long." She stares at me. "What if I had a bad belly or something?"

I wrinkle my nose. "Then I guess it would serve me right for asking."

"I was actually on the phone with Elisabetta. You remember her, my roommate and best friend?"

"Yeah. How is she?" I think of the pretty brunette.

"She's about to go out on a date."

"What?" I stare at my watch. "At this time?"

"I know, she's crazy. It's a Tinder date. They're going to go for a drink and who knows where the night, or morning, will end?" she says. "Do you have any water?"

"Of course, I have sparkling and still. Which would you prefer?"

"Ooh. Do you have Sanpellegrino?" she asks, laughing.

"I do. Would you like some?"

"You do not have Sanpellegrino." She looks surprised.

"I do. That's why I said I do."

"You're just so rich."

"I'm rich because I have Sanpellegrino?"

"Yep," she says with a giggle. I stand up and head to the kitchen and open the fridge. I take out two glasses and pour us both some water.

"Are you hungry? Do you want anything else?"

"No, I'm good."

"Would you like any more wine?"

"I don't think so." She shakes her head then hiccups. "I've had way too much wine. In fact, maybe I should get going." She nibbles on her lower lip nervously. "It's been a really fun night, but..."

"You want to leave?" I ask her, and even though this was what I'd wanted five minutes ago, I don't want to see her go.

"I think it's for the best." We both stare at each other and there's a heat in the room that is burning my skin. She licks her lips nervously and I watch as she bounces up and down.

"You haven't received your massage yet," I say softly,

hoping the disappointment in my voice doesn't shine through. I've enjoyed hanging out with Skye, and I'm not ready for her to leave, especially as I can still taste her on the tip of my tongue.

"Well, I mean, if you don't need to go to bed or anything."

"I think I can keep my eyes open for a little bit yet," I say as I hand her the water. She takes a sip and moans.

"This tastes divine."

"You'd think I handed you a glass of champagne or something."

"Almost as good." She looks into my eyes and studies my face. "You really are quite handsome, aren't you? If I was an artist, I'd want to paint you or draw you or mold you in clay." She gasps as if she's just had the best idea ever. "Maybe you'd be the new David."

"Are you saying you want to get me naked?" I lean toward her and she blushes.

"I mean, only in the most artistic of ways."

"Of course," I say. "In fact, if I were an artist, I'd quite like to paint you naked as well." I wink at her and she sips her water again.

"So are you giving me the massage in the living room or...?"

"No, I don't really think that's going to be a good workspace for me and my hands."

"Oh?" she says, turning back to me.

"Yeah, I think I'd rather have you on the bed face down on a towel, that way I can get to all the required parts quite easily."

Her eyes widen slightly. "You're taking this massage very seriously."

"I should though. I am responsible for stressing you out, aren't I?"

"You are." She nods and then grins. "If I'm one hundred percent honest, you're not the only reason why I'm stressed out, but you've definitely added some tension to my shoulders. You're so annoying sometimes."

"I know, and there's only one way I can think of to make it up to you."

"Okay then," she says. "So are we going to..." Her words drift off.

"Are we going to what?" I ask her.

"You know, are you going to give me my massage now?"

"Sure," I say. "I was wondering if you were going to offer to show me some more examples of some of the dances that go down at your bachelor parties."

"No, I wasn't even...I mean, wait. Ugh." She has a strangled tone to her voice. "What is going on here?"

"I don't know. You tell me. You didn't speak a lick of English just now."

"I wasn't showing you dances. I was just showing you how Beth picks up the hundreds, but not because..." She blinks. "Anyway, I don't want to talk about it anymore."

"You don't want to talk about how you rubbed your panties against my face?"

"Kingston." She bats her eyelashes at me. "I was drunk, let's move on from that."

"Okay. I'll move on if you want to."

"I seriously do, or I'm going to go."

"Well, we wouldn't want you to leave before you get that massage." I put my glass down, walk around the island, and grab her hand. "This way, my darling."

"You know that song?" she says, singing slightly.

"Do I know what song?"

"You know. Oh, my darling. Oh, my darling."

"No, I can't say that I do."

"Oh, it's a song that my mom used to sing to me when I was younger. She used to sing, 'Oh my darling Skye, you're bluer than a pie.'" She groans as her voice trails off.

"You're bluer than a pie?" I raise an eyebrow at her.

"Blackberry or blueberry," she says. "Don't you know what I'm talking about?"

"You are drunk. Aren't you, Skye?"

"I'm as high as the Skye with no pie." She holds her hands up and twirls around. "Do you think I've got a nice singing voice?"

"Do I have to answer that?" I say as my lips twist slightly.

"So that's a no." She suddenly stops, grabs me by the shirt, and pulls me toward her. "You've got the biggest, bluest eyes I've ever seen in my whole entire life."

"And you've got the greenest eyes I've ever seen."

"I bet you say that to all the girls," she says, closing her eyes and pushing her mouth up toward mine. "Are you going to kiss me, Kingston Chase?" I stare at her for a couple of seconds and realize she's far more drunk than I initially realized.

"I don't think so," I say. "I think you're drunk." Her eyes fly open and she glares at me.

"I am not drunk. I drink wine all the time. Do you like wine? You like wine. You drink wine with me," she says and grabs my hand. "Now, show me to your bedroom, big bad Mr. Wolf." I stare at her for a couple of seconds and think about sending her home, but I quite like seeing this side of Skye. She's lighthearted, she's fun, and she makes me feel fun too.

"Come on, let me show you to my room." We take a

couple of steps and I push open the door. I turn on the light and her jaw drops.

"Whoa. That bed is humongous."

"You like my bed, huh?"

"Yeah. I wish I could fit this size bed in my room. Wow." She runs over and jumps on top of it and bounces up and down, her eyes gleaming as her hair shakes back and forth. She leans back and rests her head against the sheets. "This bed is so comfortable." She looks up at me. "I bet you have a lot of sex in this bed, don't you?" My lips twitch again.

"I don't know if you want me to answer that question."

"Have you had sex with Angelica in this bed?" she asks me, her eyes narrowing. "Because if you had sex with Angelica in this bed, you're not having sex with me."

"I didn't realize that was on offer tonight," I say as I close the door behind me and head towards her.

"It's not," she says, shaking her head. "I mean, it's not on offer tonight or ever or anything. I'm just curious. Has that blonde bimbo been in this room?"

"She has not," I say, laughing at her use of the term blonde bimbo. "In fact, not many women have been in here. This room has not seen plenty of sex."

She looks at me in disbelief. "You're joking."

"I'm not joking. I prefer to..." I was about to say have my conquest, but didn't really think that was appropriate word to say. "I prefer to have this as my inner sanctuary," I say. "This space is just for me. And intimate moments, well, they're for other places."

"Oh, so you don't like to bring women back here because you don't want them to think that you're serious about them." She points a finger at me. "Because you don't do relationships or girlfriends, do you?"

"I take it you know me well," I say, blinking at her. "And what else do you think you know about me, Skye?"

"You think that you are the boss of me," she says, grabbing my hand and placing it on her shoulder. "But you're not the boss of me. I'm the boss of you."

"Really?" I say, reaching over and touching the side of her face.

"Yeah, I am, because..." She stills suddenly and looks at me seriously. "I'm in control here. I'm in control. I am in control," she sings. "Do I sound like Madonna? Do you think I could get a job as Madonna at a nightclub?" I stare at her for a couple of seconds and just shake my head. "What's that mean? Are you saying I don't look like Madonna?"

"You don't look like Madonna."

"Are you saying I don't sound like Madonna?"

"You don't sound like Madonna."

"Okay, what about Britney Spears?"

"Nope."

"Katy Perry?"

"Nope."

"Jennifer Lopez?"

"No."

"Halle Berry?"

"No, Skye."

"Who do I look like then?"

"You look like Skye Redding."

"I do?" she says eagerly and then pauses. "Wait, I am Skye Redding. You're a goofball, Kingston Chase."

"Are you ready for this massage or would you rather..."

"I'm ready," she says. And before I know what she's doing, she jumps off the bed, pulls off her dress, and is standing there in a bra and panties. My throat goes dry as I stare at her beautiful body. She does a little twirl. "I'm not taking off my bra and panties though. This isn't some sort of striptease. You didn't get that lucky." She runs her finger across her lips. "Now, where's the towel? I want to lie down on the bed, and I might close my eyes. And you can turn the lights off. You can maybe put on some candles and some music. Oh, I'm so looking forward to this massage." She tries to stifle a yawn. "I am really in need of it.

"You know what? Why don't you just lie on the bed?" I say. "It's okay."

"But I don't want to get it dirty or anything."

"It's okay," I say. I watch as she jumps up onto the bed and lies face down. She tilts her chin to the side and looks at me with a small smile.

"Did I tell you that you're handsome?"

"You did," I say. "Thank you."

"That's not the response I was looking for."

"Oh?"

"You're supposed to tell me I'm pretty or whatever."

"Okay."

"Okay what?"

"You're whatever, Skye."

"What?" She glares at me. "No fair."

"You're very beautiful, Skye. Very, very beautiful." My eyes wander from her face to her back and then to her ass and her shapely legs, down her calves to her feet, which are hanging off the bed. "You can shift up a little bit if you want. Your feet don't have to hang over the bed."

"It's a weird thing that I do," she says, wrinkling her nose.

"Sorry, what?"

"I like to hang my feet over the bed. I know it's weird, but it just makes me feel better. I don't know. I can't fall asleep or whatever if my feet aren't hanging over the bed."

"What about when you're with someone?" I say, frowning slightly. "Don't you..."

"Don't I what? Don't I wrap my legs between theirs and play footsie with them all night?" She grins at me. "Maybe, maybe not. Wouldn't you like to know?" I stare at her for a couple of seconds and don't say anything, because I'm very desperately trying not to picture my legs entwined with hers or our feet playing footsie.

"Okay, let me turn off the lights and see if I've got any candles."

"Ooh, yay. And what music are you going to play?"

"I don't know. What would you like me to play?"

"Something melodic. Nothing crazy. No heavy metal, no hard rock, no country, no rap."

"You're not leaving me many options."

"Maybe something classical, like an opera."

"Do you like opera?" I ask her.

"No. I mean, sometimes. But I don't know opera, so I won't sing along with it. So then I can just really relax."

"Okay then. Let's see if we can get some Carmen playing for you."

"Thank you," she says. "Okay, I'm going to close my eyes now and just relax."

"Sounds good." I head back into the kitchen and open one of the drawers and pull out some candles and a lighter. I carry them back to the bedroom and place them on the night table, then turn off the lights. I get up on the side of the bed and I knead my fingers into her shoulders. She groans immediately.

"Oh my gosh, this should be illegal."

"What should be illegal?" I ask her.

"How good this feels." She lets out a low moan. "Oh my

gosh. This feels fantastic." I can feel myself hardening as she makes the little whimpering sounds.

"I'm going to unclasp your bra if that's okay."

"It's fine," she says and giggles. "Don't try anything funny though."

"Would I do that?" I say, and she just laughs. I run my fingers up and down her back and massage her neck and her head and her shoulders. I make my way down to her waist and her buttocks. "Is this okay?" I ask softly, but she doesn't respond. "Hey, Skye." I stop for a second, and I notice that she's falling asleep. I smile as I see her lying there. "Oh, sweetness," I say.

I gather her up and pull the sheet back and place her into the bed and cover her. She has a large, wide, beautiful smile on her face as she snores slightly. I blow out the candles and head to the bathroom to brush my teeth. I should take the couch and sleep there. I want to be a gentleman.

I finish brushing my teeth, grab a pillow and a blanket, and head to the couch and lie down. I turn on the TV and watch it, but all I can think about is Skye topless in my bed, sleeping. I wonder if she hadn't been so tired and if she hadn't been so drunk just where the night would've led us. I wonder what it would be like to be sleeping next to her, her breasts pressed up against me.

But I didn't want to violate her in that way. I didn't want to put her in a position where if she woke up in the middle of the night, she'd have reason to question what may or may not have gone down. Even though I want her badly, I need her to know that I would never cross a line that she was not fully aware of.

I groan as I shift my cock in my boxers and roll over onto my side. I'm still hard. "Fuck," I mumble under my breath. I stare at the TV screen and then turn it off and just stare up at the ceiling. I am not going to be able to sleep unless I take care of this.

I take a deep breath and work my fingers down to my hardness. It's not like I'm in the bed with her. It's not like I'm masturbating right next to her. I'm lying on my own couch by myself and I'm pleasuring myself, something that I do almost daily. I'm not going to feel guilty.

I close my eyes and picture Skye's staring into mine; her parted lips, the way her breasts bounced in that dress, the way she tasted as I flicked her clit with my tongue as she hovered over my face.

"Fuck," I moan as I grip my cock and move my hand up and down. "Fuck, Skye. Fuck, I want you so badly."

Chapter Fifteen

Skye

The sound of the TV wakes me and I stretch as my eyes flutter open. I'm in an unfamiliar room and I am not wearing a T-shirt. I blink and freeze for a few moments when I realize that I'm at Kingston's apartment and I'm lying in his bed.

My eyes immediately flicker to the left and the right of me, but he's not in bed with me. A shudder of slight disappointment passes through me as I reach down to see if I have on any panties. I do. I try to think back and realize that Kingston had been giving me a massage and I must have fallen asleep.

I look over at the clock on the nightstand and it's only two o'clock in the morning. So I hadn't slept very long. I wonder where Kingston is and all of a sudden, I feel thirsty again. I slide out of the bed, look around, and head to the closet. I pull a T-shirt out and throw it on and creep down the hallway back toward the living room.

Kingston's making some weird noises and I think he's sleeping, until I hear my name coming from his mouth.

"Fuck yes, Skye," he says, and I stop dead, my jaw dropping open as I take in the scene in front of me.

Kingston's lying on the couch, shirtless, with only a pair of boxers on. His hand is surrounding his very thick and very long cock and is moving back and forth quickly. I feel my throat dry as I watch him masturbating. I am in absolute shock and I don't know if I should say anything. I take another step forward, hoping that he'll see me, but he doesn't.

"Fuck yeah. Cum for me," he moans. "Do you like it when I play with you like that? Fuck, you're so tight," he pauses and my heart jumps for a few seconds. "Yeah, Skye. Yeah, sit on my face again. Oh yeah, like that."

My jaw drops and I feel like watching my boss on his couch playing with himself thinking about me has sobered me up more than any breakfast meal has ever done.

"Oh my God, Skye. I'm about to cum," he mutters and I gasp.

He freezes and stops. His eyes move toward me and he sits up. "Skye?"

I clear my throat and lick my lips nervously. Fuck, fuck, fuck, fuck, fuck I think to myself.

"I'm just looking for some water," I say, holding my hands out ahead of me and pretending that I'm sleepwalking. "Can I have some water?"

"Skye?" He jumps up and heads toward me now.

I stare at him and then look down at his cock and then back into his face. "Yeah?"

"Were you just watching me?" He raises a single eyebrow.

I lick my lips nervously as I look back down at his still-hard penis. "Um, you want to put that thing away? It could do someone some damage."

He stares at me for a couple of seconds, confused, and then he looks down.

"Fuck," he says, as he slips his cock back into his boxers. "I thought you were asleep."

"I think maybe the TV came on and it woke me up. I'm a little bit of a light sleeper and I was just going to get some water and make sure you're okay because I was in the bed by myself and..." I realize I'm rambling. "I did not mean to stare at you doing that. I..." I lick my lips nervously. "Sorry."

"I'm sorry you had to see that," he says. "You want some more water?"

"Yes, please." I nod.

He looks at the T-shirt I'm wearing and grins. "You got good taste."

I look down and see the Metallica logo spread across my chest. "Yeah, it was the first T-shirt I found."

"You didn't want to walk out here topless?"

"Not really," I say. "But maybe you would've liked that."

"Maybe," he says. He heads toward the kitchen and opens the fridge and takes out the bottle of Sanpellegrino and grabs another glass.

I move to stand next to him, trying not to stare at his naked, tan chest. He really is built.

"Here you go."

"Thank you," I say. "I'm sorry I fell asleep during the massage."

"I mean, I guess it worked," he says. "It made you tired and that's a good indicator that you're not super stressed."

"It did feel amazing," I say. "But I feel like I didn't even get my money's worth," I tease him.

"I didn't realize you were paying me," he says with a grin.

"I didn't realize you wanted to be paid."

"Not with money," he says, winking, and I blush and look away.

"How come you left me in the bed by myself?" I ask him softly.

"Because you didn't have a top on," he says. "And I didn't want you to wake up topless just in your panties with me next to you in my boxers wondering what the hell had gone on."

I stare at him for a couple of seconds and nod. "Thank you. That was very thoughtful of you."

"I do try to be a gentleman whenever I can be." He grins. "So, I'm sorry you witnessed me..." He pauses. "Just exactly what did you witness, by the way?"

"I witnessed you on your couch playing with yourself saying my name." I grin. "So I guess I've kind of gotten into your head, huh?"

He stares at me for a couple of seconds and shrugs. "I will neither confirm nor deny those allegations."

"Uh-huh," I say. "Shall we go to bed?" I stare at him for a couple of seconds and he just stares at me.

"You want to share the same bed with me?"

"It's not that I want to, but we're both here, unless you're trying to kick me out right now."

He shakes his head. "Like I said, I'm a gentleman. I wouldn't try to kick you out."

"Well, then I don't want to take your bed. It's huge. We can share it."

"Okay." He stares at me. "So you're telling me you do not want me to sleep on the couch."

"I'm telling you I do not want you to sleep on the couch." I nod. "We can just go to bed and sleep and I will go home in the morning."

"Okay," he says. "Fine. That sounds good to me. My

couch is comfortable but it's not *that* comfortable. I only have one requirement though."

"And what's that?" He said.

"If you need to finish masturbating, do it before you get into the bed."

He bursts out laughing.

"What?"

"I thought you were going to say I masturbate and you masturbate and we just watch each other."

I stare at him in shock. "What?"

"What? You've never masturbated with someone?" he asks me softly.

"No."

"You're telling me you've never been in a relationship where you masturbated at the same time he masturbated."

"That's exactly what I'm telling you."

"Okay. Well you don't know what you're missing then."

I stare at him for a couple of seconds. "I'm not taking the bait, you know? I may be a little bit tipsy—okay, a lot tipsy—but I'm not going to masturbate while you masturbate."

"Okay. I was just saying if that was something you wanted to do, I'd be open to it. But if it's not something you want to do, then we don't have to."

"You're my boss Kingston and remember what you said to me? You didn't want me to get any ideas that—"

"Hold on a second, Skye. I said I didn't want you to get any ideas in regards to what happened between Lila and Max. I basically said I didn't want you to think that we were going to hook up and then end up in a happily ever after. I mean, mutually masturbating is not even hooking up."

"Okay, well, I'm just saying it seems to me that you're crossing some very gray lines here."

"Well, we haven't technically crossed any," he says.

"I'm tired, Kingston. Let's go to bed."

"Okay. Do you want anything else before we go?"

"No," I say as I head back toward his room, my heart thudding.

I don't know what I'm thinking by inviting him to share the bed with me. It's like I'm playing with fire and I know I'm going to get burned and I don't even care, which sounds about right for me.

I jump up into the bed and pull the sheets down so I can watch as Kingston stares at me.

"You want the left side or the right side?" he asks as I lay there in the middle of the most comfortable mattress I've ever laid on before.

"I don't mind." I shrug. "Which side do you normally take?"

"The right," he says, as he gets into the right.

I shift over slightly and he turns onto his side to look at me. "So here we are," he says.

"Here we are." I look back at him.

"You don't seem like you're super tired anymore," he said.

"I don't know. I wasn't really asleep for long, but..." I shrug. "I guess the massage really knocked me out and now I have a little bit of energy again."

"You saying you want another massage?" he asks, reaching over and squeezing my shoulder.

"No, I'm okay."

"I like the way my T-shirt looks on you," he says. "You look like a cool rock heavy metal chick."

"I'm so not a rocker or a heavy metal groupie chick. I am definitely more of a boy band girl."

"I could have guessed that," he says with a smile. "Let me guess. You were totally into Backstreet Boys."

"No, I was into One Direction."

"Ah, okay. I do know their music."

"Have you been to any of their concerts?" I ask.

He bursts out laughing then. "I am a heterosexual man. No, I have not been to a One Direction concert." He laughs. "Why? Have you?"

"I always wanted to go to one but my parents would never get me the tickets...you know how it goes."

"I guess so," he says. "Maybe one day you'll be able to go."

"They're not even together anymore." I stare at him. "You didn't know that?"

"I'm going to be honest with you here, Skye. I've heard of them but I literally could not tell you anything about them."

"What? You don't know Harry Styles?"

"Harry who?"

"Harry Styles, the dude from One Direction?"

"Prince Harry was in One Direction?" He looks shocked. "I mean I knew him and the royal family fell out, but I didn't realize it was because he was in a boy band."

"No, silly. Not Prince Harry. Harry Styles. He's an actor as well. He's been in some movies."

"Okay, if you say so."

"You really are a man's man, aren't you?"

"I guess so," he says.

"But wait, you said that you used to love to do karaoke and you used to want to be in a band."

"A rock band," he says, chuckling. "Not a boy band, but yeah, I did. I used to write songs and everything."

"You did?" I stare at him in surprise. "Like song songs?"

"What other kind of songs are there?" His eyes crinkle and he stares at me.

"Can you sing one to me?"

"What? One of my songs?"

"Yeah, one of your songs."

He groans. "I am not as drunk as you. I don't know that I have it in me to sing any songs right now."

"Come on. I've been singing to you all night."

"True. You have been, haven't you, Madonna?"

"Don't remind me. I know I cannot sing like Madonna."

"I mean, it doesn't matter though because you're prettier than her."

"Don't let her hear you say that."

"I would let her hear me if she was around," he says, touching the tip of my nose. "Okay, I will sing you part of one of my favorite songs from when I was seventeen."

"Oh, yippee," I say, clapping my hands, then I pause for a moment. "This is super weird, isn't it?"

"What?" He says.

"You and me here in your bed discussing songs you sang as a teenager."

"Why is it super weird?"

"Because we were literally just arguing the other day and you're my boss and..."

"Stop questioning everything, Skye. You know, in life, things just happen. You got to go with the flow."

"You don't think it's weird that I, your assistant, am here in your bed wearing your T-shirt?"

"No." He shakes his head. "Maybe this is just our way of getting to know each other."

I stare at him and just roll my eyes. "Okay, stop changing the subject. Let me hear the song."

"Okay. Well, the beat goes something like..." He pauses and hums for a couple of seconds before he starts singing. "There she was in the Skye, dancing in the clouds. Boom,

boom, boom. That's the drum solo by the way," he says, and I just nod.

"Continue."

"She's bouncing. Look, she's high. She doesn't want to know me, but I want to slip my arms around her."

"You were singing this at seventeen years old?"

"I was a horny seventeen-year-old boy," he says, grinning. "I was singing way worse than this."

"Oh, so you're not horny now that you're in your thirties?"

He stares at me for a couple of seconds and shifts in the bed. "Um, do you really want me to answer that question?"

"I don't know. Do you want to answer that question?" I say, as he shifts closer to me.

"I don't know. You tell me."

I swallow hard as I feel his thigh next to me. His arm reaches around and plays with my hair. I feel his hand on my hip, moving my T-shirt up slightly.

"What are you doing?" I ask, swallowing hard.

"Just checking if you still have your panties on," he says, softly, as his fingers run across the material of my panties and up to my waist.

He strokes my skin softly and I just stare at him. I reach over and touch his chest, running my fingers down the smattering of hair to his abs.

"How often do you work out?" I whisper as I run my fingers across his taut muscles.

"Every day, or at least I try. What about you?" he asks as he runs his fingers down the side of my back and squeezes my ass.

"Not that often," I admit. "Though, I always say I'm going to work out more."

"Maybe we can go to the gym sometime?" he asks, and I just stare at him.

"Maybe."

He leans forward and kisses me on the forehead, his hand still on my ass, so I run my fingers down the side of his thigh and squeeze his buttocks. He shifts closer to me, grabbing me around the waist and pulling me into him. I can feel his hardness pushed up against my belly. His leg wraps over mine and he reaches behind my head and pulls my face toward him. His lips are close to mine as he stares into my eyes.

"I hope you have a good night."

"What?" I say, blinking at him in confusion.

"I said I hope you have a good night." He kisses me on the forehead again and drops his arm away.

"You want to sleep like this?" I say, staring at him, shifting slightly.

"You want to be small spoon?"

I nod and turn around so that my back is facing him. This is way too intimate. I feel his arm wrap around my waist and he pulls me back into him so that his cock is now pressed up against my ass cheeks. His hand is now settled on my stomach. I can feel my hair pressed against his face and I wonder if it's tickling him.

"Goodnight, Skye," he says.

"Night, Kingston," I say, even though I'm nowhere close to feeling ready to go to sleep.

His fingers trail up and down my stomach as we lay there and I can feel his breath against my neck. His fingers start moving up slightly and I feel them underneath my breasts. I swallow hard as he continues moving his fingers up and down, however, not going farther than the underbelly of my breasts.

I shift back slightly and feel his hardness push between my ass cheeks. He groans slightly and shifts. I close my eyes as I feel wetness filling my panties. I lick my lips and try to close my eyes. His fingers stop moving and settle on my stomach.

I try to fall asleep, but I can't. My hand is on his before I know what I'm doing, and I move it farther up so it's cupping my right breast completely. He doesn't do anything for a couple of seconds and I feel slightly embarrassed until I drop my hand away and feel his fingers playing with my nipple. I gasp slightly as he pinches the sensitive bud then bites on my ear. He runs his hands up and down my back and I moan at the touch of him, pushing my back into him and my ass against his cock. He grunts and I feel his fingers sliding back down my stomach and into my panties. He shifts my leg backwards and I'm not sure what he's about to do, but then I feel his fingers between my legs, touching me softly.

"Are you awake?" he asks.

I nod slightly.

"Skye, answer me."

"I'm awake," I say.

"And this is okay?" He groans.

"Yes." I moan as I turn to face him.

He looks at me, his eyes dark and heavy, and before I know what he's doing, he's grabbed me and pulled me on top of him and he's pulling my head down toward him. His lips are on mine and we're kissing and I cannot believe that we've waited this long to have this intimate moment.

He slides his tongue into my mouth and I kiss him back eagerly. He tastes like red wine and Sanpellegrino and pepperoni, and I've never loved the taste of anything more in my life. I grind back and forth on him as he reaches up and pulls my T-shirt off. I watch as he throws it to the ground, then he palms both of my breasts in his hands and plays with my nipples.

I moan as he reaches down to slide my panties off. I shift to the side and watch as he pulls them off of my ankles before I reach down and grab his hardness, pulling his cock out of his boxers and rubbing myself back and forth on him. He moans as he grabs my hair and pulls me down to kiss him again, my breasts pressed against his chest.

"Oh, fuck," he says as he rolls me over so that now he's on top and I'm lying on my back, staring up at him.

He cradles my face and kisses me hard, his fingers running through my hair. I watch as he moves his fingers up and down his cock before positioning it between my legs.

"Fuck. You're so hot, Skye," he says.

He stares at me and I reach up and pull his head down to kiss him.

"Oh, fuck." He shifts his cock between my legs and rubs it back and forth on my clit, his eyes looking into mine. I nod and he pushes inside of me.

I cry out in pleasure and he groans. "Oh, fuck yes." He grows as he thrusts in and out of me and he feels better than I've ever imagined any man could ever feel inside of me.

I reach up and grab his hair as he thrusts into me faster and faster.

"Oh, fuck yeah," he says as he slams into me, our bodies writhing together.

I feel my breasts bouncing against his chest as he kisses me hard and fast. He stills suddenly and pulls out of me and I feel him cumming all over my stomach.

"Oh, fuck yeah," he says.

Before my head can come down from the high that is Kingston Chase, he slides down the bed and spreads my legs wide, his tongue on my clit and sliding inside of me, sucking and grabbing my legs and throwing them over his shoulders as he finishes me off with his tongue.

"Oh shit, yes. Don't stop, Kingston."

I scream and shout as he brings me to orgasm with his tongue. I feel myself erupting on his face and he chuckles slightly as he licks me clean then kisses back up my body and stares down at me.

"Well," he says. "That was certainly something."

I stare at him and roll my eyes for a couple of seconds and yawn loudly. "I think I'm ready to go to sleep now," I say, not able to process what I'm feeling in the moment.

"Me too." His voice is husky and he also looks disoriented.

He pulls me into his arms and holds me close and I am in bliss. That was the most amazing experience I ever had in my life and I don't know if I'll regret it in the morning, but right now I don't care. Right now is everything I could have asked for and more.

Chapter Sixteen

Kingston

I feel something warm and soft press against me and reach out to squeeze it. I realize that my hand is on someone's breast and my eyes fly open. I see Skye lying there, staring at her phone. She turns her face to me with a small smile.

"Morning, sleepyhead," she says.

I blink rapidly for a couple of seconds as I remember the previous evening. "Hey. Morning," I say more gruffly than I intend.

Her green eyes shutter for a second, and then she blinks. "Did you sleep well?"

"Yeah, you?" I realize then that I'm naked and she's naked and pressed up against me. I'm hard, and I feel it twitch against her thigh.

"I guess someone's happy to see me, even if you're not."

"What?" I blink at her.

"I mean, you don't look so happy to see me this morning." She grins. "Was I supposed to grab a cab and disappear before you woke up?"

"What are you talking about, Skye?" I say, shaking my head as I reach over and tug on her hair.

"What are you doing?" she asks.

"This," I say as I lean over and give her a quick kiss. She kisses me back eagerly and I squeeze her breast and play with her nipple. I could get used to waking up like this.

"What are you doing?" she says, mumbling as she pulls away from me, her eyes glittering.

"I was just giving you a morning greeting to let you know that I don't regret last night. Do you?" My fingers trail down the valley between her breasts to her stomach. I can feel my dry cum on her.

She wrinkles her nose. "I need to shower."

"I guess we both need to shower," I say, staring at her lips. "Do you want to go in together?"

"Maybe in a little bit," she says, grinning. I frown when her eyes go back to her phone.

"What are you doing? Are you chatting with someone or...?"

"Are you nervous that I'm telling the girls at work that we banged?"

"No. And since when do you say banged?"

"Would you rather me say fucked, or would you rather me say, 'Guess what, girls? I made love to the Kingston Chase'?" I laugh slightly at her words.

"Ha, ha. Very funny. You're not really texting them, are you?"

"No. Why? Would that make you nervous?"

"Not really, no. I just—"

"Don't worry. I'm not texting them." She shakes her head. "I'm actually looking at something."

"Okay, and what are you looking at?"

"I don't think you want to know," she says, laughing as she turns to me, holding the phone up above her head.

"Now, you have me curious. What are you looking at?"

"Something I want."

"Okay. What, for breakfast? An omelet or eggs Benedict or..."

"I mean, it's not something I can eat. But if you want to get it for me over breakfast, I don't mind."

"Okay. It's something you want me to get you."

"Yeah," she says. "It is technically something that a man gets a woman." I stare at her in confusion. What the hell is she talking about?

"Okay." I stretch the word, hoping she'll explain. "So are you going to tell me what you're talking about or..."

"Well, I was thinking..." She lies on her side and runs her finger down my chest toward my cock. She idly plays with my penis and I feel it growing harder in her palm. "Ooh," she says. "Good morning, mister." She leans down and kisses the tip and I groan. What is this woman doing to me?

"Are you going to tell me what you're looking at or are we going to fuck or...?"

"I was looking at rings, silly." She stares at me as she leans over to kiss me and snuggles into my arms.

"Sorry, what?" I blink at her.

"Engagement rings." She kisses me again and stares into my eyes. "Now that we're lovers, I was thinking you should make an honest woman out of me."

"Sorry, what?" My heart thuds as I stare at her. Is she being serious?

"Do I have a budget?" she asks. "I mean, traditionally it should be three times your monthly salary."

"What should be three times my monthly salary?"

"The amount you spend on a ring. So how much do you make per month? Or rather, I should say, how much do *we* make per month?" She laughs like she's in on some joke.

"Skye, what are you talking about? What is going on here?"

"Do you make ten grand a month? Because then the engagement ring should be thirty grand, but..."

"Skye, what engagement ring?"

"Our engagement-ring-to-be." She taps me on the tip of the nose. "I am so excited. Now that we've made love and all, I figure our relationship is moving in that direction." She shimmies back and forth. "Going to the chapel and we're —." She sings pushes her finger in my mouth.

"What?" My jaw drops.

"Why do you look like that Kingston. Can I call you my King. My future hubby. My baby daddy with the big bank account. Didn't you say that..."

I grab ahold of her hand. "Skye, we had one night together where we both drank copious amounts of wine and had some fun. That doesn't mean that we're getting engaged." The panic in my voice is clear for her to hear.

"What? You're not going to make an honest woman out of me like Max did with Lila? I mean, wasn't that what your conversation was about the other night, that..." She pouts and bats her eyelashes. "I thought this was real. I thought this was fate. Serendipity. I thought there would be a documentary on Netflix about out love."

"Skye!" Is this a case of fatal attraction?

She bursts out laughing then and shakes her head.

"Oh my gosh, I totally had you going. You should see the look on your face."

My eyes narrow as I take her in. "Is this meant to be a joke?"

"Of course it's meant to be a joke. I knew you would wake up thinking and worrying that I would think that just because we made love, I was expecting something from you. But I'm not, so you don't have to worry about it. Frankly, my dear, it was just so-so."

"Excuse me?" I stare at her, blinking.

"It was fun, but I would give you a seven out of ten." She wrinkles her nose and yawns.

"You would give me a seven out of ten?" I stare at her.

"Yeah. You came kind of fast."

I glare at her. "Because I had just been masturbating ten minutes before that and was about to cum."

"I don't care what your excuses are, but you still came kind of fast. And you came on my stomach. Cum inside of me or cum in my mouth, but not on my stomach. I mean, fuck, even on my tits would've been hotter."

I narrow my eyes at her. "You want me to cum inside of you."

"Child support, baby." She winks at me and I groan. "Dollar dollar bills."

"That's not funny, Skye."

"I'm joking. I'm on birth control. It helps regulate my periods. So even if you would've cum inside of me, it's very unlikely that you would've got me pregnant. But hey, how much would you be willing to pay me in child support if you did get me pregnant?" She licks her lips and holds her hands up. "It's a joke. Oh my gosh, if you could see your face, Kingston."

"That's not really a funny joke, Skye."

"I'm only saying it because you're acting like you think I think that last night meant something."

"I literally opened my eyes, woke up, felt your naked body next to mine, and asked if you wanted breakfast. I don't remember saying anything about me thinking that you thought last night meant anything special or..."

"Well, you don't have to worry," she says. "I know last night was just a way for us to relieve some stress and get to know each other better."

I stare at her through narrowed eyes. "You what?"

"And I am going to go home now. I'm tired and I do need a shower, and I'm hungry and—"

"Like I said, you can shower here, and I can take you to breakfast and—"

"Oh, no. You can't take me to breakfast." She shakes her head. "That's not something people in our situation do."

"Huh? What do you mean in our situation?"

"People who go to breakfast after having sex are more often than not in a relationship or have something special. You're my boss, I'm your assistant, and we just got carried away last night and we knocked one out."

"We knocked one out." I blink at her. "Really? That's the term you're using?"

"Yep, that's the term I'm using." She licks her lips nervously. "Anyway, it was fun. Could've been funner, but..."

"You don't think it was fun." I grab her hand and pull her toward me as she gets out of the bed. She collapses on me and her nipples brush against my chest. She moans slightly as I reach up and run my fingers between her legs. I let them press into her warmth for a few moments, causing her to gasp. I feel her wetness and stare at her as I trail my fingers down her thigh. "I mean, you don't exactly feel like the Sahara Desert," I say, staring at her.

She blinks at me. "Maybe because I'm not the Sahara Desert."

"You kind of feel a little bit like a typhoon," I say, licking my lips. I reach my fingers down between her legs again and rub her back and forth. She gasps, moaning slightly. I feel her getting wetter and wetter, her eyes never leaving mine, even as I slip a finger inside of her.

"What are you doing?" She moans, the sound breathy and unsteady.

I pull my finger out, bring it up to my mouth, and suck on it. "Just tasting you." I smile. "I was hungry. I needed something to satiate me."

"Okay," she says, staring down at me. I pull her hair back and she groans as she arches her back, and I watch as her breasts bounce up and down. I grab her around the waist and position her on top of me so that she's rubbing against my cock. She stares at me for a couple of seconds before I pull her face down and I kiss her hard. She moans and mumbles as my tongue slips into her mouth and my fingers run down her back and squeeze her ass cheeks. I grunt against her lips as my cock gets harder and harder and rubs against her. I can feel her wetness sliding back and forth on me. She's moaning against me now and I can feel her heart racing. I roll her over onto her back again and look down at her, kissing the side of her neck, then down to her breasts, sucking on her nipple before licking down to her belly button and down between her legs. I grab both her ankles and push them up so that I'm staring at her wetness; moist, juicy, waiting for me.

"You look like a woman who wants to be fucked," I say, grinning at her.

"You look like a man that doesn't understand his assignment," she says, sticking her tongue out at me. I laugh before grabbing my cock and guiding it to her entrance. She stares at me as I thrust inside of her, hard and fast. She screams out as I begin to fuck her in earnest, rubbing her clit as my dick fills her. Her eyes flutter back in her head and I can feel her getting closer and closer to orgasm.

"Oh my gosh, don't stop," she cries, mumbling as I pull my cock out and let it lay on top of her pussy. Her eyes open and she stares at me with parted lips.

"So...still think I'm an average lover or...?"

"Kingston," she says, glaring at me, and I laugh before thrusting back inside of her. She moans as I allow her pussy lips to close in on my cock. I grunt as I grab her hands and squeeze them tightly, lowering myself down to kiss her as I continue thrusting into her hard and fast. When I feel that I'm about to cum, I consider pulling out of her, but instead, I just stare into her eyes, grab her hips, and thrust one last time, hard and fast, erupting inside of her. She screams as she crashes down the mountain herself and I can feel her cumming, her body shaking as she grips onto me.

"Fuck," she says as I kiss her and stroke the side of her face. I lie down and stare at her, at her parted pink lips, at her wide eyes, and slide my cock out of her.

"So *now* I'm ready for you to leave," I say with a small smile.

"What?" She blinks at me.

"I mean, I couldn't have you leaving thinking I was an average lover. But now I think we both know that I warrant A+."

"Are you frigging kidding me?" Her jaw drops and I shake my head.

"No, but you said you don't want to get breakfast with me, and I'm kind of hungry. So unless you change your mind..."

She stares at me for a couple of seconds and rolls her eyes. "You know what?"

"What?" I say, snarking.

"Nothing." She jumps out of the bed, glaring at me as her hair swings back and forth. She ties it up into a bun on top of her head while I stare at her naked breasts, then she points at me. "This was a one-off. I just want you to know that."

"Okay," I say, smiling. "Technically, it's a two-off, but I'll take it."

"Ugh, you're so frustrating."

"And hot, right?" I wink at her, but she just rolls her eyes. I jump up out of the bed and pull her into me and wrap my arms around her, holding her body close to mine.

"What are you doing?"

"I just wanted you to know that even though this was a one or two-off, I still had fun." I give her a kiss on the forehead. "However."

"However what?" she says.

"I just want to ensure that we both know on Monday morning that when I ask you to do the work that you're paid to do, that you do it. And don't expect for me to go easy on you now that we've knocked one out."

"Knocked two out," she says with a little twitch of her lips. I grin.

"It was fun, you know?"

"I know," she says. "It was fun for me too. But that doesn't mean anything between us is different. I still think you're an asshole."

"As you should," I say. "I still want you to know that you shouldn't expect for our relationship to become anything like Max's and Lila's."

"Oh, don't worry, Kingston. That's the last thing on Earth I would ever want. You're not that good of a lover."

Chapter Seventeen

Skye

"Why on Earth would you say that, Skye?" Elisabetta shakes her head as she gazes at me.

I stuff another spoonful of Frosted Flakes into my mouth and just shake my head, "Because I could see the way he looked at me when he woke up. There was shock and worry." I grab the milk and pour some more into the bowl. "And I didn't want him to think that I was some loser who thought that it meant something just because we had sex one time."

"But you told the guy you were looking at engagement rings."

"It was a joke. Sue me. Okay, maybe I'm not going to be a comedian."

"That is a very bad joke to pull on a guy that you know is a commitaphobe. I mean, I don't know he's a commitaphobe, but..."

"I know. Anyway, am I crazy?"

Elisabetta just looks at me. "Do you want the truth or..."

"Of course I want the truth."

"Okay. I think that you deserve a high five for having fun last night."

"Okay."

"But I think you kind of put yourself in an awkward position by doing it with your boss, who you are already kind of annoyed by."

I stare at her and blink. "So you think me fucking my annoying boss was a mistake."

"I don't know, but we shall see," she says with a twisted smile. "Was it good?"

I stare at her for a couple of seconds and blush, thinking about how it felt to have Kingston inside of me, "Let's just say that if he showed up right now, grabbed me by the hand, and took me into the bedroom, I wouldn't say no."

"Wow. So he *was* good."

"He was." I nod. "I mean, I still think he's a jackass and I don't know if work is going to become more complicated because of this, but I don't regret it."

"Famous last words," Elisabetta says as she bites down on a strawberry. She runs her fingers through her long dark hair and leans back. "I am proud of you, Skye."

I stare at her for a couple of seconds, "What? Proud of me for what?"

"I'm proud of you for just letting loose and having a fun time and letting tomorrow worry about tomorrow."

"What are you talking about?"

"The old you would've been so focused on what was going to happen on Monday morning that you wouldn't have let anything happen."

I stare at her, my heart sinking. "Monday is going to be so awkward."

"Stop thinking about it. It's only going to be awkward if you let it be awkward."

"It is awkward! I fucked my boss and I have to go in and work for him on Monday. And just last week, he was literally telling me that he wanted me to work to finish some files that I didn't finish and now it's been a week and I'm still not done with them and I don't want to hear about it again tomorrow."

"Yeah, so? If he starts to boss you around, just grab him by the hand and close the door and get down on your knees." She giggles, knowing how ridiculous she sounds.

"Oh my gosh, no. I'm not going to give my boss a blow job just to get out of doing work."

"I mean, you don't even know if it would work, but who even cares if it works. It could be fun just to get him off in the office. Imagine the power you will feel."

"It could be kinda empowering in an I can have you whenever I want kind of way," I admit. "But no, I'm not going to do that. Okay. Enough about me. How was your date?"

"It was kind of fun," she says, staring at me and popping another strawberry into her mouth. "Let's just say that you're not the only one that had a little excitement last night."

"You did not hook up with the guy you met on Tinder," I say, shocked.

"No." She shakes her head and laughs. "If I'm being 100% honest, not really."

"What are you talking about? Not really as in not at all or not really as in we boinked all night?"

"We didn't hook up, hook up."

"And you've lost me."

"Let's just say we went for a drink..."

"Uh huh."

"And he got under the table..."

My eyes widen as I stare at her. "Uh huh."

"And let's just say I wasn't wearing any panties."

"Oh my gosh. Elisabetta, what?"

"What?" She shrugs. "You always have to be prepared for any situation."

"With no panties?"

She grins. "And let's just say this man had a tongue that was long and knew what it was doing."

"Oh my gosh. He went down on you?"

She grins and nods. "Yep."

"In the bar?"

"Yep."

"In front of people."

"I mean, there was a tablecloth."

"Okay, so no one saw?"

She shakes her head. "Well, I don't know if I'd say that." She grins at me.

"What are you talking about?"

"There were two guys sitting at the table next to us and they may or may not have realized what was going on." She grins.

"No way."

"When a guy's going down on you and he's got a tongue that knows what it's doing, hey, sometimes little whimpers and moans escape from your mouth. I can't help it if I'm loud when I come."

"Oh my gosh. You let your Tinder date go down on you at a bar and two guys watched."

She grins at me. "And I have a date with one of them tonight."

"You have a date with what? With who? With the guy that went down on you?"

"Nah." She shook her head. "Don't get me wrong, he was great. His tongue was amazing, but he was kind of boring."

"So who's the date with?"

"His name is Tombstone."

"Tombstone. What?"

She wiggles her eyebrows. "He's slightly older."

"How old?" *Please do not say he's in his 80s.*

"I don't know. I'll find out tonight."

"You're going on a date with a guy who watched you getting your pussy licked by another man?" *What sort of weirdo likes that? Stop being judgmental Skye, you're certainly not a nun.*

She laughs. "Hey, I didn't ask for his number. He just dropped it off."

I stare at her. "He watched you receiving oral sex and then gave you his number."

"So if we want to be exact, my date gave me oral sex. I came loudly. I mean, it was a loud bar, so not everyone heard me, just the two guys next to me. My date gets up from under the table, says he's going to go and get us some drinks. I smile. I look over at the two guys who both grin at me knowingly. I'm sure they expected me to be embarrassed, but nope. I'm a modern woman and if a guy wants to go down on me, I'm going to let him. Anyway, the very good-looking guy—"

"Tombstone?"

"Yeah," she says. "He stands up and he walks over to me and hands me a business card. Then he takes out a pen and says, 'If you want to have an even better night than you've had tonight, call me.' So I stare at him as I take the card and I'm like, 'How do I know this is really your number?' And he says, 'Give me your phone.' So I do."

"You what?"

She grins and nods. "I gave him my phone and he called himself."

I stare at her.

"And then he pulls out his phone and he texts me and hands me my phone back. And you want to know what he said in his text?"

I shake my head. "I don't know if I do, actually, but we've come this far. What did he say?"

"He said, 'Send me a photo of your tits.'"

"No. What? That's crazy."

"It was kind of crazy. But you want to know what's even crazier?"

"What?"

"I undid the buttons of my shirt."

My jaw drops as I listen to her.

"And..."

"Oh my gosh, you did not."

She grins. "I undid the buttons of my shirt. I wasn't wearing a bra. And I take a photo of my tits and my date comes back and he's staring at me and he's like, 'What's going on?' And Tombstone says, 'Don't you worry about it.' And my date says, 'What the fuck is going on here?' And I just smile. And then Tombstone leans down and gives me a kiss on the lips and then I feel his fingers playing with my nipples." Her eyes widen. "I know. Slutty, right?"

"Elisabetta, what the fuck?"

"I don't know what to say," she says. "Maybe it was the tequila shots. Maybe it's because I haven't been laid in a while. I don't know. Anyway, my date is pissed off. Tombstone chuckles and says, 'Let's go out tonight.'" And I nod, then do my top back up and make my way out to the street and catch a cab home."

I stare at her. "You had a crazier night than I did."

"I think we both had crazy nights," she says. "You hooked up with your jackass of a boss."

"You let a stranger go down on you and then let another man play with your boobs in front of him. That's crazy."

"We're young," she says with a shrug. "Isn't now the time we're supposed to be having fun?"

"I guess so." I laugh. "What is going on?"

"I don't know," she says. "Maybe we've been good girls for too long."

"I guess so. Shit, so you're going to go out with him tonight? Where are you going?"

"I don't know," she says. "But if all goes well, I might invite him over tonight, if you don't mind."

"I don't mind, but are you okay with me being here or..."

"Of course," she says. "As long as you're okay being here."

"I mean, I think I'll be okay being here, right? Nothing crazy's going to go down, is it?"

"I cannot promise anything," she says as she takes another strawberry. "All I can say is that I'm going to let the night take me where it will. Are you going to text Kingston?"

"Oh, hell no," I say, shaking my head. Though, as I say that, my phone beeps. I stare Elisabetta and she just smiles at me and stands up.

"I'm getting in the shower."

"Okay," I say as I pull out my phone. I see I have a message from Kingston. I open it.

"**About those files...**" I groan as I read it.

"**It's not Monday morning yet,**" I send back immediately.

"**I need you to finish them first thing tomorrow.**"

"**Um okay. You could have told me this tomorrow.**"

"**No, because I need you to come in early.**"

I roll my eyes. "**How early is early?**"

"**I think 5 A.M. should do it.**"

"**Keep dreaming, Kingston.**"

"**Nah, I'd rather keep fucking,**" he responds.

I gasp. "**Totally inappropriate.**"

"**Sorry. You're right. So I'll see you at 5:00 in the morning?**"

I just stare at the phone before responding. "**Unlikely. Goodbye.**" I power the phone off and shake my head, then place my bowl in the kitchen sink and run my fingers through my hair. I don't know what the fuck I'm doing, and I don't know what the fuck Elisabetta is doing either. We've both lost our minds. Absolutely lost our minds. And the crazy thing is, I don't even care. I feel like I'm finally living. I feel like I'm finally experiencing life.

I power my phone back on and call Lila.

"Hey," she answers, gasping for air. "What you doing?"

"I was just calling to see what you're up to today. I'm not interrupting you, am I?"

"Oh, I was just on the treadmill, so I'm very grateful for the interruption," she says, giggling. "I don't have plans today. I think Max is meeting up with Gabe, and Marie might be interviewing with him or something? So if you want to hang out..."

"Perfect," I say. "I have so much to tell you."

Chapter Eighteen

Kingston

My phone beeps at 10 PM and I frown when I see that it's a notification from work. Someone has entered my office. I immediately sit up and bring up the cameras. My jaw drops when I see Skye on the screen grabbing something from my desk.

"What on Earth?" I mumble to myself as I quickly dial her number. The phone rings a couple of times before she answers.

"Hello, this is Skye."

"I know it's you. I called you."

"What's going on, Kingston?" she says, sounding annoyed.

"What are you doing at the office? Are you trying to steal trade secrets or something?"

"Yeah. I am stealing all the trade secrets to sell to the Russians for millions and billions of dollars." She lets out a sigh. "You said you wanted the files taken care of, right?"

"I said you could do it tomorrow morning."

"Yeah. Well, it turns out that I had some time tonight."

"It's ten o'clock at night."

"You think I don't know it's ten o'clock at night?" she snaps.

I pause. "Hey, is everything okay? You're not mad at me because of—"

"No, I'm not mad at you because we had sex, Kingston. I'm not mad at you, period. I just can't be at home right now."

"Why can't you be at home right now?"

"My roommate has someone in the apartment, and they're in the living room..." She pauses. "Anyway, I don't really think I need to say more than that."

"Wait, Elisabetta? She has her Tinder date back in the apartment?"

"No, it's not her Tinder date. It's another guy. Anyway, I really shouldn't be spreading her business. I'm just working, and I want to make sure that I have everything done tonight so I can prove myself to be a great assistant, so you can come in tomorrow morning and have everything done because I know how important it is to you."

"Okay. Thank you, I guess."

"You're welcome."

"So you're planning on staying there all night doing this?"

"Well, until I get a text message from Elisabetta that it's safe to come back to the apartment. I don't really want to be in my bedroom listening to my best friend bang some random dude."

"Oh," I say.

"Is that all you're going to say?" she snaps again.

"Hey, I'm just saying that that does sound like it sucks. I don't have a roommate, so that's not something I've had to worry about. But I guess if I did, I wouldn't appreciate them banging in the living room, either. Look, if you are homeless for the evening, you can come back over to my place."

"No, thank you. I don't need your pity."

"It's not pity. You slept here last night and—"

"And look how that turned out," she says sarcastically.

"You're not trying to say that you did not enjoy last night, are you?"

"I'm just trying to say that last night was last night, and it's already in my past."

"Really? Because this morning it wasn't in your past."

"You know what I mean," she says. "Do you want me to get this work done for you or not?"

"I do want you to get this work done, but I didn't expect you to be at the office on a Sunday at ten PM. It makes me feel bad."

"Why does it make you feel bad?"

"Because I don't want people to think that I'm a monster."

"Really? You don't want people to think that you're a monster in the office, yet you're always bossing people around and—"

"Hey, I'm reasonable, though, don't you think?"

"I guess."

"Hey. Look, Skye, are you upset with me because of what happened this weekend? Are you upset because you're in the office working? Are you upset because your roommate has someone in the apartment and you can't go home? What's going on?"

"Nothing." She lets out a deep sigh. "I'm just frustrated."

"Why are you frustrated?"

"It's nothing that I can talk to you about," she says. "Or at least it's nothing I *want* to talk to you about."

"Fair enough. Hey, why don't you come over to my

place? Bring the files with you and we'll go through them together and drink some wine."

"Are you out of your mind? I am not coming over to your place to drink more wine."

"Why not?" I say innocently.

"Because I don't want to wake up tomorrow morning with you inside of me."

"Well, you didn't wake up this morning with me inside of you," I say, laughing. "Though, if that's something that's a kink of yours, I'm sure we can make it happen."

"Really? That's so inappropriate."

"What? You're telling me that you haven't thought about last night and hoped that it would happen again?"

There's silence on the line.

"Come on, tell me the truth."

"Was last night fun? Yes. Do I think you're an asshole? Yes. Do I think it's going to be awkward tomorrow morning? Yes. Do I want to repeat what we did? I don't know."

"Why do you not know?"

"Because it's already going to be complicated, Kingston. I'm your assistant. You don't really respect me. You don't think I do an amazing job. And, yeah, while we had great chemistry, I don't want people in the office thinking that I got the job, or I'm keeping the job, because I'm banging you."

"Okay," I say softly. "Are you upset because this is not going anywhere super important?" I ask awkwardly.

"Dude, I don't want to marry you. I don't want you to propose to me. I'm not looking for a long-term relationship with you. You're not the dream guy I've always had in my head."

"Well, thank you," I say. "That makes me feel great."

"I'm just being honest. Yeah, it was fun hooking up.

Yeah, I'd do it again, but I don't want that to make my position more complicated."

"What if we had rules?"

"What sort of rules?"

"What happens in the office stays in the office, and what happens outside of the office stays outside of the office."

"So what, you're trying to come up with an arrangement?"

"I mean, other people have them. It could work. We both enjoyed making love, or knocking one out or banging or whatever you want to call it, and I think we'd both quite like to do it again."

"Maybe once, just to see if it was good or not," she says seriously, like she is weighing her options.

"So come over tonight. Bring the folders."

"But isn't that blurring lines if I bring work over?"

I pause. "I think it's okay for you to bring work to my home, but it's not okay for you to bring our sex lives to the office."

"So I can work with you at your house, but I cannot do anything in the office," she says softly.

"Yeah. We don't want word getting out that anything is going on. And I'm sure that we can both agree that what we're having is fun, and as long as it stays fun, it's fine. But when either one of us is over it—"

"You mean if I get a boyfriend or something?"

"Well, I guess." I frown at the thought. "Why? Is there a potential out there that—"

"I'm not looking to have a friend with benefits for the rest of my life. I am looking for a relationship. Remember I told you I want to travel around the world."

"So, sure, when you meet the guy that wants to travel

around the world with you, we stop things. Or when things are no longer fun."

"Or, I guess, if you find a woman," she says.

"Yeah. Or if I find a woman." I chuckle. "Which I don't anticipate happening. But you have to promise not to catch feelings for me."

"Well, *you* have to promise not to catch feelings for *me*, Kingston."

"I can pretty much assure you that I don't catch feelings for women."

"And I can pretty much assure you that I don't catch feelings for jerks," she counters.

"So are you coming over then?" I ask.

"You want me to bring these folders?"

"Yeah, because maybe we finish the work tonight, then neither one of us has to get to the office tomorrow at five AM."

"Okay," she says, "I'll bring them. But..."

"But what?" I ask.

"I just don't know that I want to carry the folders onto the subway."

"I'll send a cab to pick you up."

"Okay, thank you."

"Are you hungry? Do you want me to order a pizza or something?"

"I think I've had enough pizza for a lifetime," she says, giggling.

"Chinese food? Indian? Ethiopian?"

"I'm okay, but thank you." She pauses.

"Tell me. What is it?"

"I mean, I could go for some tacos. Like, real Mexican tacos with corn tortillas and carne asada and cilantro and onion."

"Okay, I can get some authentic Mexican tacos for you. You want some tequila shots as well?"

"Tequila shots make me do bad things, Kingston."

"So then that's a definite yes to the tequila shots," I laugh.

"You're bad," she says.

"Well, if we're going to follow through with this arrangement, we might as well do it to the best of our ability."

"What does that mean?" she asks.

"It means that if we're going to have fun, I want to make sure that I show you the most fun you've ever had in your life."

"Okay. Like how?

"Like, have you ever had anal?"

"I'm not doing anal with you, Kingston."

"Have you ever had anal? I didn't ask if you want to do it with me."

"No," she says. "I don't want—"

"Aha. So you don't know the joys of it."

"Kingston."

"What? I'm just saying," I chuckle. "Have you ever been tied up?"

"Like you mean with handcuffs, or a tie, or...?"

"I'm talking about with rope and hanging from the ceiling."

"What? You're not for real."

"Maybe I am, maybe I'm not. But if you're open to exploring, so am I."

"Kingston, I think we're going to have to have a chat while I'm there because I think you and I are thinking about this in two different ways."

"Oh yeah? And how are you thinking about it?"

"I'm thinking about we just have some casual sex every now and again. You're acting like you're Christian Grey."

"Really? I make Christian Grey look tame. Trust me."

"Trust you?" she says, laughing. "I don't know if I would be wise to trust you."

"Maybe you are smarter than you look," I say.

"Really?"

"I'm just joking. I'm going to send the cab over now. It should be there in ten minutes, okay?"

"Sounds good," she says.

"Good. I'll see you later." I hang up the phone and I walk into my bathroom. I stare at my reflection in the mirror.

What have you done, Kingston? I shake my head. Even though it had been my suggestion, it's not something I've ever contemplated in my life before. I don't believe in messing around with people who work for me, even if we're keeping it separate.

But there's just something about Skye. Hearing her voice sounding so sad and desolate, it made my heart pang. And seeing her in that office all alone with those files, it made me feel guilty. And hearing that she couldn't go back to her apartment because her roommate was banging it out with someone else, it just doesn't sit right with me. And if I'm being honest, I thought about her all day and missed her company, missed her laugh and smile.

I'm looking for a relationship, and I don't want this to go anywhere, but it would be fun just to see where it could lead.

Chapter Nineteen

Skye

"Hi, thank you so much for picking me up," I say to the cab driver as I slide into the back seat. I stare at the stack of files on the seat next to me and let out a deep sigh. "I am guessing you know the address."

"I do," he says with a nod. "Settle in."

"Thank you," I say as I buckle my seatbelt.

I take a deep breath, and for a couple of moments I think about telling the driver to stop and let me out. I'm not really sure that I'm making the best decision, but a part of me just wants to go with it and see how it works out.

I hear my phone beeping and I look down to see Elisabetta has texted me. "**Oh my gosh, Skye. I am so sorry. I got carried away. Where are you?**"

I stare at the phone and smile slightly. I don't really want to tell her that I walked in on her on all fours with a strange man behind her doing Heaven knows what while she was screaming. That was a sight that I want to forget for the rest of my life.

I text back quickly. "**Hey, no worries. I actually**

got caught up with some work and I'm still working. So see you tomorrow?"

"**Are you sure?**" she messages back immediately.

"**I'm sure.**"

I look at my screen and lick my lips. I want to speak to Elisabetta. I want to ask her if she thinks I'm making a mistake, but I don't know if she's still with the guy. I don't know where her head space is at.

I decide to call Lila and she answers on the third ring.

"Hey, what's going on?"

"I didn't wake you up, right?"

"No, it's not that late."

"You and Max aren't doing anything intimate or anything?"

"Max is in the office," she says, giggling. "I was just about to watch *Love is Blind UK*. The new episodes just came out."

"Oh? Is it good?"

"Oh my gosh, girl, it is so good. The men are adorable. Even better than the US men. There's this one guy that if I wasn't with Max, I would want to be with him."

"Oh? Really?"

"Yeah. His name is Benaniah, but he goes by Ben for short. He is so dreamy. He has these blue eyes and this blonde hair and oops. I should probably keep the excitement out of my voice."

"Man, I'm going to have to check it out."

"You know what I was thinking?" she says.

"No. What?"

"I was thinking you should go on a dating show."

"What, like *The Bachelor*?"

"No, like a *Love is Blind* or something like that. I think

you'd do really well. You have such a bubbly personality and you're so fun, and then when they meet you, they would be absolutely astounded because you're also drop-dead gorgeous."

"Oh my gosh, Lila. I am so glad we met in the street that day. You have done so much for my self-esteem."

"What? I'm just telling the truth."

"I know, and you're going to think I'm absolutely crazy right now."

"Um, why would I think you're crazy?"

"Because of where I'm going."

"You're confusing me. What's going on Skye?"

"So I was at the office working..."

"What? On a Sunday evening?"

"Don't ask. Anyway, I guess somehow Kingston found out and he was alerted to the fact that I was working."

"Oh, and he got upset?"

"No, he loved it." I giggle. "He wanted me in the office tomorrow morning at five AM."

"Five AM? Is he crazy?"

"I think so, but guess what?"

"What?"

"You have to promise not to tell Max."

"Okay."

"I mean it, Lila. No one can know what I'm about to tell you."

"Oh my gosh, you didn't steal like a million dollars from the vault at the law firm, did you? You're not on the run to the Bahamas or Mexico or something."

"Lila, you watch too many movies. Does the law firm even have a vault with a million dollars?"

"I don't know," she says, laughing. "If they do, Max hasn't trusted me enough to tell me about it yet."

"Exactly. So if your fiancé, the love of your life, has not told you about the vault, how on Earth would I know?"

"True," she says. "So what's going on?"

"I'm headed over to Kingston's place," I say in a whisper.

"But it's ten o'clock at night."

"I know. We're going to do some work."

"Oh, wow. He is a really hard boss. No wonder you wanted to be a part of the Annoying Hot Bosses Club."

"But he also had a suggestion for me and..." My voice trails off. "I kind of think I'm going to say yes."

"What are you talking about?"

"He thinks that we should..." I pause to think of the right words. "I guess be friends with benefits."

"What?"

"I know. I know. It's an awful idea, but he's so handsome and it's not like I'm dating anyone. It's not like I'm even meeting anyone and sex with him was so good and I do want to do it again. And he has this idea that we keep the bedroom in the bedroom and work at work. So we're not going to discuss anything physical or intimate in the office."

"Um," she says, but doesn't say anything else.

"You think it's a bad idea, don't you?"

"I just think it's going to be really hard to keep sex in the bedroom and work at work. I mean, what if you see him in the office and you just want to rip his clothes off?"

"Well, then I'll wait until I see him the next time out of the office and I'll do it."

"What if you want him to take you on the desk? What if you want to have a quickie in the bathroom? What if—"

"Lila."

"What? I'm just saying keeping sex in the bedroom sounds like a great idea. I just don't know that it's possible."

"So you think I should say no?"

"I don't think you should say no if that's something you want, I just wonder if it's something that is actually feasible and well-thought-out."

I lick my lips as I listen to her words. She has a point. I've never been a proponent for friends with benefits because I've never actually thought that it could work. I'd always thought that people would catch feelings, but I don't really see me catching feelings for someone like Kingston and I sure don't see him catching feelings for me.

"I mean, I think it could be really fun, and if at any time it's not fun, we won't do it anymore. Maybe, in fact, I'll do it and then I'll try signing up for a dating show and then when I get cast, I can just end things so that it's not messy and I can just give myself wholeheartedly to the process of the show without feeling horny because I haven't had any in a long time."

There's silence on the other end.

"Are you there, Lila?"

"Um, I'm here, but I'm still trying to process what you just said."

"What? I think it's reasonable. I bet you a lot of times the people who go on those shows end up with someone that's not that great because they're so horny and in lust so they go by physical attraction. But if I've been getting some with a really good-looking guy, then I can really focus on personality and ensuring that we're a good fit outside of just the physical attraction. So maybe you're right. Maybe *Love is Blind* is the show for me."

"Skye, you are saying that you're going to enter into a friends with benefits situation with a boss you find quite annoying so that you can have better luck on a reality TV dating show that you haven't even applied for, that wasn't even in your mind ten minutes ago until I spoke to you on the phone?"

I chuckle. "You know me. I'm quick on my feet and fast in my brain."

"I think that you will use any excuse to enter into this arrangement and I'm going to be honest; it sounds fun. It sounds exciting and Kingston is gorgeous. He has the bluest eyes I've ever seen in my life and that dark silky hair? Shit, he could be a Greek god. He could be a Roman god. He could be a movie star. I understand why you're attracted to him. I understand why you want to have some fun." She pauses. "I just don't want to see you getting hurt, you know? You're my friend and I love you and I care about you and I want to ensure that all your dreams come true. And I know you want to meet a great man."

"I do," I say softly. "I was thinking about it earlier today. I want to find true love."

"And do you think you're going to find true love by banging your boss?" she asks. "I'm sorry. That was crude and I don't like to be crude, but..."

"But nothing. It's a valid question. No, I don't think that I'm going to find true love by entering into an arrangement with my boss. But it's fun. And you know what I've decided?"

"No. What have you decided?"

"I've decided that I'm going to live for the here and now. If tomorrow I meet a great guy and I think there's potential, I'll just look Kingston in the eyes and I'll say, 'While what we had was fun, it's time for me to move on because I've met someone that can maybe give me what I really want.'"

"Do you really think it will be as simple as that?" she asks softly.

"I do, and I don't know if I'm lying to myself or not, but I really and truly do."

I look out the window and stare at the people walking down the street as the cab zooms down the road and I wonder if I'm lying to myself. I wonder if I really and truly can be in an arrangement with someone like Kingston without developing feelings, without it going haywire or getting awkward and messy.

"And I mean, honestly, Lila, it's not like this is my dream job. If everything goes to shit, I'll just quit and I'll find something else to do. I'm nothing if not resourceful."

"I know," she says. "And I understand, and trust me, if at any time it feels like it's too much or too messy or you just want to chat, I'll be here. Okay?"

"I know, and that's why I love you so much. You're always there for me. So maybe we can grab lunch this week?"

"That sounds great."

"I think we're about to pull up to the building, so I'll see you soon? I'll talk to you later, girl. Bye."

I hang up and sit back in the seat, closing my eyes. My heart is thudding at the thought of seeing Kingston again. The cab pulls over and stops and the driver looks in the rearview mirror.

"This is the address I was given. You sure you want to get out?"

I stare at him and nod slightly while grabbing my folders.

"I don't know you and you don't know me," he says. "But friends with benefits usually ends up as enemies with nothing."

I stare at him for a couple of seconds before giving him a

wry smile. "I mean, I guess the good thing is he and I aren't really friends."

The guy blinks. "What?"

"Me and Kingston, the guy I'm entering this relationship with," I say, having no idea why I'm telling this stranger my story. "We're not really friends. So if it blows up, it's not like I'm losing a great friendship. It's just me going back to my old life. But thank you."

He nods and turns around to look at me. "For what it's worth," he says, looking me up and down. "I'd want to enter a relationship like that with you as well." I stare at him for a couple of seconds in shock as he winks. "I have a wife, but what she doesn't know." He grins. "You know, 'when the cat's away, the mice will play.' He pulls out a business card and hands it to me. "If you're ever looking for a second non-friend with benefits."

I stare at the card in his hand and blink. "But you just said you're married."

"And?" He raises an eyebrow and I just shake my head.

I jump out of the cab with the files and slam the door behind me.

He rolls the window down and grins. "I'm just saying, if you like to give it up."

I press my scowl and head toward the building. I'm mortified and pissed off and wish I'd taken the card so I could research the guy and contact his wife and tell her that her husband is a philandering pig.

I step inside the lobby of the building and my heart jumps for joy when I see Kingston standing there, a smirk on his face as he heads over to me.

"You made it. I wasn't sure if you were going to come."

"Well, I want someone to help me with all these files," I

say with a small smile. "It's not every day your boss offers to help you do your work."

"True," he says. "And it's not every day your boss invites you to spend the night."

"I know. Crazy." I grin. "Hopefully I don't have to do anything to earn the pleasure of sleeping in his bed."

"I don't think you have to do anything you wouldn't enjoy doing."

"Ah, but how do you know what I would enjoy doing?"

"I've got a pretty good idea," he says as he takes the folders from me. "In fact, why don't we head up to my place right now and see if I can guess one of the things you enjoy doing."

I look into his eyes and my heart races and all I can do is nod. We walk toward the elevator in silence, and as we step in, he presses the button to his floor then takes a step back.

"I wish I didn't have these folders in my hand," he says as he licks his lips.

"Oh? Why is that?"

"Because I'd love to press you up against the wall, lift your leg up, and pleasure you."

"Are you really saying what I think you're saying?"

"Depends on what you think I'm saying. Do you understand direct statements?" He grins. "You ever had sex in an elevator?"

I shake my head. "Have you?"

"Perhaps," he says. "But not this elevator." He grins. "There are plenty of places I haven't had sex that I would love to have sex with with you."

"So we're doing this then." I stare at him, my heart racing, my stomach flipping.

"If this means we're going to embark on a sexual journey together, I think so. That's why you're here, right?"

"You're not worried that this is going to blow up in our faces? You're not worried that..."

"Worried that what? Worried that you will fall for me?" He shrugs. "I am devastatingly handsome with a personality to match."

I groan. "So modest."

He grins. "But you seem like you've got your head on straight and I feel like I've got my head on straight. I think we both see this for what it is."

"And what's that?" I said.

"Us satisfying each other." He grins.

"I hope that—." My phone rings and I frown as I see Elisabetta's name on the screen. "I have to take this." I answer the phone quickly. "Hey, is everything okay?"

"Can you come home?" She whispers. "I did something stupid."

"Oh, Lord, what happened?"

"I can't talk right now. I'm in my closet whispering to you."

"Okay, I'm coming right now. I'll be there as soon as I can." I look over at Kingston with wide eyes. "Elisabetta is in trouble. I have to go."

He stares at me for a few moments, his eyes darkening as he nods. "I'm coming with you."

"What? No, I don't need you to—."

"The guy is still there?"

"I think so." I admit.

"I'm not letting you go into a potentially dangerous situation by yourself. I am coming with you." He gestures me into his apartment. "Let me get dressed and grab my car keys."

"You drive?"

"I'm not just a pretty face." He grins, but then stops as

he notices that I'm shaking. "Hey, it's going to be okay. She's okay right? Should we call the cops?"

"I don't think we need to call the cops, but I'm scared. I've never heard her sound like that before."

He nods and races to his bedroom and is back out within minutes, holding up some keys. He grabs my upper arms and looks me directly in the eyes. "I am here for you and your best friend. We will take care of whatever the problem is, okay?"

"Okay." I nod weakly. Never have I been more grateful for Kingston being so dominant and bossy. "Thanks."

"No worries. I always take care of my own." He says softly and my heart races slightly at his words. I have no idea what he means by that, but the sentiment makes me feel ecstatic.

* * *

"You really don't have to come with me," I say to Kingston as we make our way up the stairs to my apartment. "I know that you probably had other things going on this evening and—"

"No, it's fine," he says. "I was not going to allow you to go back to the apartment by yourself. You don't know what's going on."

"I mean, I don't think she's being murdered or anything. She sounded more tearful, not scared." I look at him and blink. "But I am grateful that you've come with me. Thank you."

"You're welcome," he says. He smiles at me, and we share a look for a few moments as we head towards my door. I'm not sure what we're going to enter and see, and I'm nervous. I'm really grateful that he's here beside me. Even though Kingston can be a jerk, I've quite liked seeing this protective side of him. It reminds me of when we were in Club Z and Whitaker Matlock had tried to feel me up. It had been uncomfortable, and I was slightly out of my element, and knowing that Kingston had seen that and stood up for me had meant so much.

I grab my key and open the door. "Hey, it's me," I say as I step inside. Kingston hurries in behind me and closes the door. "Hey, Elisabetta. I'm home," I call out again, and I hear thuds walking toward me. A guy in his late twenties with dark brown hair glances up at me in surprise.

"Yo, what's going on?"

"Hi," I say, frowning. I look over at Kingston. "That's not the guy that I saw her with earlier," I whisper, and he makes a face. "Sorry, who are you?" I ask him.

"I'm Radium." He grins. "You're Elizabeth's friend?"

"Elisabetta," I say. "Yeah, I'm her best friend and roommate. You know where she is?" My heart's pounding. I really hope he hasn't done something to her.

"She's in the bathroom, I guess." He shrugs. "I guess she's showering or something."

"Okay. And you're leaving or..."

"I mean, she told me she wanted me gone, but I wanted to tell her it's no big deal. You know?" He looks over at Kingston. "I'm sure you agree. It happens."

Kingston stares at him, then looks at me. "What's he talking about?" he asks softly.

"I have no idea." I shake my head. "I'm going to go and see how Elisabetta is. Kingston, will you stay here with Radium and just make sure everything's okay?" Kingston nods and I hurry toward Elisabetta's bedroom, open it, and make my way to the bathroom. I knock.

"Who is it?" she calls out, slightly annoyed.

"It's me. It's Skye."

"Oh. Hold on." I hear footsteps, and then she unlocks the door and opens it. She's wearing a white towel and her body is still wet. "Oh my fucking gosh," she says, shaking her head. "Never fucking again. I'm so fucking embarrassed."

"What happened? You're making me nervous. Who the hell is Radium? That's not that dude I saw you with earlier."

"Oh my gosh, Skye. I'm an idiot. I totally screwed up."

"He's not dangerous, is he?"

"Who?" she says, blinking.

"Radium."

"Not that I know of. Why? Isn't he gone?"

"No, he's in the living room with Kingston."

"Kingston?" She raises an eyebrow. "Your boss?"

"Yeah. He was concerned that something bad happened and didn't want me to come here alone."

"Oh, that was nice of him. Much nicer than I would've expected from a jerk like him."

"I know. I kind of felt the same way," I say with a little giggle. "But what is going on here? You called me and you sounded really upset. And I'm not going to lie, I came home earlier and you were with a different guy. Who is this?"

"Oh my gosh. So, remember Tombstone?"

"Yeah, I remember what you told me about him."

"He came over and, you know, we were going to have some fun, but then he couldn't get it up." She rolls her eyes. "I guess he had a lot on his mind or something." She shrugged. "Anyway, he said, 'If you want me to go, I can go.' And I was like, 'Sure, go.' And so I was just kind of hanging out and I was like, 'You know what? Fuck, I feel horny.'"

I stare at her. "Elisabetta, really?"

"What can I say? So I went on the app and I matched with Radium and hey, he was feeling horny too."

"Okay, and what happened?" I say softly. "Can we sit on your bed or something? I feel awkward just standing here in the bathroom with you."

"Sure," she says. "Do you think we should go out there and speak to Kingston and Radium first though?"

"No, I'm sure it'll be okay," I say as we walk and sit down on her mattress.

"So anyway, Radium comes over over."

"Yeah, and?"

"We're hooking up."

"You don't even know him."

"I made sure he had protection. Come on now, Skye. You've never just been horny for horny's sake?"

"Of course I have, but that doesn't mean I meet a random dude on a site and invite him over, especially after another guy had already been here."

"It's not like I fucked Tombstone. Come on. It's not like I'm fucking two different guys on the same night, which would not be the worst thing to ever happen in the world, by the way."

"I'm not judging you. You know that, Elisabetta." I let out a deep sigh. I have no idea what's going on with my best friend, why she's all of a sudden lost it. All I know is that I can just be there for her. "So what happened?"

"He gets here and he's cute. You know I like that surfer look."

"Yeah, he does kind of look like a surfer or a skateboarder."

"Anyway, we're in the bed and he's like, 'How adventurous are you?'"

"Okay?"

"And I was like, 'I'm more adventurous than Christopher Columbus.'"

"What?" I stare at her.

"You know, Christopher Columbus, the explorer."

"Okay."

"Maybe I should've said Marco Polo, huh?"

"Elisabetta, stick to the story."

"Sorry," she says, grinning. "Anyway, he's like, 'You want to do anal?' And I was like, 'I don't know.' And he's like, 'I've got lube.' And I should've been like, 'Why do you have lube?' But anyway. I'm like, 'He's hot and what the fuck, let me just go with it.'"

"Okay?" I say, blinking, not wanting to ask my best friend why she thought anal with a perfect stranger was a good idea.

"Anyway, he's fucking me pretty good."

I stare at her. "Okay."

"And then I feel his fingers all over me and he does this move."

"What move?" I ask her.

"Girl, I'm not even sure because everything that happened next happened so quickly." She makes a face.

"What happened next?"

"I shit on his dick."

"You what?" I almost scream and then lower my voice as we hear footsteps. The doors open and I see Kingston standing there.

"Is everything okay?" He looks concerned.

"Yeah, she's fine. She's just telling me what happened. Sorry."

"Okay." He nods. "Because I'm going to get this dude to leave because I don't really think he sounds like he is mentally with it." He looks at me and then he looks at Elisabetta. "Are you okay? Do you want me to call the cops? Do you want—"

"No, I'm fine. I'm just mortified," she says. "Absolutely mortified. That has never happened to me before."

He blinks in confusion. "Sorry, I don't really know what you're talking about."

I stare at Elisabetta and she looks down in shame. "You can tell him later, only because he's here and he's going to want to know, but I do not want to be a party to the conversation when you tell him."

"Okay," I say. "Everything's fine, Kingston. Will you just get Radium to leave?"

"Okay," he says, nodding. "If you say so." He closes the door again and I look over at Elisabetta.

"Girl, that's not that bad. I know it's happened to other people."

"I shit on a rando while he was doing me up the ass." She stares at me. "Not just a little shit. A lot of shit. I never want to see that man again."

"Okay." I nod. "And you never have to see him again. We can make sure of that."

"And now I feel guilty."

"Why do you feel guilty?"

"Because freaking Tombstone sent me a text message saying that he wishes he could be the man that I wanted and he was sorry about tonight. And I feel like a slut."

"You're not a slut. It's not like Tombstone's your man."

"I know, but...what's going on with me?" She stares at me. "I just feel stupid."

"Girl, you're not stupid. You obviously were hornier than you thought and you just wanted to get laid. It happens."

"Yeah, I guess."

"And it's not your fault you shit on this dude. I mean, he was kind of asking for it if he wanted to do anal."

"What?" she says.

"It's never happened to me per se, but I've heard of plenty of people who have shit when doing anal."

"Really?" Her lips twitch, and I nod.

"Yeah." I give her a hug. "You did wash, right?"

"I'm wet. Of course I washed."

"Just checking. I don't want to be hugging my shitty best friend."

"I'm no longer shitty," she says, giggling. "Though the sheets under this duvet may—"

"Ew." I jump up. "Are you freaking kidding me?"

"I didn't have time to rip them off, but it's not like I was doing it on the duvet. We were doing it on the sheets. The duvet is covering anything that..."

"Oh my gosh. Elisabetta, this is gross. I am going into the living room. Put on some clothes and join us."

"I don't even want to stay here tonight," she says, shaking her head. "I want to go to the Ritz or something and just relax in a big king-size bed that doesn't have remnants of shit or cum." She wrinkles her nose. "Because you know he came, right?"

"Honestly, I don't want to know," I say giggling. "I really don't. This is like the grossest story I've ever heard."

"I guess I could be on a poster for why you do not want to engage in anal sex with strangers," she says, joking, and I have to stifle a snort. It's really not a laughing matter. I am not going to make a joke about adult diapers.

I don't think she will appreciate it.

It's too soon. Way too soon.

"Why don't you put on some clothes and I'll see if Radium's gone? And maybe I'll ask Kingston if he can take us to a hotel."

"You don't have to stay with me," she says. "If you want to be with him tonight..."

"What?"

"I called you and you were obviously at his place because he came with you."

"Yeah, and?"

"And it's late. Maybe you were going to have your own fun tonight."

"No, we were just going to work. We—"

"Maybe you were going to work. Maybe something else was going to happen." She shrugs. "But he doesn't seem like he's that bad of a guy."

"What are you saying?"

"He came here with you to make sure you were going to be okay to make sure I was okay. That's a pretty stand-up thing to do."

"Sure, he has his moments," I agree. "But I don't want to just leave you at a hotel and—"

"Trust me. I just want to be by myself for the rest of the night. I want to lie in. I want to get room service. I want to just have a bath for four hours and scrub my entire body clean." She takes a deep breath. "And then watch Netflix."

"Are you sure?"

"Yeah. I mean, I'd be grateful for the ride to the hotel, but I want you to enjoy your night. Just be careful."

"What does that mean?"

"We don't want two shitty stories in our friendship, right?"

I burst out laughing and hug her. "I love you."

"I love you too."

"I'm worried about you though, you know?"

"I know," she says. "I'm just going through some shit, but I'll figure it out."

"I'm always here for you. Whatever you need, whatever you want."

"I know," she says. "That's why you're my best friend and that's why I love you. And tell Kingston that I'm very grateful that he accompanied you as well."

"I will. Okay, let me go out and make sure Radium's gone," I say as I head toward the door.

"Okay. I'm just going to get some stuff together in a bag as well."

I head out into the living room and find Kingston sitting on the couch. He looks up at me with a query in his eyes. His dark hair is fluffy and he looks slightly tired.

"Everything okay?"

"Yeah. She just kind of had a little bit of a crazy night."

"Yeah, that's what I gather."

"Oh?" I ask him as I sit next to him on the couch.

His lips twitch slightly. "Yeah, Radium kind of told me what happened." His eyes widen and he smirks. "I mean, she shouldn't be embarrassed. That's something that does happen when...you know."

"That's what I told her," I say, blushing. "She wants to stay the night at a hotel though," I tell him.

"Oh, okay. And are you staying there with her?"

"No." I shake my head. "I told her that we had work to do."

"Oh, yeah. We have so much work to do." He grins.

"Yeah, we do have work. I know. That's what I said."

"So we'll take her to a hotel, and then we'll go back to my place and do some work?"

"That sounds like a good idea to me."

"Great," he says, and we just stare at each other awkwardly. I can feel the heat pulsing between us. He rubs my leg and I stare up at him in surprise. "You're a good friend," he says.

"Thank you. You're a good boss."

"I am?" he asks in surprise.

"Don't let it go to your head, but yes, tonight you were. I appreciate you coming with me."

"I know that you think I'm a jackass, and maybe sometimes I am, but deep down inside, I'm a kind of good person."

"Yeah, very deep down inside," I say, teasing him.

"You know, I could take that comment somewhere else, but I'm not going to." He winks at me and we both start laughing.

Chapter Twenty

Kingston

My adrenaline is still at an all-time high as we make our way back to my apartment. I'm grateful that we got Elisabetta checked into a luxury hotel so that she can relax and unwind. I'm also grateful that Skye decided to come back with me. I could tell that the whole ordeal had really worked her up and I wanted to make sure she was okay.

I quite liked being her protector and I had felt like a knight in shining armor when she'd looked to me to decide what to do. She'd even backed me up when I'd given Elisabetta a small lecture about doing drugs and inviting strange men back to her place. I'd been angry at the thought of how badly the night could have ended. She'd not only put herself at risk, but Skye as well.

"So I just want to say before we go into your apartment that I'm not here necessarily for the arrangement that you have offered me," Skye says, staring me down with bright eyes.

My lips twitch for a couple of seconds and I raise an

eyebrow. "Okay. So we will conveniently forget I just rescued your best friend and whisked you away in the night."

She squeezes my hand. "I am grateful for that, but we both know the other conversations we've had."

"We do." I nod, though all I really want to do is pull her into my arms and devour her.

"I'm here because you said you were going to help me with these files, and I don't want to go to work at five o'clock in the morning to finish them. So I took you up on your offer. I have been weighing up whether or not I would like to enter a friends with benefits or enemies with benefits arrangement, but..."

"Hold up a minute," I say as I open the door to my apartment. "Enemies with benefits?"

"I mean, are we really friends? You're my boss and I don't know if one night of eating pizza and drinking wine makes us friends."

"True," I say. "So you're saying that when we get into the apartment, you don't want me to show you the 101 ways my tongue can make you cum?"

She laughs lightly and shakes her head. "No, I don't need to learn or know the 101 ways that you can do that," she says. "That's also quite impossible, I believe."

"Oh, trust me when I say it's not." I grin. "But come on. Let's go inside and we can do some work."

"Okay." She looks at me cautiously. "And that's okay?"

"Is what okay?" I ask.

"Just working and not, you know, hooking up."

"I didn't invite you here just to hook up," I say seriously. "Sure. We had fun the other night and I would love to repeat it, but that's not what this is about. I didn't hire you, nor did I invite you over tonight, for the sole purpose of us making love or doing whatever. These files are very important. We have a lot of cases that we need to get to summary judgment and—"

"Okay, okay," she says. "Remember, I'm not a lawyer. I don't even know what you're talking about."

"I know. Come on. Let's take a seat at the dining room table and go through this stuff. Once we're done, we can chat about the other stuff."

"Okay." She nods softly.

I close the door behind her and place the files on the dining room table. I watch as Skye takes a seat and looks at me.

"Would you like something to drink? Water, wine, coffee?"

"I think I'll have a cappuccino if you are able to make it. I feel like it's going to be a long night going through all of these."

"I do have an espresso machine. Two cappuccinos coming up," I say, as I head to the kitchen.

She grabs the folder at the top of the pile and I watch as she pulls out a yellow legal pad and pen from the small satchel she's carrying.

"What's this about anyway?" she asks as she starts scribbling notes on the pad. "Who are all these people?"

"You want to know what the case is about?" I ask, very surprised. She hasn't really shown much interest in anything before. Just done the work.

"Yeah. These are a lot of people that we're suing and I'm just curious why."

I pull out two small cups and saucers and turn on the espresso machine. I listen as it grinds the beans and turn toward her.

"Well, we are representing a bank."

"A bank in New Jersey, right?" she says.

I nod. "Yeah, and that bank was the financier for several car dealerships in the area."

"Oh, okay." She nods.

"And one of the car dealerships was a Toyota car dealership and they went out of business. Do you want sugar and milk?" I ask.

"It's a cappuccino. Doesn't it already have milk?" She frowns.

"Oh, yeah. Sorry. Would you like sugar?"

"Yes, please. Brown if you have it."

"I believe I do," I say, opening a cupboard.

"Okay, so we're representing a bank that represents a car dealership?" she says, frowning. "Sorry, I'm confused."

"No, we're representing a bank that lent money to a car dealership and the people we're suing are customers from the car dealership."

"Oh, okay. Like, they didn't pay their car loan?"

"Exactly," I say with a smile.

"Wow. There are so many of them." She licks her lips. "That's kind of sad. The economy sucks."

"Yeah, the economy is pretty bad right now, but many of them are not happy that they are being sued by the bank."

"Why not? If you don't pay, you don't get your car."

"Well, the fact of the matter is they didn't receive a car."

"What?" She looks at me in confusion.

"So many of these customers purchased cars from the dealership and were meant to come and pick up their cars. Either they were in transport or the car was being serviced and being prepared."

"Okay." She frowns.

"The car dealership went bankrupt. However, they had

all signed contracts taking on the loan of the car, so the bank did transfer the money to the dealership."

"Wait, hold on a minute. But they never got the car, you said."

"And that's correct. However, when they signed the contract with the bank, they agreed to pay back the loan and the loan was given to the car dealership."

"But they never got the car from the car dealership," she said. "What?"

I shrug. "Unfortunately, they shouldn't have signed the loan until they took possession of the car."

Her jaw drops. "You're joking, right? That doesn't sound horrible to you? I couldn't imagine buying a car thinking I was picking it up on Monday. The car dealership goes bankrupt and I don't get the car and then the bank's suing me for the money. Shouldn't the bank sue the car dealership?"

"The contract was with the customer. It wasn't with the car dealership," I say, shrugging as I head to her with her cappuccino. "Would you like some biscotti or something with it?"

She stares at me as she shakes her head. "It just feels wrong. It feels really, really wrong. I feel for those people."

I shrug. "Unfortunately, when it comes to the law, there are many things that may make you feel like it's not fair, but the black letter of the law is what it is. The Constitution and the laws of the land apply to everyone and without them we..."

"Oh my gosh. You're not lecturing me about the law of the land," she says, rolling her eyes. "Give me a break. It's just not right."

"I'm just saying," I say, as I take a seat and grab a file from her.

"You're telling me it doesn't make you feel bad whatsoever?"

There's passion in her eyes as she looks at me incredulously. I want to tell her that I'm not paid to care whether or not I think something is right. I'm not paid to act on my emotions. I'm paid to argue the law. I'm paid to get my clients what they're due. Yet, somehow, it doesn't feel like enough. Somehow, I don't want to disappoint her.

"I'm just saying that you work for a corporate law firm, not legal aid." I take a sip of my own cappuccino.

"Maybe I should get a job at legal aid," she says, rolling her eyes. "Maybe then I'll meet people that actually care about other people and what's right and..." She stops. "Anyway, I guess this is why I never wanted to be an attorney because I think that actual human beings and their stories should matter more than what some arbitrary law says."

"The laws are important, but if you want to change them, maybe you should think about getting into the House of Representatives or Congress or..."

"Yeah, why don't I just run for senator or governor while I'm at it," she says, rolling her eyes. "Maybe I can become the next president of the United States of America." She holds her hand up high. "I feel like I'd be great at the job."

I stare at her for a couple of seconds and just laugh. "Well, if you decide to run, you've got my vote."

"Well, thank you. I just need a couple million more." She grins. "You know, when I was in school, I really did like history and the government classes we had to take."

"Oh, yeah?"

"Yeah. I can even still remember some facts I learned."

"Oh, why don't you tell me a couple?"

"Do you know how many senators there are?"

"Um, I believe there are two senators in each state and there are fifty states, so 100 senators?"

"Yeah," she says, nodding admirably at me. "Okay. That was an easy one. Do you know who would become president if the president was no longer fit for the job?"

"The vice president," I say, grinning.

"And you know who would become president if it wasn't the vice president?"

"The speaker of the house," I say quickly, and she rolls her eyes.

"You know everything."

"I am an attorney. I also like to keep up with politics." I shrug. "Ask me a couple more questions."

"Okay," she says. "Do you know who wrote the Constitution?"

"I believe that was Thomas Jefferson." I grin at her.

"Okay. Do you know who freed the slaves?"

"I believe Abraham Lincoln signed the Emancipation Proclamation, which freed the slaves."

"So you're a history buff too, huh?"

"I mean, I did enjoy history and I'm a bit of a trivia buff."

"Huh," she says. "There has to be something I know that you don't."

"Try a couple more questions and let's see."

"Okay, um..." She licks her lips and taps her finger against her legal pad. "Man, I'm trying to remember what I know that you might not know."

"Okay."

"Okay. I've got one for you. Can you name some of the original colonies?"

"Well, there were thirteen original colonies," I say, grinning at her. "Some of them were in New York, New Jersey, North Carolina, Massachusetts."

"Fine," she says, holding up her hand. "You are a smarty-pants. I get it. I wish you would use your brains for good and not evil." She grins.

"Hey, it's not like I'm a dictator or a tyrant running a country. I'm just representing my clients."

"I know," she says. "I'm just teasing you, but you do have to admit it does seem wrong that the bank is suing these poor people."

"I will say that it is unfortunate that they signed a contract stating that they would repay money without taking possession of the collateral first." I nod.

She stares at me and rolls her eyes. "Maybe you should run for president of the United States because that was such a non-answer it's not even funny."

"Oh, I have no interest in politics," I say. "Though, I do care about the laws passed, of course."

"I would ask you how many justices are in the Supreme Court, but I guess you already know."

"Nine, and the Chief Justice is John Roberts." I grin at her.

"And the Chief Justice is John Roberts," she says, laughing. "Man, maybe I should be on your trivia team. I feel like we'd win."

"Maybe," I say. "So what is it that you want to do with your life?" I ask her as we continue going through the folders.

"What do you mean?"

"I mean, you told me that you want to travel around the world and you want to meet the love of your life and write a book about your adventures, but what then?"

She blinks at me. "I don't understand what you're saying."

"Are you planning on being a nomad for your entire life or...?"

She stares at me, realization lighting up her eyes. "No, not my entire life. I know I don't want to be a nomad. I guess I never thought past the traveling around the world." She licks her lips. "That's actually a really great question. Maybe I'll get married and have kids and become a yoga teacher."

"Oh, so you're saying you're flexible, are you?"

"I know some downward dog." She shakes her ass.

"You want to teach me some yoga?"

She stares at me for a couple of seconds and twitches her nose again.

"What is it? Tell me."

"So, I've only been to two yoga classes," she admits.

"What?" I stare at her. "How are you going to teach yoga if you've only been to two yoga classes?"

"I don't know. Maybe when I go to India I'll learn under a yogi and then become a teacher. Or, you know, I could teach Zumba. I did ten Zumba classes five years ago and I love Zumba. I thought I was quite good."

My lips twitch. "Okay, so a yoga and a Zumba teacher."

She smiles. "I know. I sound like I'm all over the place, don't I?"

"It's okay. You've got your entire life to figure out what you want to do."

"I guess that's true. What about you? Do you plan on being an attorney for the rest of your life?"

I stare at her for a couple of seconds and nod slowly. "It's what I was made to do, be an attorney and make lots of money."

"And how much money do you need before you want to

do something else?" she says. "What's the ultimate goal? What do you want to buy with all that money?"

I stare at her for a couple of seconds and my heart thuds at her question. She's hit upon something that has been in the back of my subconscious for a long time. What is the pinnacle of my success to be?

"I don't know," I say. "I guess I have just always wanted to be a top attorney making a lot of money."

"I mean, you don't do girlfriends or commitment, unless you're planning on getting married at fifty and then popping out some kids later in life."

I stare at her for a couple of seconds. "I can honestly say I've never thought about getting married. And the kids?" I shrug. "Take them or leave them. It's not been a life goal of mine."

"So your life goal is just to make money and win cases for crappy ass banks and other corporations that don't give a shit about the people?"

"Well, I don't want to say they don't give a shit about the people. They did put out their money, right, to help them purchase cars and to help them buy things. Should they really have to take the loss?"

She stares at me for a couple of seconds. "I guess that's a gray area."

"It is, and a judge will decide," I say. "I'm not the final decision maker here. I just represent my client, which is the bank. Those customers will have attorneys. Maybe they'll argue a good case and they'll beat us."

"You don't want them to beat you though, do you?"

My lips twitch. "I very rarely lose cases, Skye."

She nods slowly. "I think you very rarely lose anything," she says softly.

"And what is that supposed to mean?"

"I mean, I bet you any woman you set your eyes on that you want, you get her."

I stare at her for a couple of minutes and shrug. "I don't know. I guess I've never thought about it."

"You're one of those winners in life, aren't you Kingston Chase? You're smart, you're handsome, you're rich. It seems to me that everything you want, you have. So what else do you want?"

You pops into my mind and I blink rapidly before dismissing the thought. I have no idea where it came from.

"I think I would like to have some cheese and crackers," I say, jumping up. "Would you like some?"

"Yeah. What cheese do you have?" she asks.

"I believe I have some brie, some Gouda, some cheddar, some goat's cheese."

"Wow. You're a connoisseur of cheeses."

"I wouldn't say that, exactly, but I do like a little cheese. I may also have some meats. Some chorizo, some prosciutto, some salami."

She licks her lips. "You're making me hungry."

"Well, it looks like we have a long night ahead of us."

"Yeah," she says. "I guess so."

"I don't just mean these folders," I say, turning to look back at her.

"Oh?" She raises an eyebrow.

"I think that we should address what we talked about earlier."

"We don't have to. I mean there's not much to talk about, right?"

"We should talk about us," I say. "Well, not us, but any physical acts that may happen again between us. Maybe we should come up with some rules. That way nothing is in the gray area, so to speak, like you said before. It'll be black and white and hopefully we'll both be on the same page."

"Okay. So what are you suggesting?"

"I'm suggesting that we don't mention this arrangement inside the office whatsoever. That way no lines could ever be blurred."

"Okay," she says, nodding. "That works for me."

"I am suggesting that we alternate the activities that we do each week."

"I'm not following here," she says, frowning. "What activities?"

"I think that we should hang out and not just have sex."

"What? Why?"

"Because I don't want you to ever think that this is just a sex thing."

"But it *is* just a sex thing."

"No, it's an us enjoying each other's company and having sex thing. I don't want you to consider me your enemy with benefits." I frown. "I think we can still be friendly and have fun and in the night have some good sex and I don't want to be the only one coming up with ideas and things to do. So maybe we alternate."

"Okay, so like a date night?"

I nod slowly. "It won't be a date. It will be a fun night."

"A fun night," she repeats after me. "Okay, so we alternate planning fun nights?"

"Yeah," I say. "Maybe once a week?"

"Okay," she says. "The same night every week or...?"

"I don't know. What works for you?"

"I mean, yeah, maybe. I don't know," she says. "Is it weird if we have a scheduled fun night?"

"What if we say Saturdays?"

She stares at me for a couple of seconds. "I volunteer on Saturdays in the morning at an adult literacy organization, so I wouldn't be available all day, but—"

"I didn't know you did that," I say softly, looking at her with admiration.

"You don't know everything about me just because you think you do."

"That's true. I don't. So why don't we say Saturday afternoon and Saturday evening?"

"Okay." She nods. "And you want to do it every Saturday or every other Saturday or...?"

"Let's start with every Saturday and just see how we feel."

"Okay," she says. "But..."

"But what?" I ask as her voice trails off.

"How do we ensure that we don't catch feelings or let stuff get complicated or..."

"I don't know. What do you suggest?" I ask her.

"Maybe we have to make sure we go on dates with other people as well so that we're not the sole focus of each other's mind."

I stare at her for a couple of seconds. "You're asking me to go on dates with other women?" I laugh. "Well, that's a new one."

"I am not saying that I think you should sleep with other women because that's nasty," she clarifies.

"Excuse me?"

"You and I, we didn't use protection and I'm assuming that going forward we're not going to use protection, but I'm not going to do that if you are sleeping with other women because I don't know what you may or may not pick up."

"That's fair," I say. "So no other sexual partners?"

"Yeah," she says. "You can go on dates and flirt, but if it

comes to a point where you want to have sex with them, you have to let me know and vice versa. And that way we just end whatever we have."

"Sounds about right to me. I can work with that."

"Okay," she says. "And we don't mention anything that happens on fun night in the office, period. When we're in the office Monday through Friday, fun night doesn't exist."

"Okay," I say. "That won't be a problem for me. Will it be for you?"

"No," she says, shaking her head. "Not at all."

"Well then, I think we have a plan." I carry a small wooden board filled with cheeses, meats, and crusty baguette and crackers back to the table. "Now we shall feast and continue working."

She nods and yawns slightly. "Sounds good to me."

"You're tired," I say, narrowing my eyes. "Are you sure you want to do this now? Are you—"

"I'm fine. Once the caffeine kicks in, I'll be good to go." She gives me a small smile. "But I don't think that I have energy to do anything more than work tonight."

"I understand," I say, disappointment filling my heart, but I shrug it off. "Let's just work on these folders and then we'll go to bed."

"I can leave when I'm done. I don't have to—"

"You'll stay here tonight," I say.

"But..."

"But nothing." I shake my head. "You'll stay here tonight."

"Okay," she says, reaching for a piece of bread. "Thanks."

"You don't have to thank me," I say, smiling widely as I reach for a piece of salami. The salty meat feels like Heaven on my tongue. I grab another folder. "Now, let's see if we can get this done tonight so I don't have to make you wake up at four o'clock in the morning."

"Yay. How sweet are you."

"I like to think I'm pretty sweet," I say, grinning. "But maybe not as sweet as you."

"Ha ha," she says, blushing, knowing exactly what I'm talking about as I lick my lips and stare at hers.

Chapter Twenty-One

Skye

I stretch my arms and legs as my eyes flutter open, then look around the room to see if Kingston is here. The curtain has been drawn and I can see that it's definitely morning. I look over to the clock on the nightstand and gasp when I see it's nine AM.

"Oh no," I moan, as I sit up, my hair tousled. I hear footsteps and the door opens.

Kingston steps in with a cup of coffee in his hand. "Morning, sleepyhead."

"Oh my gosh. I slept so late. I'm so sorry," I mumble quickly and he shakes his head.

"Don't be. We finished all the folders last night, so you're actually on schedule."

"I know. I just..." I yawn. "Oh my gosh. I can't believe I'm yawning and I just woke up."

"It's because we didn't get that much sleep." He grins as he sits on the edge of the bed and hands me the cup. "I wish I could say we didn't get much sleep because of all the love we were making, but I am pretty satisfied with the fact that we finished all those files.

"Thank you so much for your help." I sip on the coffee gratefully. I feel his eyes on my lips and don't miss it when they move to my chest. I'm wearing another one of his T-shirts without a bra and I can feel that my nipples are poking through the thin material.

He licks his lips and stands up. "I think I'm going to head to the shower and then we can go into work."

"Aren't you nervous that people are going to ask questions as to why we are arriving together?"

He looks at me and shakes his head. "Why would I be nervous about that? We were working late."

"I know we were working late, but what if people think we were doing something else?"

"That's not my concern." He shrugs. "We weren't."

"Yeah, but we said we were going to keep personal personal and business business and if we show up together and I am..."

He stares at me and lets out a small sigh. "You can go home. You can put on some fresh clothes and then come to the office when you're ready." He shrugs. "Does that make you feel better?"

I stare at him for a couple of seconds and nod. "It should make you feel better too."

"I don't care what people say about me around the office," he says. "The rule is there to keep us safe, not because I'm afraid of a little gossip." He shrugs and heads out of the room. "Let me know if you want me to make you some eggs or something for breakfast."

I shake my head as I slide out of the bed. "I'm okay. Thanks."

He looks down at my long legs and then gives me an

impish grin. "Okay," he says, as he stands there looking back at me.

I'm slightly disappointed that he didn't attempt to make a move, which is what I thought he'd do. I sip the coffee and walk out of the room into the kitchen area.

"You can turn on the TV if you want," he shouts from the bathroom.

"Thank you," I say as I head into the living room.

I place the coffee cup down on the coffee table and take a seat on his luxurious couch before reaching for the remote control. I power it on and settle back into the couch. It is so comfortable. When I am rich and successful and have a place that is large enough to accommodate such a large couch, I will get one just like this. However, it may be in a different color.

I switch the channels until I find reruns of *Reba* and grab the coffee cup again. About ten minutes later, Kingston walks out with damp hair and a wry smile on his face as he looks at the TV.

"What is this?"

"You've never seen *Reba*?" I ask, staring at him incredulously.

"Um, I can't say that it's a show I would have been interested in watching, no."

"Oh, it's so good. It's about this single mom who works two jobs who loves her kids and never stops." I laugh. "Oh my gosh. Did I just repeat the lyrics to the theme song?"

"I don't know." He shrugs. "Did you?"

"Well, I don't know. Anyway, she was married to this guy, Brock, who's a dentist, and he cheated on her with Barbara Jean, who he's now married to and they have a son, but he still has three kids with Reba. And weirdly enough, Barbara Jean, who's his mistress-turned-wife, is best friends with Reba, which is kind of weird because there's no way I would be best friends with the woman that my husband cheated on me with. But I guess Reba's living her best life now because she met this guy and—"

He holds a hand up. "It sounds like a soap opera. Are you watching *Days of Our Lives?*"

"No, goofy. I mean, it does kind of sound like it's a soap opera, but..." I shrug. "I love it. I always thought that if I made it as an actress, I'd love to star in a show like this."

"You'd love to star in a show about your husband cheating on you with your best friend?"

"No, I'm saying like a sitcom. I think I can be pretty funny and, you know."

"So is that one of your dreams then? To become a successful actress and star in your own sitcom? What would you call it, Skye?"

"No. Acting isn't the love of my life. Not like Lila. It isn't something I feel like I was born to do, you know? I enjoy it. I love going on auditions and well, if I made it, I wouldn't be unhappy. But it's not like an end goal of mine. You know? It's not like I want to see my name on a movie poster with Brad Pitt or George Clooney or Henry Cavill. Though I might not say no if it was Henry Cavill."

He grins. "Okay then. So you're telling me Henry Cavill is competition."

"He could be," I say, laughing. "So, you know what you didn't tell me?"

"What didn't I tell you?" he asks.

"You didn't tell me who's planning the first fun night next weekend."

"Oh, I figured I would unless you want to."

"No, I want you to." I grin. "That way I know just how much I need to step it up or not."

He stares at me for a couple of seconds. "Uh, step it up? Please explain."

"If you fly me out to Paris for chocolate croissants in a little French cafe and take me shopping at Hermes and to a hotel where we make love looking at the Eiffel Tower, I'm not going to plan a picnic in my living room." I giggle. "I mean, I'm not going to plan a trip to London or Spain or anything. I don't have that kind of money, but—"

"Skye, what are you talking about?"

"I'm just saying, if you plan a really cool date..."

"So a really cool date for you would be me flying you to Paris for chocolate croissants to make love watching the Eiffel Tower. Noted." He grins. "I'm not going to lie, that wasn't on my list of potential fun night activities, but I will keep it in mind." I laugh.

"What? You don't want to spend thousands of dollars on me just to get some?"

"I would spend thousands of dollars on you to not get some," he says softly.

I just stare at him for a couple of seconds and his lips twist and he turns away. "Anyway, I'll plan the first date. I will let you know what time to be ready."

"Also let me know what to wear," I say.

"Well, the less clothes, the better." He grins.

"No, I'm serious. Like, I need to know if I should wear strappy heels or sandals or boots or sneakers."

"Boots?" he asks.

"I don't know, like mountain hiking boots if you're going to take me on some sort of rugged adventure."

"Where in Manhattan would we be going on a rugged adventure?"

"I don't know. Maybe if you flew me to Montana or to Colorado or even to Canada."

"Why do all of the dates you're thinking of have me flying you somewhere?" he asks. "Are you hoping to travel the world with me?" He blinks. "Are you hoping to write your next book about me?"

"Well, I've never written a book, so it wouldn't be my next book. It would be my first book. And I wanted my first book to be about my adventures around the world with the love of my life and you're not the love of my life. You're my..." I pause. "Well, you're my boss with benefits. I think that's what I'll call you."

"I like it," he says. "So you don't want to write a book about your boss with benefits?"

"I mean, I could," I say. "Well, let's see how the first date goes first. Then I'll decide."

"Oh, so then maybe I really do need to step it up."

"What? You want to be in a book that I write?"

"I wouldn't say no unless you're an absolutely shitty writer." He laughs. "Are you a shitty writer?"

"Would I say if I was a shitty writer?" I tease him. "Who would say that? 'Oh, I'm a shitty writer. I'm writing a book.'"

He laughs and runs his fingers through his hair. "I guess not you." He looks at me thoughtfully for a moment. "Okay, you should shower and head home so you can change and I'll meet you in the office later."

"What? You mean I can't spend the rest of my day watching TV?" I grin.

"Nope, because it's Monday morning and you're already late for work." He raises an eyebrow at me. "And you know what they say."

"No. What do they say?"

"You don't want your boss to catch you coming in late to work too many times or you might get fired."

"But I don't think my boss would fire me for that, would

he?" I jump up off of the couch and turn the TV off before taking a couple of steps toward him and stopping when I'm a few inches away. He only has a white towel wrapped around his waist and I place my fingers against his chest and touch a droplet of water on his nipple. I place my finger to my lips and lick it, staring into his eyes as he looks back at me.

"Are you telling me that you do not want to go to work right now?" he asks, his eyes darkening as I reach up and wrap my hands around his neck.

"I'm not saying that," I say softly as I stand on tippy-toes and press my lips against his.

He reaches down and grabs me around the waist and I feel his pink is sliding down into my panties and pinching my ass. I moan slightly as I press myself against him. He lifts me up and I wrap my legs around his waist as he pushes me up against the corridor wall and I feel his lips against my neck.

"What are you hoping will happen right now?" he asks as his lips move to mine.

"Not much," I say as I run my fingers through his hair and kiss him.

I feel his tongue slipping into my mouth and I hold on to him for dear life as he gyrates against me. I feel his towel fall down to the floor and the length of his hardness presses up against my panties. I moan against his lips as he reaches one hand up under my T-shirt and plays with one of my breasts.

"Fuck, I don't want to go into work," he says as he rubs his hardness against my panties.

I swallow hard as my fingers run down his neck and squeeze his shoulders.

"I know," I say, staring into his eyes as he takes a step back and lets me down.

He pulls my T-shirt off and it drops to the ground, leaving me standing there in just my panties next to his very naked and hard body. He pushes me up against the wall and leans down to kiss me again, his chest pressed up against my breasts as he runs his fingers up and down the side of my body. I run my fingers all the way down his back and squeeze his buttocks and moan as we stand there caressing each other.

In the distance, I hear a faint beeping and let out a small little sigh as he steps back and curses under his breath.

"One second," he says as he strolls to his bedroom and grabs his phone and answers it. "Hey, what's going on?" He snaps into the phone, and I wonder who he's talking to. "Yeah, Max. I'll be there soon. I didn't forget." He rolls his eyes as he stares at me.

I walk over to him with a wicked little smile and he looks down at me with curious eyes. I drop to my knees and look up at him.

"I think that I can get that paperwork done by..." He pauses as my lips touch the tip of his cock. His eyes widen and I wink before I open my mouth wider to swallow him.

"Uh, Max, can I call you..." He pauses as he reaches down and runs his fingers through my hair. "Look, I'll be back in a moment," he says, and drops the phone to the floor.

He looks down at me with humor in his eyes. "What are you doing?"

"What do you think?" I say as I look up at him and grin.

I swallow him yet again, my head bobbing back and forth as I try to take him deep into my mouth. He groans as he holds onto my hair and I feel him getting harder and harder, his body stiffening as I suck his glorious, salty cock. I know when he's about to cum because he stills completely. I don't stop. Instead, I suck on his tip and gently run my fingers under his balls and squeeze.

"Oh, fuck," he says as he pulls out slightly and then slams his cock into my mouth.

I feel him spurting his thick cum and I swallow fast, licking my lips dry as he finally finishes.

I stand up and stare into his face, giving him a quick kiss on the lips.

"I think it's time for you to go to work," I say. "Try not to think of me too much."

He looks befuddled, dazed and confused, and I grin as I head into the bathroom and close the door behind me. *Holy shit,* I think as I stand here recalling what I've just done. I had never done something like that before in my life, and yet it was one of the hottest moments I can remember having.

* * *

"I just love Girls' Night." Elisabetta says as we dance in sync as we walk down the street.

"You sound like you're in a good mood." I say, looking at her in surprise. The last few times we'd hung out, she'd been slightly down and I was happy that we were going to have some fun, just the two of us.

"I am. I mean, I'm young, I'm single, I have the best, best friend in the world, and tonight we're going dancing. What more could I ask for?"

"Yeah, I love you too, and I'm excited to dance, though let's make a rule."

"What's the rule?" She asks, groaning.

"No hooking up in bathrooms with random men."

"Okay, I can promise that." She grins. "I'm surprised that your hot boss allowed you to go dancing with me tonight."

"Excuse me? What's that supposed to mean?"

"He seems pretty possessive of you, and I'm sure if he saw you right now in that slinky silver dress, he would want you to be over at his place."

"Maybe, I guess, but like I told you, we have an arrangement."

"Yeah, yeah, yeah. How long is that going to last?"

"I don't know, but we'll see."

"I just never expected my best friend to be boinking her boss."

"Really, Elisabetta?"

"What? I'm just saying. I didn't see you as a *Fifty Shades of Grey* sort of girl."

"I'm not in a *Fifty Shades of Grey* relationship. He doesn't whip me, he doesn't tie me up. Okay, that's a lie. He's definitely tied me up."

"Ooh, la, la. Skye's a dirty bitch."

"Shush." I say, laughing as we walk past two guys who stare at us with eager glances. "You don't want to give anyone any ideas."

"No, you only want to give your hot boss ideas."

"Are you jealous?" I ask her, joking.

"I'm not going to lie, he's fucking hot, and I would be lying if I said he wasn't. I would be lying if I were to say I wouldn't also enter into a sexual relationship with him if he asked me." She winks at me. "So you do you, girl."

"I am going to. And thank you so much for buying me this Fuji max camera and these rolls of film, that was so thoughtful of you."

"Well, I wanted to thank you again for rescuing me that night from Radium and not judging me for the craziness that went down. Plus, if you're going to do a selfie business and charge money, I really don't think you can use people's phones. They can grab their phone and go running and not pay you. This way, if they want to get the cute little snap you take of them, then they have to pay."

"I know. This is why you are so brilliant."

"Girl, I'm not brilliant because I thought it was a good idea to buy you a Polaroid camera and take photos."

"Yeah, you are."

"You thought of it too," she says.

"Yeah, but I didn't have the money to spend on it." I motion to my handbag.

"So what's going on with Whittaker Matlock?" she asks. "Did he ever come into the office or...?"

"He keeps making appointments, but he hasn't yet come." I shrug. "Kingston hasn't said anything about it, but I can tell that he gets a little bit aggravated every time I let him know that Whittaker's business manager has contacted to reschedule."

"Yikes. Do you think that's a bad sign?"

"All I know is that Kingston said at least he's not canceling the appointment."

"Oh, I like a guy that thinks that the glass is half full and not half empty," she says with a nod. "To be honest, when you told me what went down that night, I was shocked that Whittaker even made an appointment."

"Me too," I say. "But I'm just the assistant, I don't really know how this sort of business goes."

"Yeah, and I don't think I want to know," she says. "Let's think about fun things."

"Okay. Like what?"

"Like are you going to buy some sexy lingerie for the next time you're with Kingston?"

"Oh my gosh. I'm not talking about Kingston anymore tonight."

"Why not? He's such a fun topic of conversation."

"I feel like I talk about him all the time. And no, I'm not going to buy lingerie just to have sex with him. He would just rip it up and there would go my money."

"But didn't he say he wanted to give you a credit card?"

"He suggested it, but I'm not going to use his credit card to buy lingerie for him to rip up, it's a waste of money."

"You're far too practical, Skye, you do realize this? If you're in a love affair like this, you've just got to go with the flow, roll with the punches. Shit, if he wants to pour $10,000 champagne on your ass crack and lick it up, let him."

"I don't think we should be talking about ass cracks right now," I say, giggling.

"Hey, that should be my joke." She laughs. "But you're right. I'd much rather he drank $10,000 champagne from your you know what."

I blush as she winks at me. "Elisabetta, we're going out to dance and get our flirt on with random hot men in the city. We're not going to talk about my hot boss, who may or may not make me come in a million different ways, because I do not want to think about him tonight. I do not want to think about him at all.

"You like him though, right?"

"It's just so complicated. I don't even know what's really going on. I don't even know how I feel about him. Some days I hate him, some days I..." I pause. "Like him a lot."

"You kind of love him some days too, don't you?"

I glare at her. "I'm not even responding to that. I just know that this is a situation where I do not feel like I know the ins and outs completely because it's so fluidly changing.

Sometimes when I'm with him, I feel like the Earth is moving."

"That's what she said." She giggles, and I just glare at her. "Sorry. You know I had a couple of vodka shots before we left."

"I know. It's just weird, you know? I just don't even know him. Sometimes he seems like he's all about the money and will do anything to make as much money as possible, and then other times he seems like he really cares about people and my feelings and doing what's morally right."

"He's not the devil. He is not a psychopath, right? He does care about good and bad, right?"

"Yeah. I mean, do I think he's evil? No. Do I think he can be a jackass sometimes? Yes. Do I enjoy him being a jackass sometimes? Yeah. I don't think he's like the snake trying to make me eat the poison apple or anything, I just think that it's complicated on both our ends. It makes my brain hurt to think about it."

"Your brain's not thinking about it when he is inside of you though."

"Really?"

"What? You said he's great sex."

"He is great sex, and that's why it makes it so hard. Do not say, 'That's what she said' again."

"That's what she said," she says under her breath, and we both start laughing. "So are you going to see him tonight or...?"

"No, it's not our scheduled night, thank you very much."

I'm grateful when we arrive outside the nightclub.

"So let's get some drinks and just dance. Are you going to take pictures before or after or..."

"Actually, look at those girls over there," I say, nodding at two girls taking selfies in front of the sign.

"Go on, girl, go."

"Okay." I say. "Sorry, I don't want to hold us up."

"Just go, Skye."

I run over to the two girls who are giggling and taking a selfie.

"Hi. How are you doing tonight?"

They look up at me suspiciously. "We're fine. Why, what's going on?"

"My name is Skye and I am an official photographer."

"You what?" They stare at me. "What are you talking about?"

"To be clear, I'm not an official photographer. I am an unofficial official photographer of the night." I grin at them.

"Sorry, what are you talking about? What does that mean?"

"I saw you girls were trying to take a selfie, and I wanted to offer my services."

"What services? Where's your camera? Are you paparazzi?" The girl with the blonde hair says. "Because I'm not going to talk about what went down with me and Tennessee River last week."

"Sorry, what?" I blink at her. I'm the one that's confused now.

"You probably saw me on TMZ, but I am not a groupie. I did not have sexual relations with that man," she says, laughing.

Her friend collapses in laughter. "You're too funny, Eastern."

I stare at them both trying not to roll my eyes.

Idiots.

"I'm not quite sure what you're talking about, I don't read

TMZ and I've never heard of Tennessee River, but I am a photographer, and if you girls want a cute shot"—I hold up the small little camera in my hand—"I can take one for you, and I have little Polaroids so I can give it to you to keep as a keepsake."

"Oh, I see." Eastern says, blinking. "You want to take a photo of us, what, for the New York Times?"

"No." I say, shaking my head. "I don't work for the New York Times, and I very much doubt they would want to publish my Polaroid pictures in their paper."

"So the New York Post? Tacky."

"No. I'm not sure if you understood what I said. I am an unofficial official photographer of the night, meaning that—"

"I don't really understand what this girl is saying, do you?" the blonde asks her friend.

The friend shakes her head.

"I can take a selfie for you."

"No, we don't want you in our selfie, we don't know you. Oh my gosh. I can't stand these claim-to-fame whores."

"What?" My jaw drops.

"You recognized me, and now you want a photo with me so you can post on your socials that you know me. But you don't know me just because you saw me on the street. I don't know you, I don't want to be on your Instagram account. How many followers do you even have, ten?"

"No, I actually have like 105 followers on Instagram."

"Oh, 105, so many." The girls laugh. "Be gone."

I stare at them and blink. "What did you just say to me?"

"I said be gone, paparazzi."

I look around and shrug before heading back over to Elisabetta, who's standing next to the wall, typing something on her phone.

"Hey, how did it go? How much did they pay you?"

"I didn't even get to take a photo." I say, shaking my head.

"What? What do you mean?"

"I went to offer my services and they thought I was the paparazzi."

"The paparazzi, what? Who is it? Don't tell me that's Gigi Hadid or something."

"Girl, I've never seen those two nobodies before in my life," I say, laughing. "One of them was going on about how she slept with Tennessee River. Have you ever heard of anyone called Tennessee River?"

"Never before in my life," she says, giggling. "Are you sure they weren't joking?"

"I am absolutely positive they weren't joking. I am still kind of confused as to what just happened." I burst out laughing. "Am I living in an alternate reality here? What the fuck was that?"

"I don't know, but don't let them discourage you, girl. I'm sure there are plenty of people that want you to take random-ass Polaroid photos of them and are willing to pay $20 each." She laughs lightly.

"Elisabetta."

"What?" she says, holding up her hand. "I did tell you I didn't think it was the best idea in the world."

"What are you saying?"

"I mean, I don't think I'm being unclear, Skye. Like I said, I don't think it's the best idea in the world. I don't think you're going to make much money from this.

I stare at her for a couple of seconds and giggle.

"You know what? I think you're right. I don't think it's my best money-making idea that I've ever had."

"Me either," she says.

"Then why did you buy me this camera and all this film?"

"Well, we can take selfies of ourselves," she says, grinning. "Plus, I wanted to be supportive."

"You bought me a camera and film even though you didn't believe in the idea?"

"But I believe in you," she says, grinning. "I think you can do anything you set your mind to."

"Why are you so sweet and nice to me, and why do you encourage me on stupidness?"

"Because that's what best friends do. I'm not going to let you walk across a train track when a train is coming, because I don't want you to die, but I will let you have different money-making ideas and run with it until you realize they're not the best."

"Thank you," I say. "I appreciate it."

"That's kind of why I'm letting you have your fun with you know who."

I just blink at her. "I told you, we're not talking about him tonight."

"I know, but I'm just saying. Do I think it's the best idea that you've ever had? Do I think there's potential for your heart to be broken?" I just stare at her, and she links her arm through mine. "But that's life. We miss a hundred percent of the chances we don't take. Maybe it's also going to be amazing. Maybe he's going to be the one that makes you rethink your entire being."

"I don't know that I want someone to make me rethink my entire being," I say to her. "I mean, I'm pretty set on what I want from life."

"I know," she says. "You want to travel, you want the love of your life, and you want to write a book about your epic love story."

"Yeah. Those are the goals. I'm not that close to them, but—"

"But you're closer than you were last week, right?"

I nod slowly. "Yeah. Shall we go in and dance?"

"Let's do it." She says. "And you know what?"

"What?"

"I'm going to give you $100."

"What? Why are you giving me $100?"

"Because I would like at least five amazing photographs of myself tonight."

"What? You can't pay me to—"

"That's how much you charge per photo, right? $20?"

"Yeah, but—"

"So five amazing photos is $100."

"You bought the camera and the film. I am not—"

"I'm your best friend and my dad is loaded. Please let me support you, even if I'm your only customer of the night."

I reach out and give her a big hug and kiss her on the side of the face.

"You're the best friend I could have ever asked for. You know that, right?"

"I learned from the best," she says, pinching me on the ass. "Now, come on, let's get inside and dance and get our flirt on."

"Okay," I say, laughing. "Let's do it."

Chapter Twenty-Two

Kingston

"Good afternoon, Mr. Chase."

There's a knock on my door and I look up to find Skye standing there with an innocent, polite smile.

"Yeah. Can I help you, Skye?" I say in my best informal fashion.

"There's someone here to see you about a potential new lawsuit," she says.

"And you know their name?"

"He says his name is Javier Estes."

"It doesn't ring a bell." I shake my head.

"He said he would like to see you."

"You know I'm busy." I stare at her. "So that's a no." I shake my head. "Get some more information about the lawsuit from him and tell him I'll give him a call when I have time."

"Yes, sir," she says. "Certainly."

She closes the door and I try not to smile as she walks away.

The fact of the matter is, I'm not busy, but seeing as

today is Friday and tomorrow is our first fun night and I still have no plan, I'm trying to figure out what to do. The entire week has gone by super professionally. Even I had almost forgotten that Skye and I had been intimate. Even I had almost forgotten that we had a plan for the weekend.

She spoke to me informally, sometimes distastefully, and hadn't so much as touched my shoulder, let alone tried to kiss me or give me another blow job. However, that didn't stop me from thinking about the blow job she'd given me the last time I'd seen her outside of the office. Fuck, it had been hot.

I stare at my laptop and think about date night ideas. Even though it's not technically a date, I want it to be fun. I don't want her to feel like I'm only using her for sex, even though that's definitely where the night is going to end.

I think about booking a hotel room someplace that will blow her mind and impress her, but then I don't want her to feel cheap, which is weird because I've never had that thought before and she's already slept at my place anyway. I mumble under my breath, "Which is also weird." She's the only woman that has spent the night, more than once now. I have two T-shirts that smell of her that I haven't washed, but I'm trying not to think too hard about that.

There's another knock on the door, and this time she opens it, steps inside, then closes it behind her.

"So, Mr. Estes says that he's here about a potential torts case in regards to a pharmaceutical product."

"What pharmaceutical product?" I ask.

"A cream that is meant to stop cramps but actually burns people. He says that he works at a local emergency clinic and they've had several clients in the last couple of months come in with second-degree chemical burns due to using this cream."

"I don't really do torts cases. We're not a torts law firm," I say frowning. "But that does not sound good. Do you know the name of the product?"

"He says he doesn't want to say the name unless he speaks directly to you."

I nod. "Hold on," I say, picking up the phone.

"Hey, Max," I say when my partner picks up.

"Yeah, what's going on, Kingston?"

"We have a potential client here with a tortious claim against a pharmaceutical company for producing a cream that may or may not be burning those who use it."

"What's the name of the company? What's the name of the cream?" he asks.

"He doesn't want to say."

"You know, if it's related to Gold Nugget Pharmaceuticals, we cannot take the case. That would be a huge conflict of interest."

"I know," I say. "That's why I wanted to ask you if you've heard of anything related to this with any of their products."

He says, "I don't know. Hold on. I know Remington's been working on some of their stuff for me. Let's get him on the line."

"Okay."

I look over at Skye and I can tell she's trying not to listen to the conversation.

"Hey, Remi, I've got Kingston on the line with us."

"Hey, what's up? I'm about to head into court. Can this wait?"

"No," I say quickly. "We've got a potential client here with a lawsuit against a major pharmaceutical company. We do not know which pharmaceutical company it is. Apparently, they're making some sort of cream that's meant to relieve cramps but it is actually giving people second-degree burns."

"Fuck, it's not with Gold Nugget, is it? Shit, I told them that."

I sigh. "So they have a cream that is burning people?"

"They took it off the market," he says. "But they did not have it withdrawn from retail stores that it was already in, even though I told them to. However, they did not want to take on any..." He pauses. "Look, I've got to go."

He hangs up. Max swears under his breath.

"You're going to have to send that guy away."

"I know," I say. "But you do know we have a problem here because another firm is going to take this case."

Max lets out a deep sigh. "I know. I'll speak to Remington and we'll have to speak to John Schneider, the CEO, and figure out the next steps."

"Okay. Tell him that there is a local emergency walk-in clinic that has a lot of clients, so he'd better come up with a settlement number."

I hang up and look over at Skye. There's a frown on her face.

"What's going on?" she says.

"You're going to have to let Mr. Estes know that we're unable to take his case and that he should find himself another law firm."

"But he has proof. He showed me photos. He—"

"We cannot take this case, Skye," I say bluntly.

"So what? You don't want to help these victims get money because we may or may not represent the pharmaceutical company that made this product."

"Obviously, we cannot sue ourselves."

Her jaw drops.

"What? But you don't even know the company! Are you...?"

She shakes her head.

"Every time I think you guys cannot be any lower, you are."

"I don't really know what I'm meant to make of that."

"What'd you think you're meant to make of that?" she says. "It means you're representing scumbags. We represent a large pharmaceutical company that makes thousands of different products that help people, but they're also making products that don't help people, that are hurting people."

"That's just the way the cookie crumbles, Skye. They will make good on any products that they've created that have harmed people." I shrug. "Please go and inform Mr. Estes that I'm not available to talk to him and that he should do some research for tortious firms that would be interested in taking a case like this."

"You're not even going to tell him yourself? You don't think you owe him that courtesy?"

"I'm a busy man, Skye, and I have a lot of work this afternoon." I blink at her. "Is that all?"

She stares at me for a couple of seconds after I dismiss her then shakes her head. "You're such a jackass," she says under her breath.

"What did you just say?" I stand up.

"Nothing, sir," she says, rolling her eyes and leaving my office, slamming the door shut behind her.

"I guess I have to plan a really good fun night tomorrow," I say under my breath.

I know that she doesn't understand why I'm unable to take the case, or rather, she *does* understand, but she doesn't agree with it morally. She doesn't understand that when it comes to the law, morals have nothing to do with it.

I sigh. *That's not your problem, Kingston.* I lick my lips and sit back down again, pulling up the travel website and searching flights to Paris. I sit back, smiling, wondering what she would say if I did fly her out to Paris for the weekend so that we could stroll arm in arm down the Champs-Élysées, eating chocolate croissants and drinking espressos in the City of Love.

Maybe we take a boat ride down the Seine, then go for dinner and feast on escargot and bone marrow before taking her back to a palatial room where we'd make love all night long. The thought seems ridiculous. There's no way in Hell a friend with benefits or a boss with benefits would plan such a romantic, delightful date, especially as it wasn't even meant to be a date.

I take a deep breath and exit the site. As much fun as it would be, I'm not flying her to Paris. I don't want her to get any ideas.

My email screen pops up with a new notification and I click on it. I see I have an email from Skye so I open it quickly and read.

"Dear Mr. Chase,

I just wanted you to know that you are a horrible lawyer. You have no qualms about taking advantage of the little people and you make me ashamed to even work for you. I hope that you are able to sleep well tonight knowing that you're giving another win to the corporations of the world that take advantage of people like me."

I stare at her email and roll my eyes before hitting respond.

"Dear Ms. Redding,

Thank you so much for your email. I'm not really sure how you want me to respond to this, so instead I will attach a copy of my recent bank statement, and yes, it is seven figures, and yes, I will sleep well tonight. Have a good evening."

The reply comes almost instantaneously.

"Dear Mr. Chase,

I think it's obnoxious of you to send me a copy of a bank statement showing you have over $5 million in the bank. Number one, I don't even know if that's true. And number two, if it is, I don't think it's smart to have that much money in the bank, but what do I know? I'm just simply your assistant.

Miss Redding."

I grin and respond back.

"Dear Miss Redding,

You are my assistant, and as such, you're being a little bit obnoxious yourself, not to mention rude and disrespectful, seeing as I sign the checks that pay your salary each month. The simple fact of the matter is, I have this money in an account because it was going to be used to purchase a commercial building in another state. I would love to inform you that I have the majority of my money in mutual funds and real estate and I do know what I'm doing. Just in case you didn't know, I have an MBA as well as a JD.

Your boss, Mr. Chase."

I sit back and wait for her response. I smile when I see it pop up a couple of minutes later.

"Dear Mr. Chase,

Good for you that you have an MBA and a JD. I guess it's true what they say. People can have brain smarts, but they don't always have common sense or a heart, which is sad. You can't actually think money makes you a decent person. In my eyes, money is the crux of all evil."

She didn't sign her name to this one. I respond.

"Dear Ms. Redding,

Are you saying that you think I'm evil?"

The response comes quickly.

"Dear Mr. Chase,

I didn't say that, but if you think you are."

I respond.

"Dear Ms. Redding,

Just so you know, I have a heart and I volunteer as a big brother with the Big Brothers Big Sisters program, and I donate a substantial amount of money each year to causes I think are worthy, so hopefully that means I'm not as evil as you might think I am."

She responds.

"Dear Mr. Chase,

I'm not the one that you have to be worried about. The people that Mr. Estes represents and is fighting for are the ones that should be on your conscience."

I roll my eyes as I read her reply. Why is she not going to let this go? I respond.

"Dear Miss Redding,

I am going to pick you up at 2:00 PM tomorrow afternoon. Please wear something comfortable."

I hit send and sit back. No response comes and I can feel my shoulders getting tense. What if she changes her mind? What if she no longer wants to do this? What if she's so upset at the work that I do that she's going to call it off?

My breath catches as I see her response come through.

"Dear Mr. Chase,

I sure hope tomorrow is fun because I'm pissed off at you right now."

I grin as I stare at the email. She's still in. That's all I need.

I turn my laptop off and I jump up and head out of the office. I walk over to Skye and look down at her as she stares at her computer screen so intently that I realize she hasn't even noticed that I'm here.

I clear my throat and she looks up, blushing slightly.

"Doing something important?" I ask her.

"I was just waiting for your response," she says, glaring at me.

"Okay. Well, there will be no more email responses this evening as I am leaving for the day."

"You are?" She stares at her watch. "But it's only three o'clock."

"I am aware of the time. I'll see you tomorrow," I say softly, lowering my voice.

She nods. "I guess so."

"Wear something sexy," I say.

"Excuse me?" She raises a single eyebrow.

"I said, wear something sexy."

"You can't tell me to wear something sexy," she says, shaking her head. "That's against the rules."

"Against what rules?" I ask, chuckling.

"Against the rules of this boss with a benefits relationship. You don't get to tell me what to wear."

"Okay, then don't wear something sexy. Wear whatever you want." I grin. "But I'll see you tomorrow, okay?"

"Okay," she says with a nod.

"I'm looking forward to it," I say.

She licks her lips nervously and I head out.

Chapter Twenty-Three

Skye

I step out of the shower in my towel with my long dripping hair and head toward Elisabetta's room.

"Hey," I say as I walk inside. "What do you think I should—" I pause as I notice Elisabetta is on the bed with a strange man.

"Oh, sorry. I..."

"Hey," Elisabetta says with a wide smile. "No need to apologize. We were just relaxing. Tombstone, this is my best friend and roommate, Skye. Skye, this is Tombstone."

"Hi," I say with a small nod, pretending that this is the first time I'd ever seen Tombstone. I am grateful that this time he's not buck naked and neither is my best friend. They do appear to just be lounging around on the bed. I wonder if he knows about her experience with Radium.

"Hey," he says, sitting up and looking me over, and I'm suddenly self-conscious that I'm just in a towel. "Nice to meet you." He steps forward and gives me a hug. I feel him pressing me close to him and holding me tight for longer than is polite.

"Nice to meet you too," I say as I offer him another wan smile.

His hair up close is sprinkled with gray and his blue eyes are not as warm as I would've liked to have hoped. He's definitely older than I thought he was going to be. He has to be in his late forties. I wonder what Elisabetta is doing with him.

"So what was your question, Skye?" she asks, as if everything is perfectly normal.

"I was just going to ask you what I should wear for my fun night with Kingston this evening," I say, blinking at her. "I don't know what we're doing, but he said make sure I am wearing something sexy and relaxed."

I lick my lips nervously. "But I don't want to disturb you. I didn't realize that Tombstone was going to be here."

"Yeah, well, when you told me you had a date, I was like, I don't want another Saturday evening by myself." She grins. "So I asked him what he was doing."

"And I decided to come on over," he says, nodding. "I figured I couldn't let a beautiful woman like Elisabetta spend a Saturday evening alone."

"How very gracious of you," I say politely, though I really want to roll my eyes.

"I try," he says. "Plus I got a little something for us to share tonight." He looks over at her and she looks excited.

"What?" she squeals. "Tell me."

Is he about to propose to her? Is he as crazy as I think he is?

"I don't know. Is your friend here a narc?"

I raise an eyebrow. "A narc? Why would I be a...wait, you brought drugs?"

I stare at him, then look at Elisabetta. Please tell me she's not going to encourage this guy.

"We don't do drugs."

"Oh, chillax, Skye," she says. "What did you bring? Not Molly. I don't do Molly. It gets people way too fucked up."

"No, just a little coke," he says, looking over at me. "You want some before you go on your big date?"

"It's not a date. It's a fun night, and no, I don't want any coke." I look at Elisabetta. "And you don't want any either, right?"

She shrugs. "I've been a good girl all my life. What's a little coke between friends?" She grins. "Plus, I know Tombstone will take care of me."

"Hey, can I talk to you in private?" I say, grabbing her hand and pulling her out of the room.

"Be right back, Tombstone," she says with a little wave.

I drag her into my bedroom and close the door.

"What the hell is going on, Elisabetta?" I say, glaring at her. "That dude is old as fuck. Not trying to be rude, but he is."

"He's older and he's distinguished and he is hot and he's packing and..."

"And what?"

"And I'm bored and I'm lonely and you never have time. You are always working and now you're freaking hooking up with your boss. Like, I need something to do too."

"You are not blaming me for the fact that you are about to do coke with some creepy old man."

"He's not creepy. He is good looking and he is not that old. He's only forty-two."

"He's got a head full of gray hair."

"It's salt and pepper and it's premature," she says.

"Really? Is that what he told you?"

"I saw his driver's license, Skye. What, do you think I'm going to fuck a sixty-year-old man because I'm bored?"

"I don't know. You're about to do coke with a granddad because I'm going on a freaking hookup with my boss. I can cancel it right now if that's going to stop you from doing drugs with this loser."

"He's not a loser. And we have fun. I know what I'm doing."

I look at her and shake my head. "But do you really? We don't do drugs."

"A little coke is not going to hurt anyone. And honestly, I didn't want to tell you this before, but this is not the first time I've done coke."

"What?" My jaw drops. "What are you talking about? We've never done hard drugs."

"*You've* never done hard drugs." She shrugs. "I may have dabbled in some things."

I sit on the bed, my brain processing a million miles a minute.

"When? And what drugs have you done?"

"Well, I've done coke a couple of times. I've done some Molly. I've..." She licks her lips. "Done some Oxy."

"What? When? How did I not know?"

"Maybe when you were studying and I was going to parties that you didn't want to go to. We weren't joined at the hip."

"But we've been best friends forever. We've lived together forever. You've never even told me."

"Because I knew you would act like my freaking mom and freak out and I didn't need that. It was just for fun."

I try not to show her how offended I am by her words. Does she really think I'm that judgmental? And that much of a stiff? "So is there anything else you've done for fun that you've never told me about?"

She stares at me for a couple of minutes and shrugs. "I don't need you judging me, Skye."

"I would never judge you, Elisabetta. I'm just curious as to what else you haven't told me."

"Well, maybe now's not the time. I've got a man waiting in my bedroom and you've got a man about to pick you up. Who, by the way, is your freaking boss that you can't stand."

I feel my face form into a hard scowl.

"What? I can't tell you what to do with your life," she says, raising an eyebrow. "I mean, you came home yesterday telling me how your boss practically sold his soul to the devil for money, and yet you're going out with him tonight to bang him."

"It's not like that," I say. "What he does is a job and yeah, maybe ethically I don't agree with his choice of clients, but..."

"But what?" she says. "He takes shitty-assed clients that do bad things to good people for money. And I do drugs, so sue me. It's not like I'm freaking popping pills every week. He brought some coke. We'll do some coke and then we'll fuck and do whatever we want. I'm an adult."

I stare at her, my heart sinking.

"Are you mad at me?"

"No, I'm not mad at you." She sighs and leans back on the bed. "Look, maybe I just feel lost. Maybe I just don't know where my life is going. I'm in my frigging mid-twenties and I don't have any dreams. I don't have anything. I don't have a job. I don't have a man."

"I mean, you've got Tombstone."

"Really, Skye?" she says, her lips twitching.

"What? I thought you liked him."

"You know he's not the man I'm going to be with for the rest of my life, Skye. Just like you know your boss is not going to be your forever."

"I know, but..."

"But what? We're both just making do right now."

I lick my lips. "Okay. I guess that's true." I shrug. "I won't judge you and you won't judge me."

"Exactly," she says. "Also, there's something else you don't know."

"What?"

"I'm not going to tell you right now because I think if I do, you're going to flip a switch and I don't want you to flip a switch before your date."

"Um. Now, you cannot not tell me."

She grins as she stands up and heads to the door. "Oh, I totally am not telling you."

She pauses for a second and looks over the dresses I have displayed on my bed.

"Wear that slinky black dress. No panties. No bra."

"What?"

She grins. "And borrow my silver pumps. It will look great. Again, no bra and no panties. Girl, this is your boss that you are fucking for fun. You might as well literally bang the living daylights out of him because that's what this is all about, right? I mean, it's not like he's taking you on dates so you guys can fall in love. It's literally a preamble to sex. Just like the coke is."

She shrugs. "And if you're going to do something like this, you might as well just go all the way. Totally. Be a vixen, be a bombshell, be a seductress. Do all the things in your mind that you've always wished you could do, but you felt too nervous to do."

"But..." I start, and she shakes her head.

"That's what I'm doing right now. We're in our twenties. Let's live our lives. We have plenty of years to be the good girls and do the things everyone expects of us. Right now, we're in a place where we're having fun and I know tonight I'm going to have fun." She pauses. "You're not coming back tonight, right?"

I frown. "Why are you asking me that?"

"I will have company and I just want to know if—"

"I won't be back tonight," I say, groaning. "Be safe, okay?"

"I'm always safe," she says. "I promise."

I let out a deep sigh.

"And I can't talk you out of doing the coke?"

"There are a lot of things that you're going to wish you could talk me out of tonight," she says, grinning. "And you'd be wasting your breath to try."

"Why do I not like the sound of that? You're not going to do heroin or anything, right? Please tell me no. You know, people freaking get addicted to heroin. And don't do meth and—"

"I'm not stupid. I'm not going to do heroin. I'm not going to do meth. I'll do a couple bumps and have some fun. That's it."

She steps forward and she gives me a hug.

"I know you're probably questioning our friendship right now, Skye. I can tell from the look in your eyes and I know that a part of you wants to stay here and protect me and make sure I don't do anything crazy, but I'm not going to. I know what I'm doing. And tomorrow, when you get back, we'll have brunch and I'll tell you all about my crazy evening and you'll tell me about yours. Okay?"

I stare at her and nod slowly. "I'm worried."

"What are you worried about?"

"You. I've never seen you like this. I..."

"It's okay. You don't have to be worried about me. To be honest, I'm kind of worried about you, too."

"Why?" I ask.

"Because I'm mentally equipped to deal with craziness like this. Whether or not you believe me."

"I don't know that you are."

"What does that mean?"

"It means I was pretending I was innocent for years. You were actually living the innocent life and now we're both going buck wild. The only thing is I know if the stallion knocks me off, I'm going to get back up again. I don't know about you."

She squeezes my shoulders. "Please, if at any point you feel like you don't want to go through with this, leave. Call me, do whatever you need to do."

"It's fine. He's not going to do anything crazy. He's not going to make me take drugs."

"I'm not talking about that," she says, kissing me on the cheek. "I love you. I just want you to protect your heart. Have fun tonight. Do everything that I would do."

"Well, it seems to me that you would do absolutely everything."

She grins and nods. "That is true. Here's to us and here's to tonight."

"Here's to us," I say, and hold her tight.

"I love you."

"I love you too," she says, then opens the door.

"Now let me get back to my man. I don't want him thinking that I've disappeared."

I stare at her for a couple of seconds. "And what would he do if he thought you disappeared?"

"I don't know," she says. "Maybe he'd call another

woman." She shrugs. "Not that I'd care if he has another woman, of course, but I am pretty dead set on the plans we have tonight." She grins, her eyes twinkling. "And yes, I will tell you all about it tomorrow."

And with that, she leaves the room.

Chapter Twenty-Four

Kingston

I can sense that Skye is distracted as we sit in the French restaurant waiting for our appetizers. "Hey, is everything okay?" I ask her, taking in her worried expression. She looks up and nods, but leaves it at that. I wonder if she's still mad at me about what happened at work yesterday. "Remember what we said, Skye?" I remind her.

"Sorry. What?" She blinks as she sips her water.

"We said that business was to stay in the office and fun nights were for fun."

"Yeah. Okay."

"And it seems to me that you're still upset about the pharmaceutical case that I couldn't take because of the possibility of a conflict of interest."

"Oh," she shakes her head. "It's fine. Whatever. You do you."

I lean forward and grab a piece of the crusty baguette and take a bit of the butter. "Are you okay?"

She nods, then makes a face. "I'm sorry. I am just really distracted right now."

"No need to apologize. You want to talk about it?"

"It's just Elisabetta. I am worried about her."

"Why?"

"When I was leaving, she had this older guy in the apartment and he brought cocaine and I guess they're going to do coke tonight and have sex and do something crazy. And she wouldn't tell me exactly what the crazy thing was, but now all I can think about is her jumping off buildings or doing something that might put her life in danger." She stares at me. "I'm sorry. I didn't mean to—"

"Hey, don't apologize," I interrupt her. "Who is this guy?" Elisabetta seems to be making poor decision after poor decision and I'm not impressed. Though I'm not going to tell Skye that. I don't want her to think I'm judging her best friend.

"Remember the guy I told you about from her date that was sitting at the other table? Tombstone?"

"Oh, yeah. You said she went on a blind date with some guy called Captain, right?"

"Yeah."

"And he went down on her, right?"

"Yeah." She makes a face. "And these two guys were watching from the next table and one of them gave her his card and that's who's at the place right now. And he's creepy. Really creepy. And I don't understand why or how she can't see it. And I feel partially guilty."

"Why would you feel guilty?" I frown.

The waiter approaches and we pause. "Here you go," he says, putting the plate down on the table. "And have you decided what you would like for your entrées yet?" he asks in what I can only guess is a fake French accent.

"I am ready. What about you, Skye?"

"Can I get the pommes frites with béarnaise sauce?"

"Oui, madam. And you monsieur?" he says, looking at me.

"I'll have the same."

"And how would you like your steaks cooked?"

"I'll do medium," Skye says.

"And I'll do rare."

"Rare? You like it bloody, huh?"

"I guess I do," I agree.

"Anything else before I put in your orders?"

"No, this is good. Thank you." He nods and walks away. A man in the corner starts playing the guitar and singing and we both glance over at him.

"This is a nice place," Skye says. "Thank you for bringing me here."

"I figured it's not as good as Paris, but maybe almost as good."

"Yeah." She gives me a small little smile and nods.

"Hey." I reach over and grab her hand. "You're not responsible for your best friend's choices. If she decides she's going to do drugs and have crazy sex with this guy tonight, that's on her. You cannot take on any guilt for that."

"I just feel bad. I've been living with her for free and I know she's been bored and lonely and I know she's wanted to do more stuff and I just haven't had time. I've been working so much. And now this thing with us..." She raises her hands in the air, clearly frustrated with the situation. "Maybe if I would've just told you no and tried to make plans with her, none of this would've happened."

"You really believe that?" I ask her softly.

She sighs. "No, I guess I'm just hurt."

"Why are you hurt?"

"Because she told me that this is not the first time that she's done drugs. I thought she and I...well, I thought we both had never done drugs, but she's done lots of drugs before and she said there's a lot of stuff I don't know. And I just feel like if I'm her best friend, why didn't she trust me enough to tell me?"

I stare at her for a couple of moments before slowly nodding in understanding. "I understand what it is to be hurt by secrets. I understand what it is to be hurt by knowledge of the fact that the people closest to you haven't told you everything that you hope they would have. She didn't tell you because she didn't want you to treat her differently."

"But I wouldn't look at her differently. I would never judge her."

"I know, but maybe she wanted you to feel like she was this ideal of a person that you had in your head, kind of like me."

"What are you talking about?"

"You didn't respect me as your boss because you thought I was grumpy and annoying, which is kind of cute in its own way, but once you realized the sort of cases that the firm takes, I can tell that your opinion of me has changed." I can hear the sadness in my voice because it's true. "You think I'm all about the money. You think that—"

"No, I don't," she says, shaking her head and leaning forward. "I know I reacted poorly and I know that I've been judgmental. And you're right. I don't know that I would take those cases as a lawyer, but I'm not a lawyer. And I guess you don't get to cherry-pick your clients. And I guess it's like people who are public defense attorneys or prosecutors. Sometimes prosecutors prosecute the wrong people and sometimes defense attorneys get guilty people off the hook, but it's the job. You can only do your job to the best of your ability. I do understand that. I mean, ethically, it would make me feel like shit. But I guess when you go to law school, there's no class on moral compass."

I smile at her. "I don't want you to think that I only care about money. Also, I did take a professional responsibility class."

"What else do you care about in life? Everything that you're working for is in regards to money, right?"

I stare at her for a couple of seconds, the harsh truth settling into my brain at her words, "I guess, yes. Technically, I work for money. We all do."

"You could take on worthy cases and really help people in need, you just wouldn't make as much money. Right?" She shrugs and I nod.

"That's true."

"So, at the end of the day, it's all about money. I'm not judging you. I work for you, right? Sure, I also dance at bachelor parties. It's not like I'm super proud of that, but I do it for the money. I mean, I wouldn't give lap dances or pick up hundred dollar bills from men's faces, but we all have a line of what we're willing to go up to. I guess our lines are just different."

"I don't want you to judge me for that though. I don't want you to think I'm a bad person."

"Why not?" she says. "Why do you care what I think?"

"I just care. You're my employee with benefits. I want you to think that I'm a good guy."

She smiles at me. "I don't know you super well. I know you kind of well, because you've been inside of me and I had your penis in my mouth, but..." She pauses and blushes. "I don't know you like your family, or your long-term friends, or even your partners at the law firm, but what I do know is that you're caring."

"Really? You think that?"

"You kind of rescued me on my bad date, I'd say," she says, grinning at me. "And that kind of meant a lot to me. Even though it led to me in your bed. I mean, I think we both wanted it. You didn't rescue me from the date just to get me into your bed, did you?" She raises an eyebrow and I shake my head.

"It wasn't even on my mind," I say honestly, then I pause. "So yes, I thought about sleeping with you, but I wasn't thinking about sleeping with you when I said, 'Let's leave the restaurant.' You know what I mean?"

"I do," she says, grinning.

"And you know what? We're here, let's have fun. Let's not think about Elisabetta and all the bad decisions she's making tonight."

"Exactly. We have some bad decisions that we should make ourselves."

"Oh, yeah? Like what?"

"Like what we're going to do after this dinner."

"You mean you're not just going to whisk me off to a hotel or your apartment?"

"No. What would be the fun in that?"

"I can think of a million things we could do that would make it fun." She grins at me and I chuckle.

"You're a good friend, you know that?"

"Thank you," she says. "And you are too."

"Wait."

"What?"

"Are you saying that I'm not an absolutely horrible person?"

"I'm saying that you're not an absolutely horrible person. And I'm also saying that I redact the comment I made recently."

"What comment is that?"

"Where I said that you weren't my friend."

"I don't remember that."

"Well, I kind of said we weren't friends with benefits because we weren't friends. But even though you're my boss, you've also been a really good friend to me. You listen to me, you take care of me. I just wanted to say I noticed that and I appreciate you."

"Oh no, you're not getting all emotional on me, are you?"

"Don't worry. I'm not going to start looking at engagement rings again," she says with a quiet laugh. "I don't want to scare you off a second time."

"You didn't scare me off."

"Uh-huh. You weren't about to have a heart attack that morning?"

"I don't think I was about to have a heart attack. Maybe a stroke." I laugh. "Especially when you started asking me my monthly salary so you could figure out how much of a ring you could get."

"That was hilarious," she says. "You should have seen your face."

"Yeah. Well, I'm sure you had fun with it." I lean back in the chair so I can stare at her and she smiles back at me. I'm not really sure if I'm supposed to be feeling the happiness that I'm feeling in this moment. I'm not really sure if I should be enjoying the camaraderie that we're experiencing. I don't really know what you're supposed to talk about or feel when you're in an arrangement like this, and I guess I don't really care because this is the most alive I've felt in a long time. This is the most at ease, open, and happy I've felt.

"You know something, Skye?"

"I know many things, but I'd like to know what you're about to tell me."

"You've made me question myself and my life goals more than anyone else in my life ever has. And for that, I thank you."

"Oh, wow." She looks taken aback. "So have you decided on what your life goals are?"

"No," I say with a small smile. "But the simple fact of the matter is, it's something I'm now analyzing and thinking about. It's something I'm giving real thought. Where are we going? What do I want? And for you, I want you to know that I don't know that I would've thought about this for a long time if you hadn't asked. And I don't want to be sixty or seventy years old wishing that I'd done X, Y, or Z but hadn't because I didn't even realize it was something I wanted."

She smiles at me. "Well, then I'm glad I'm making you question yourself and think about what you want from life."

"So, what about for now?" I say. "Shall we dig into this brie? It looks delicious."

"Yeah, let's do it," she says. "Thank you for arranging this. It's nice."

"You're welcome," I say, grinning at her. "I just hope the rest of the night continues just as great as it started."

Chapter Twenty-Five

Skye

"Oh my gosh. I'm so full," I say as I rub my stomach.

Kingston and I leave the French restaurant and I look up at him with a small smile.

"Thank you so much. Delicious dinner and those profiteroles were to die for."

"I'm glad you enjoyed them." He grins. "Thank you for sharing.

"You're welcome." I stare at him and feel a lightness in my step that I haven't felt in a long while. "So what's next?"

"Would you believe me if I said we're off to the airport?"

"Say what?" I say through narrowed eyes.

"No, no," he says, laughing. "Sorry. Bad joke."

"Oh, no worries. I didn't actually think we were off to the airport."

Disappointment floods through me and I look away. I don't want him to think that I'm that gullible.

"Hey," he says. "I do have something really fun planned though. It's a surprise. I hope you'll enjoy it."

"I'm sure I will," I say, nodding. "And also, thanks for being a great listener at dinner. I appreciate it."

"You're welcome," he says. "I just want you to know that lots of us experiment in life with sex, with drugs, with rock and roll." He chuckles. "And it's okay. It's a phase we go through. Some of us do it in our twenties, some of us do it as teens. Shit, some of us wait until we're geriatrics and realize we haven't experienced life. I just want you to know that if there's anything that you want to experiment with, I'm a safe place. You can confide in me anything, ask to do anything, and I will see if I can make it happen."

I look at him in surprise. Is this really Kingston Chase, the most infuriating, annoying man I've ever met in my life, telling me that he'd be my safe place? What is happening in the universe?

"You look shocked," he says.

"I just don't know what to say. That's really touching. Thank you." I nod. "To be honest, I've never wanted to experiment with drugs, and sex is something I am enjoying with someone I know right now," I say, and then I groan. "Okay, that came out really awkwardly."

"It's okay. I think I know what you mean. You up for a walk?"

I nod vigorously. "Yeah. I mean, depending on how long, but I could sure walk off that steak and those profiteroles."

"It should only be about twenty minutes."

"Sounds good," I say.

We walk down the streets of New York and watch the traffic pass us by. A gaggle of girls walks past us, giggling and laughing about some restaurant they just dined and dashed in. Kingston and I share amused glances. Then comes a group of three guys, talking about starting a band and hitting it big.

"My uncle says he knows a manager," a skinny kid with spiky hair says. "And he can get us signed. This time next year we'll be millionaires."

"Sounds rad, dude," another guy with purple hair says. They high-five and Kingston and I share another amused glance.

Then comes an elderly woman muttering to herself. "Three eggs, a loaf of bread, jam. Three eggs, a loaf of bread, jam." She blinks as she looks up at us. "Grocery list." She smiles. "Three eggs, a loaf of bread..." She pauses. "Oh gosh, darn it. I've forgotten it."

"Jam," I say with a smile.

"That's it. Thank you, dearie. Three eggs, loaf of bread, jam," she continues.

I look up at Kingston and find him staring at me with an inscrutable expression on his face. I wish I knew what he was thinking.

"You know something, Skye?"

"No. What are you thinking about?"

"I was thinking that you're such a pleasure and a blessing to people. You're always so helpful."

"Thanks, I think. That's not your way of telling me you want me to do more work tonight, right?"

"No," he says, laughing. "Though, I mean, maybe."

"Oh my gosh. I do not want to go through any more folders or files." I groan.

"I don't mean the legal work."

"Then what sort of work do you mean?"

"How can I be clear? On top work."

"What?" But it dawns on me what he means. "Oh, you want me to be on top?"

"If you'd like to ride." He grins. "A stallion."

I stare at him for a couple of seconds then nod slightly. "I'm a pretty good rider."

"Well, then this horsey can't wait to be ridden."

"Oh my gosh. That sounded gross."

"I know. It didn't sound as cool as I thought it was going to."

We turn onto Third Avenue and he grabs my hand. It feels nice holding hands and walking down the street, but surprisingly, it feels like we're a couple. I don't know if I should mention that to him, but I don't want to. I don't think it's a good idea for friends with benefits to be holding hands, walking down the street on a Saturday night. But at this moment, I don't want to think about the do's and the don'ts and the can's and the cannots of this arrangement. I just want to enjoy it.

"Do you know something I'm scared of?" he asks out of the blue.

"Spiders, I guess."

"No."

"Snakes?"

"No. Actually, I quite like snakes."

"You like snakes? Oh my gosh, you're disgusting. Who likes snakes?"

"I think they're kind of cool creatures. They can be so long and they can eat things so humongous."

"They can eat you," I say and he chuckles.

"But no, not snakes. I'll give you a couple more guesses."

"Um, alligators?"

"I don't like alligators, but I'm not scared of them," he says.

"Losing cases in court." My face lights up as he wrinkles his nose.

"I don't like losing cases in court, but I'm not scared of that, either."

"I give up. What are you scared of?"

"Going through tunnels," he says.

"Going through tunnels?" I look at him in confusion.

"Yeah, driving through long tunnels. It triggers me. It activates a deep-seated fear inside of me."

"What do you think is going to happen in a tunnel?"

"I feel like it might collapse and the earth and the cement and the concrete will cave in on me and cars will crash and pile up and I'll be stuck.

"Oh, wow. Why do you have that fear? Is it something that's happened to someone you know?"

He looks at me for a few seconds and shakes his head. "No, it's because I was a stupid kid."

"You were? Tell me more."

"When I was younger, there was this movie and my parents told me not to watch it, but of course I watched it. And there was a scene where some miners went underground and they were traveling to a different part of the mine in a little train in a tunnel and it caved in. They were stuck there for, I think, a few days and they ended up all dying from lack of oxygen, lack of water, and lack of food. I've never been able to forget that movie or that scene.'

"Oh, that sounds traumatic."

He nods. "I mean, if I'd listened to my parents, I wouldn't have watched the movie, but I did, and now every time I drive through a tunnel, I think to myself, what would I do if it caved in?"

"Oh man." I stare at him. "Do you drive through a lot of tunnels?"

"No, not anymore." He shakes his head. "So what about you? Any fears?"

"I hate spiders. I hate snakes. I hate cockroaches." I shudder. "Oh, boy do I hate cockroaches."

"That sounds like you've had an experience. Want to tell?"

"Well, my grandparents used to live in Florida and I remember one summer we went to visit and I was lying in bed and I was feeling comfortable and smiling and laughing."

"Smiling and laughing?" he says.

"Yeah, I was speaking to my cousin. We were talking about the previous day when we were at Disney."

"Oh, okay. Disney's fun."

"Yeah, it's a lot of fun. Anyway, we were joking around and then I started to fall asleep. Then I felt something tickling me and I was like, 'Lucy, stop.' But no one responded and she continued tickling me. So I was like, 'Lucy, stop.' And then she wakes up and she's all groggy and she's like, 'What?' I'm like, 'Stop tickling me, Lucy.' And she was like, 'What are you talking about? I was sleeping.' So I turn on the light..." I stare at him and I shudder. "And there was a big ass cockroach running across my body." I almost scream again. "Oh, the memory of it, it makes me want to die."

He stares at me, his lips twitching. "That does sound traumatic."

"It's not funny. It was awful."

"I'm sure it was."

"That's why I say I could never live in Florida."

"Oh?"

"Because the cockroaches, they love that heat. They don't love cold places."

"You know we have cockroaches in New York as well."

"I know. Don't remind me." I wrinkle my nose. "But yeah, I hate them. I hate them so much."

"Well, I can certainly understand that." He stops suddenly and squeezes my hand. "Wait here."

I look up and I see we're outside a laundromat. "We're picking up your laundry?" I ask him in confusion.

"No, silly," he says, shaking his head as he pushes the door open.

I see a big bulky guy standing to the side. "Got any laundry tonight?" he asks.

"Three loads," Kingston says, and I stare at him.

"You have three loads of laundry that you're picking up? Oh my gosh. Do I have to carry this laundry back to your apartment? How far away is—"

"No, silly," he says, shaking his head.

The bulky guy looks at Kingston, then looks at me. "Three loads, huh?"

Kingston nods. "Yes, sir."

"Any dry cleaning?"

"Yep. $250 worth."

"Sounds good, sir."

The guy steps to the side, grabs something from behind him, and hands it to Kingston, who hands it to me. It's a ticket that looks like it's to pick up dry cleaning.

"So we're picking up your dry cleaning as well?"

"No, goof. We're at a speakeasy. This is just a front."

"Oh my gosh. This is a speakeasy?" I say excitedly. "Disguised as a laundromat?"

He nods slowly. "Yep, but you have to put that little ticket over here and the door will open."

"Oh, this is so cool." I beam at him. "Because you know I was going to kill you if you brought me to a laundromat to pick up your laundry."

"I wouldn't do that," he says, laughing.

"Yeah, well, you never know with some guys."

"Oh? It sounds like you speak from experience."

"Oh, trust me. I went on a date once with this guy in college and we went to grab a burger, then we went back to his place and I thought it was because he wanted to sing his song to me because he said he knew all of Jack Johnson's songs and I said I love Jack Johnson. But when we got back to his place, he handed me a basket. He was like, 'Here's $5. Will you go to the laundry room and I'll meet you there?'" I stare at Kingston, who's laughing. "It's not funny. It was horrible."

"I mean, did you do the laundry or not?"

I stare at him for a couple of seconds. "I'm not going to answer that question."

"Oh, Skye, you did his laundry?"

"I did one load, but he never came back." I blink and shake my head. "I know. I sound like an absolute loser."

"No, you just sound like a really nice girl that was taken advantage of."

"You could say that again."

I put the ticket into the slot and then a door opens to the right of us. I can hear jazz music playing from the bottom of the stairs and I glance at him with wide eyes.

"Oh my gosh, this is so cool. I've never been to a speakeasy before."

"Well I'm glad that I'm your first," he says as he leads me down the stairs.

We make our way into a small room and there are about twenty other people there sitting at small little circular tables. There's a stage at the front of the room where a saxophone player, trumpet player and someone on the keyboard is playing. A beautiful, tall woman with long curly hair steps onto the stage and starts singing a song about New Orleans.

"This is perhaps the coolest moment of my life," I say, looking at him. "I'm not even mad that we're not in Paris."

"Really?" he says. "You like it that much?"

There is a happy look on his face and I nod. "Yeah, this is the best fun night I've ever had."

"Oh, yeah? Better than date nights even?" he asks, grinning.

"I'm not even going to answer that question," I say as we make our way to a table and sit down.

Within moments, a tall man with a buzz cut stops by. "Welcome to the Laundromat. Would you like two of the specials tonight?"

Kingston looks at me and I nod. "Sure. Thank you."

"Great. They'll be right out."

He disappears and I look at Kingston with wide eyes. "We don't even know what they are."

"I know we don't, but isn't that part of the excitement?"

"Yeah," I say, sitting back. "This is so cool."

I look around me at all the other couples and I feel like I'm part of something. I feel like I'm experiencing a moment on a checklist that I hadn't even been aware that I should have on the list.

"You know what's crazy?" I say, as I look over at Kingston.

"No. What?"

"This is so cool and this is the sort of moment I expected to have on my travels around the world and I didn't even think that I could experience something like this right here in New York. It just reminds me of how little I really know The City, how little I've explored. Shoot, how little I've explored the country."

"So what? You don't want to travel around the world now?"

"Oh, no. I definitely want to travel around the world, but I guess I can do more exploration and travel within the state as well."

"Yeah," he says, with a nod. "And maybe other states."

"Yeah. I mean, I have to see how much money I have, but..."

"Stop thinking about money," he says. "You tell me that I'm obsessed with money, but almost everything you talk about comes down to money and how you don't have enough to do it. Sometimes in life, you have to make the opportunities. You have to make things happen. You can't wait until you have the money."

I stare at him for a couple of seconds. "True, but I don't want to be homeless or living in the streets or have nothing to eat."

"You can always count on me. You can always call me. No matter when, no matter why, no matter how, I'll be there for you, Skye."

I blink rapidly, trying not to cry. "That doesn't seem very professional."

"Are you saying I'm not professional?" He scowls slightly.

"I'm saying you seem really caring toward me right now and is that really an emotion that you should have toward me?" Why do I sound like I'm begging him to tell me he has feelings for me?

He stares at me in confusion. "What do you mean by that?"

"Just that, in the day, during the week, you're my boss and we have a boss-employee relationship and that works. And then on fun nights once a week, we're able to have fun as a preamble to hot sex and we both know that this isn't leading anywhere serious and we both know that we don't want the other one to catch feelings. So maybe we don't want to do things that could come across as caring, because then that indicates more of a deep relationship and we don't want that. Right?"

He licks his lips and nods slowly.

"Don't get me wrong, I'm very grateful for the offer, but I just don't want to complicate everything."

"Noted," he says.

"And this is only our first fun night," I say. "It's fine for us to define what is and isn't acceptable."

"Okay," he says.

"You look pissed off at me."

"I'm not pissed off. I'm just taken aback. I was trying to be..." He pauses. "You know what? Let's don't even have this conversation. Let's enjoy the music, wait for our drinks, and have a good night."

I can tell he is annoyed, but I don't know what else to say. I don't know why he's annoyed. He was the one that had initially told me that I wasn't to expect anything. Now he's trying to tell me that I could expect him to be there for me at any time for any reason? Shit. That's something only your parents or your very best friend in the world says, not your friend with benefits at the beginning of the friends with benefits relationship.

I lick my lips nervously and just stare at the stage. There's an uncomfortable silence between us, but I'm going to ignore it for now. The singer changes the song to one I know and I start clapping my hands.

"Oh my gosh. I love this song. I love Nina Simone."

"It's a good one," he says, and I try not to sigh deeply.

I'm not going to let his pissy mood annoy me. Not after the evening started out so nicely.

The waiter hurries back to the table with our drinks and a little bowl of peanuts. "I'll be back," he says. "Enjoy."

"Excuse me?"

"Yeah?" he says, looking at me.

"What's the name of the drink?"

"It's called the fruity peacock."

"Oh, okay. And are you going to tell us what's in it or..."

"Oh, no. Our mystery drinks, we never say what's in them. We don't want anyone to steal them." He grins. "Enjoy."

He heads away and I look over and at Kingston, who shrugs. We pick up our glasses and cheers before both taking a sip.

"Oh my gosh, this is delicious." I lick my lips. "But I have absolutely no idea what's in it."

"I think it has rum and maybe pineapple juice." He takes another sip. "There's something else in here, but I just can't tell what it is."

"Right? But isn't it delicious?"

"Very," he says, nodding.

I take another sip then close my eyes and listen to the singer. I feel like I've been transported back in time to the 1940s and I'm here with my mobster boyfriend, doing something illicit and illegal. It feels kind of cool. It feels kind of fun and I realize that I've missed this in my life. I've been so focused on trying to save money to go and see the world that I haven't been enjoying the here and now.

My eyes fly open and I look over at Kingston. I'm surprised to see that he's staring at me, a weird expression on his face.

"Hey, everything okay?" I ask him.

"Yeah. I was just listening to the music," he says, as if I hadn't just caught him staring at me.

"You know what I realized?" I say, as I take another sip of my drink.

"No. What?"

"I realized that I don't live life for now. I live life for tomorrow and I don't want to do that anymore."

"I'm glad to hear it."

"You know what I want to do right now?" I ask him.

"If you say you want to make love, I can make it happen. I'll just—"

"Nope. I want to dance."

"You want to dance." He wrinkles his nose slightly and I laugh.

"There's a small little dance floor over there. I'm sure they wouldn't mind."

"I'm sure they wouldn't." He nods. "But I'm not much of a dancer."

"Isn't tonight meant to be our fun night where we just do things that we wouldn't normally do? Wasn't that the whole point of this?"

He nods slowly. "So, you're saying if I dance with you tonight, I can take your anal cherry?"

"No," I say, blushing and laughing. "That's not exactly the same thing."

"I know." He grins. "Come on." He puts his drink down and stands up before heading over to me. "May I have this dance?

He offers me his hand and I beam up at him. I take his hand and stand up and he whisks me over to the little dance floor. I can see that all the band members are excited and happy that we started to dance.

He pulls me into his arms and we slow dance back and forth to the sounds of the jazz singers singing. The saxophone player has a solo and it reverberates through the room in a warm, melodic way. I press my head against his shoulder and close my eyes. I can feel the alcohol hitting my brain.

This is nice. His body feels warm and hard and comfortable. I smell his cologne and try not to shiver at how it makes me feel inside.

I'm falling for Kingston Chase.

It hits me suddenly, with a crashing impact, like a freight truck on a highway crashing into you headfirst, and I'm not sure what to do. It's our first official night out together and I'm falling for him. I'm seeing him in a completely different light and I don't know if that's a sign for me to pull away and run as far as I can, but I don't want to.

I know he and I are not going to end up like Max and Lila. I know that he's not my future husband and I know he's not looking for a relationship. I'm not going to lie to myself and pretend that he is. But I also know that I've never felt like this before in my life. I've never been with someone that made me feel so many different emotions and so many different firsts. And I didn't want it to end. Not yet. I don't want to run away because I'm scared he could break my heart. I don't want to run away from what could possibly be a life-defining relationship.

Maybe I need a broken heart to really feel like I'm living. Maybe this is going to be the start of my journey. Maybe this is where my life actually begins. Maybe it doesn't matter how long it lasts, but maybe it only matters that I have this moment.

Chapter Twenty-Six

Kingston

"So how's everything going with your new assistant?" Remington asks as I walk into his office on Tuesday morning.

"Everything's fine. Why?" I take a seat in the leather chair across from his desk and he just gives me a knowing look. My heart pounds for a second and I wonder if he does know.

"I don't know. She's just looking cuter and cuter each day," he smirks.

"I haven't noticed that she's looking cuter and cuter?" I shrug and pretend like I haven't been paying close attention to her every single time I see her.

"Well, I feel like she's wearing shorter and shorter skirts and more revealing tops and there's a certain look she gives you when she sees you."

"Er? A look of hatred," I say and he chuckles.

"Yeah, something like that. So it's working out then?"

"Yeah. Why wouldn't it be working out?"

"Just checking." He grins and nods toward the desk

outside his office where his secretary, Juniper, sits. "This is the secret to having a long-lasting assistant."

"What is?" I ask him.

"Not being attracted to her. And you can do that in one of two ways. Either you get someone that's older. I mean, unless you have a fetish for older women or you like cougars. There are some very attractive older women, but I'm just saying, as a general rule, that works."

"Okay. And the other?"

"The other one is if you're going to go with a younger one, make sure you don't want to bed her."

I stare at him. "Is this your way of telling me that you have or haven't bedded Juniper?"

"No way. I would never do that. We have too much of a mutual understanding."

"And what understanding is that?"

"Neither one of us is interested in the other," he says with a grin. "She...well, I don't even think she dates," he laughs.

"Okay, so she's not interested in you and you're not interested in her."

"Exactly. Kind of like you and Skye."

"Exactly," I say, nodding. "I have zero interest in her."

"Which is surprising to me," he says. "Because she's very attractive."

"She's okay if you like redheads."

"You know something I've always wondered about redheads?" he asks.

"No. What's that?"

"Come on. You have to know what I'm thinking, Kingston."

"If you say if the carpet matches the drapes, I will stand up and leave your office."

"Then I won't say it," he grins. "But don't you sometimes look at her and wonder?"

I stare at him for a couple of seconds and I just keep my lips pressed together. One, because I already know that her carpet matches her drapes, and two, because if he keeps up this conversation, I'm going to smack him because I do not want him wondering about Skye whatsoever. I haven't seen her in a personal manner since Sunday morning, and while I'm grateful that we've decided to separate the personal and the business, it's still odd having her act so professional in the office, as if nothing else is happening.

"So anyway," he says. "Shall we start going through these continuances? I need to get Juniper to contact Judge Warren to see if there's any update on when we can go to trial for the Altadena Electronics case."

"Okay. Well, let's see," I say, leaning back. He mumbles about something related to one of his cases and I feel my mind wandering off. I wonder what fun night Skye is going to plan. I wonder if she's racking her brains for something really fun and exciting. Hopefully she doesn't spend too much money. I realized then that I need to have a conversation with her. I'd feel awful if she was spending a lot of money on me. Maybe it would be a smart idea for me to give her a credit card. That way she wouldn't have to pay for the dates out of pocket, but she could choose what we did. That's actually a great idea.

"So yeah, what were you thinking about that, Kingston?" Remington says, and I look up at him.

"Yeah, sounds good to me," I nod.

"Well, that was easy," he says with a smirk.

"Yep. You know me. Easy Kingston Chase."

"Actually, things are never this easy with you, but I'm not going to argue. Also, by the way, Max wanted to know if you're interested in going to Atlantic City with me, him, and Gabe in a couple of weekends?"

"Yeah, sounds like fun. When were you thinking?"

"I'm thinking the third Saturday next month."

"Saturday?" I pause as I stare at him.

He nods. "Yeah. Saturday. Why? You got big plans for some distant Saturday next month?"

"No, no plans," I say quickly. "But I will need to check my calendar. I may or may not have something scheduled with an old friend."

"Really?" he says. "And you can't get out of it?"

"It's been scheduled for a while. I'll check and see."

"Okay, well let us know. We can change it to another Saturday."

"Can't we go on a Friday?"

He stares at me for a couple of seconds. "I guess we could, but traffic out of The City will be horrid and we want to stay the night." He stares at me. "We were thinking of getting some sort of suite and..."

"I'd prefer it to be a Friday. Of course, I can check and see if I can do a Saturday if absolutely necessary," I say quickly when I realize he's looking at me suspiciously.

"Okay, well, you check your calendar and let me know." He leans forward. "Is everything okay Kingston?"

"Yeah. Why are you asking me that?"

"You've just been acting funny."

"Erm, funny how?"

"I don't know. You haven't said one thing about any of the five cases I've just been speaking about. You now have random plans with a random friend for a Saturday. Let's be real. I haven't heard you talk about any friends other than your law partners in a really long time. You're not dating someone, are you?"

"What? No, of course not," I say quickly. "Me? Are you kidding?"

His eyes narrow. "Are you dating someone? Holy shit. Who are you dating?"

"I'm not dating anyone. There may be someone that I'm having some fun with, but that's it."

"Holy shit. Who is it? Oh my God. Not Natasha."

"Natasha?" I stare at him.

"Your last female of the month."

"Oh, Natasha. No, no, no, no," I say and shudder. "Definitely not."

"Huh? Who is it? Can we meet her?"

"Why would you need to meet her when she's nothing?"

"Well, she's obviously something if—"

"Hey, Remi, do I ask you about your women of the weekend?"

"No, but there's no point because it's a different one each weekend." He grins. "Actually, that reminds me. Hold on a second." He presses the intercom on his phone. "Hey, Juniper."

"Yes sir?" she responds immediately.

"I need you to contact Bruno at the local flower shop and have him send a dozen roses to Camilla, and another dozen to Lily Anne. Oh, and a dozen to Charity as well."

Juniper clears her throat. "And what color roses would you like me to send, sir?"

"All red. Or wait, do you think I should send yellow or pink or—"

"Red sounds fine, sir."

"Great, and you'll do that now?"

"Certainly, sir. And what would you like the card to say?"

"You can just say, 'Looking forward to seeing you soon. Always yours, Remington'"

"Yes sir. Anything else, sir?"

"That sounds good." He presses the intercom button and grins at me. "Thank you for that. I nearly forgot I needed to send those roses."

"Are you kidding me?" I stare at him. "You're sending a dozen roses to three different women."

"Yeah, I met them all within the last couple of weeks and I don't want them to think I've forgotten them."

"So you're dating all of them?"

"No, but I plan to see one of them this weekend and I'm not sure which one I want to see yet. Camilla was a blonde, but her hair was a little short and I'm in my long hair phase." I roll my eyes and he grins. "What can I say? I just love pulling on long hair, especially when I'm behind."

"Really, dude? I do not care to hear about your prowess in bed or your preferences."

He chuckles. "I know, but sometimes I like to share."

"Anything else?" I say, standing up. "I really have got work to be doing."

"No, I guess we're good for now. So you'll check your calendar and see about next month?"

"I'll do that." I walk over to the door and look back at him. "You really are a dog, aren't you?"

"Hey, it takes one to no one," he grins. "Woof, woof."

I step out of his office and close the door behind me. I look over at Juniper, who's scribbling something on her notepad. "How are you doing this morning, Juniper?" I ask, looking down at her.

She peers up at me through her thick glasses, her hair in a tight bun on the top of her head, her lips a pale pink. She's wearing a baggy, oversized shirt and she gives me a small smile. "I'm fine today. Thank you for asking Mr. Chase. How are you?"

"I'm doing good. I just wanted to say that even though you don't work for me, I'm appreciative of the fact that you put up with Remington. I know it's a lot having to deal with him."

Her smile widens as she pulls off her glasses for a second and rubs the arch at the top of her nose. As I stare down at her face without the glasses, I realized that she's really quite pretty, or at least could be if she did something with herself. "I appreciate that comment Mr. Chase. It's always nice to be in high regards at the law firm you work at." She puts the glasses back on and they swallow her entire face up again.

"Well, you're welcome. Keep up the good work."

"Thank you," she says with a nod. "I better order these bouquets now."

"Yeah." I roll my eyes. "Good luck with that."

I head back to my office and I see that Skye is busy texting someone. I stop next to the desk and clear my throat. She looks up and blushes slightly. "Oh, what are you doing?" I ask her, lowering my voice slightly.

"Nothing. Why do you ask?" she says far too quickly.

I pull out my phone to see if she's been texting me, but I have no missed messages from her. "Were you sending someone a dirty pic or something?"

"No, of course not. I don't send dirty pics."

"I know, unfortunately." I grin. "So then what were you doing?"

"Well, not much. I was just checking something."

"You were typing into your phone rather rapidly," I say. "You can tell me."

"I mean, can I?" She wrinkles her nose.

"Yeah. Why wouldn't you be able to tell me?"

"I was applying for a reality dating TV show," she shrugs and licks her lips.

I frown slightly. "You what?"

"I was applying for a reality dating TV show. *Love is Blind*. Have you heard of it?"

"You mentioned it to me before, but I thought that was because you wanted to watch it, not because you wanted to be on it."

"Well, you know." She clears her throat and looks away. I can feel myself getting angry.

"Okay, well good luck," I say, though I don't really mean it.

"Thanks." She blinks as she looks up at me. "So is there any work that you need me to do? Because I was actually hoping that I—"

"Yes, I have a lot of work that I need you to do. Did you finish transcribing the recordings that I gave you this morning?"

"No, but you said you needed them by Friday and it's only Tuesday and—"

"Well, I need them by the end of the day."

"But there's five hours of transcription for me to do."

"And is that a problem?"

She lets out a huge sigh. "No, I guess not."

"Good. If you can get them done by five PM today, I would be grateful."

"But you said Friday when you handed it to me and now you're—"

"I know you're not talking to me like that."

"What?" Her jaw drops.

"I'm your boss and I demand respect." I know I sound like a jerk, but I just can't stop myself.

J. S. Cooper

She narrows her eyes and takes a deep breath. I can't keep my eyes off of her lips. She looks so sexy when she's mad.

"You're such a freaking jerk," she mutters under her breath.

"Sorry, what did you say?"

"Nothing, Mr. Chase."

"Oh, I didn't think so. Also, by the way, you've got to let me know the plan for Saturday."

"Really?" She looks indignant. "You're going to bring up Saturday now?"

"Why wouldn't I? I need to know what to wear and what time to be ready, right?"

"Really, after you just told me to spend the rest of my afternoon transcribing recordings that you told me weren't due till Friday, you're going to now ask me about Saturday?"

"The two are not related, are they?" I grin. "Oh, and I'll have a credit card for you by the end of the week."

"What are you talking about?"

"For the dates, the fun nights that you plan. I don't want you having to spend your money on the dates that we plan."

"They're not dates," she snaps.

"Well then on the activities that we partake in before we bang."

"Oh, wow. Way to make me feel like a classy woman."

"What would you rather me say, Skye? Would you rather me say dates? Would you rather me say activities? Would you rather—"

"I would rather not talk about it in the office." She gives me a stare. "Thank you very much."

"Okay then. So you want to talk about it later?"

"We can talk about it on Friday afternoon," she says. "When I figure out what we're going to do."

Not The Boss of The Year

"You haven't figured out where you're taking me on our fun night yet?"

"No, I have not," she says. "And if you keep this up, there's not going to be another fun night."

"Oh, so you use me for one fun night and that's it?" I grin at her.

She just shakes her head. "I have work to do Mr. Chase, so if you don't mind." She picks up the headphones on the side of her desk and places them over her ear then gives me the sweetest smile. "If you have any other questions in regards to work, please let me know." She puts the headphones over her ears and presses play on the digital recorder I'd handed her earlier and begins typing into her laptop.

I stare at her for a couple of seconds and just smile before heading back into my office. I sit at the desk and watch her typing outside the tall window. I wonder if she's really mad at me or she is just faking it for work. I have a feeling it's a little bit of both. I'm curious what date she's going to plan. Even though technically they're not dates, that's how I like to think of them.

I probably shouldn't. It most likely puts me in a mental place I shouldn't be in, but I don't care. I'm having fun and I hope she's having fun too.

I scowl as I remember that she said she'd applied to be on *Love is Blind*. I type the name of the show into Google to check out what it's all about. As I read about the premise, I'm not impressed. I do not want her going on that show. I do not want her looking for love with a stranger. I do not want any of it. For a few moments, I think about applying myself.

How funny would that be if we both got on the show and she didn't even know I was in the other pod? I grin to myself. I wonder if we would connect then. I freeze as I realize what thoughts are crossing my mind. It shouldn't matter if we connect in the pods because the pods are about finding a connection and I'm about physical intimacy.

"Remember what you're doing, Kingston," I chastise myself as I click out of the website and open my emails to see if I have anything that I need to send. I take a deep breath, close my eyes, and rub my temples as I realize this is getting far too complicated, far too quickly. You just need to remember what this is about. Sex and fun. Fun and sex. I open my eyes again and my heart races slightly as I see that I have an email from Skye. I grin as I open it eagerly, and I burst out laughing as I read what it says.

Chapter Twenty-Seven

Skye

Dear Sir/Madam,

I would like to nominate my jerkface of a boss, Kingston Chase, for the worst boss of the year award. I don't know if that's a category at your esteemed paper as yet, but if not, it should be.

Yours Sincerely,

Skye Redding

Skye,

You do realize you sent this to me, your boss, right?

Not Amused,

Kingston Chase

Kingston,

Maybe if you cracked a smile some days, you wouldn't be the monster that you are.

Skye

P.S. And of course I realized. I was just giving you a heads up before I actually submit something.

Skye,

Just so you know, you never have to let me know before you want to give me ~~head~~...a heads up.

Kingston

Kingston,

You will never get head from me again.

Skye

Skye,

You wanna bet? Also, what newspaper am I to expect my prize from? Wondering if it's an esteemed paper that I should expect to add to my resume under the accomplishments section.

Kingston

Kingston,

If you want to lose ALL of your money, then sure, let's make a bet.

Skye

Skye,

You really do seem to have your eyes on my money, don't you? Is that your way of saying that you will accept a credit card from me?

Kingston

Kingston,

I don't need or want your credit card.

Skye

Skye,

Only for dates. And sexy outfits. And toys. 😜

Kingston

Kingston,

Get a life.

Skye

Skye,

A life or a hardon? Because I have both.

Kingston

Kingston,

I have work to do and my boss sucks, so I have to stop emailing you.

Skye

Skye,

Want to grab dinner tonight?

Kingston

Kingston,

Nope. We only see each other on fun nights. Those are the rules.

Skye

I exit out of my email account and lean back in my chair. Kingston is driving me crazy. I can't quite figure him out, or exactly what our relationship is, or even what I want or how I feel. When we're together, it's fun and exciting and I feel a thrill of happiness that I haven't felt in years.

Chapter Twenty-Eight

Kingston

"Are you ready?" Skye gives me the sweetest smile as we stand outside my apartment building, and I nod slowly. She's wearing a yellow sundress and her hair is hanging down her back in soft curls.

"I love your hair," I say, wanting to touch her silky coils.

"Well, it's wavy, but I curled it up this morning," she grins. "You like it?" She spins around and I nod slowly.

"I do." I'm surprised at how happy and light she is this morning, especially considering how the work week went and how early in the day it is. I ask her, "I thought you couldn't do early dates?"

"I can't, normally," she says with a grin. "But I wanted today to be special."

"You ducked out. Weren't you volunteering?" I ask her.

"No," she shakes her head. "You're coming with me." She grabs my hand and starts pulling me to the right. "If we're not fast, we're going to miss the beginning, and I know Mr. Johnson and Mr. Brown are not going to be happy about that."

"Who are Mr. Johnson and Mr. Brown?"

"They're my favorites," she smiles.

"Wait, so we're going to the literacy organization now?" I look down at my jeans and my blue shirt. "Am I dressed appropriately or—"

"You look fine. You look casual and you look professional, so I think you're winning."

"Okay, I'm going to take that as a compliment."

"What? Do you want me to say you look devastatingly handsome?"

"I mean, I wouldn't frown if you did." She laughs.

"We'll be there for a couple of hours."

"A couple of hours?" I raise an eyebrow. "Do I have time to get a coffee or—"

"We can get something from a cart on the street if you want, if you really need the caffeine."

I nod. "I think I'm going to need the caffeine. I didn't have any coffee this morning."

"Oh, how come?" she asks.

"Because I thought we were starting at brunch."

"Oh, I guess that makes sense."

"But it's okay," I say quickly. "I'm glad to go to this volunteering event with you. I don't really know much about literacy organizations or anything, but..."

"You're just going to read with them, and write, and listen, and provide feedback," she explains. "Trust me when I say it's not that hard."

"Okay, I believe you. You're so brilliant. You might be the best teacher ever."

"I don't know that I would say that."

I chuckle as we make a right.

"Did you have a good week?" I ask her in an attempt to

make small talk. She looks at me with an upturned nose and narrows her eyes.

"Is that a joke, Mr. Chase?"

"I'm guessing that your boss was kind of hard on you this week."

"My boss was a jerk with capital J, and a capital E, and a capital R, and a capital K." She sings and I laugh.

"Is this what I'm expected to do once I get to volunteering? Sing my sentences?"

"No, but you can if you want to, if you find that works for you."

"We'll see. Seriously though, do you think I'm too hard on you at work or—"

"It's fine," she says. "If you treat me the same way you treat most of your employees." She pauses. "Wait. I mean, your assistants don't seem to last very long, so maybe you shouldn't treat me the way you normally treated the others." I stare at her for a couple of seconds to see if she's serious and then she giggles lightly. "It's fine. You're not that horrible. At least you're not Remington."

"Oh? What's wrong with Remington?"

"Let's just say he does not seem to respect Juniper. Did you hear he had her order a whole bunch of roses for a whole bunch of different women?"

"Wait, that is not acceptable."

"If you ever did that to me, I would tell you where to stuff those roses." She sniffs as if she's smelling something distasteful. I debate sending her roses to see what she'd do with them. I think she'd love them.

"Oh, so are you saying you want me to date several women and send them roses?" I tease her, wanting to see the fire in her eyes.

"All I'm saying is that you're not sending *me* roses."

"I didn't know we were dating..." I say, and she stops dead in her tracks. Her mouth pulls into a thin line and her eyes look down for a second before she glances back at me with a wide smile that appears to be quite fake.

"True, we're not dating, so I guess I am the only one that's not getting roses."

"No one's getting roses," I say softly. "I'm not dating anyone." Though, the more time I spend with her outside of the office, the more time I feel like we are actually going on dates and doing ourselves a disservice by calling it something else. We continue walking in companionable silence for about ten minutes before stopping to grab two coffees and two bagels.

"Oh my gosh, this is so good," she says as she bites down into the buttery crisp bagel. "I love street food."

"So do I," I say. I take a bite of my bagel and we continue on the way until we stop outside of a small building.

"Come on, let's go in," she says, turning to me. I notice immediately that her shoulders seem to be stronger and she strides with more purpose as she walks inside.

"Hey. Morning, Skye," an older woman with gray hair says.

"Morning, Patricia. How are you today?"

"Great. We were wondering if you were going to show up today."

"Yeah, of course. You know I'm here every Saturday."

"I know, but I did tell you last week that you should take a break. You don't have to come every Saturday."

"I love this," Skye says sincerely. "If I can come, I'll make it." She turns to me. "Hey, Patricia. I want you to meet someone. This is—"

"Oh, is this your boyfriend? He's dishy," Patricia says, grinning as she looks me up and down. "Wow. I've wanted to meet the person that's made Skye smile recently." I raise a single eyebrow and look at Skye.

"No, Patricia," she says quickly. "This is Kingston Chase. He's my boss at the law firm."

"Oh," Patricia looks confused for a second. "Just your boss?" she says, noticing our close body contact. I watch as Skye blushes, but shrugs it off.

"I would say we're a little bit more than boss and employee." I step forward and take Patricia's hand.

"I am delighted to make your acquaintance. I hope you don't mind me crashing today."

"Oh, we're always looking for more volunteers," she grins at me. "We would love to have you come every week if you feel like you have the time and the energy. What is it that you do again? Are you at the restaurant?"

"No, I lost that job," Skye says quickly. "He's an attorney. Remember I told you I got a job at a law firm as an assistant?"

"Oh, yes." Patricia looks me up and down again. This time, more carefully. "You are the partner at a law firm. "Well, I do have some paperwork I can give you if you're interested in being one of our corporate sponsors. I mean, no pressure or anything."

"Sure. I'll take it," I say.

"Oh, you don't have to do that," Skye says quickly. "I didn't bring you here to get you to volunteer money. I brought you here for—"

"It's fine," I say, grinning at Skye and then Patricia. "If we can be of any service, I'd love to see how we can help." Patricia grins and grabs some paperwork and hands it to me.

"We have different levels of sponsorship. Feel free to ask any questions if you have any."

"Will do," I say as I take the paperwork.

"This way," Skye says, looking back at me with a wry smile. "Hey, I'm sorry about that. I totally didn't bring you here because—"

"It's fine," I say, staring at her. "If there's a way that I can financially help this organization, I will."

"No, you don't—"

"If it's important to you and you feel they do good work, I'm happy to." I shrug.

"That's so nice of you," she says softly. "I didn't..."

"What? You didn't expect me to be a nice guy?"

"Well, it's not that. I know you're a nice guy. Sometimes I just..."

"You just what?" I say frowning. "Do you think I'm miserly? Do you think I'm cheap?"

"Not at all. I just..." She shrugs. "I don't know. It's just weird having you here."

"Oh, why is that?"

"This is like my safe space, and, well, you are my boss and I don't normally mix the two."

"Are you saying that I make your safe space not so safe anymore?"

"No," she says, shaking her head. "I guess what I'm saying is you feel like part of my safe space as well."

"Even though I'm a jackass of a boss."

"Yeah. Weird, right?" We walk into a large room and I see an elderly man jumping up.

"Skye, there you are. Bobby and I were just wondering if you were going to come."

"Oh, Arthur. Of course I was going to come," she says, rushing over to the elderly man and giving him a big hug. "So good to see you, Arthur, and I brought someone with me."

"Who's this?" Arthur asks, frowning as he looks at me.

He's got dark eyes and dark skin, and I can tell he's sizing me up. "Is this your gentleman friend?"

"No, he's my boss."

"Give her a raise," he says immediately, and Skye starts laughing.

"Don't, Arthur."

"What? I'm sure you deserve a raise, and he looks like he can afford it."

I grin.

"Nice to make your acquaintance. My name is Kingston."

"Good to meet you, Kingston. I'm Arthur and that's Bobby." Bobby is an elderly white man who's still seated. There's a chess set in front of him and he's studying it.

He looks up at me with a scowl, "Trying to decide if I should move this knight or not. Morning, Skye."

"Morning, Bobby," she says. "This is—"

"I know who he is. I heard." He looks over at me and grunts, and I'm not sure if that's a sign of approval or disapproval.

"Shall we start with you guys reading books this morning or...?"

"I have a letter that I wanted to write," Arthur says. "To my granddaughter, and I was hoping that we could go through it to make sure that it makes sense." He stares at Skye. "If you don't mind."

"Of course," she says. "I'd love for us to work on that." She looks over at me. "Do you want to sit with Bobby?"

"Sure," I say, walking over to the man who's sitting at the chess set.

"You play chess?" He looks at me.

"I haven't played in a while," I admit. "I have a feeling you'd beat me."

"Huh," he grunts, but there's a smile on his face. "What are we going to do?"

"Well, this is a literacy organization, right?"

"Yes, and your point is?"

"Well, shall we read, or write, or..." I lean forward and whisper slightly. "I don't really know how this works. This is my first time."

"I know. I've never seen you here before." He leans back. "You are Skye's boss?"

"That, I am."

"I hope you're treating her well."

"Of course, I—"

"She's more than just an employee, huh?"

"I don't really know what you mean."

"I see the way you two are looking at each other, way more than a boss-employee relationship. Don't worry. Back in the day, I had a little thing with a secretary myself." He winks at me.

"Oh, your secretary?" I'm surprised. If he had a job where he had a secretary, why is he at a literacy organization?

"I know what you're thinking. What's this schmuck doing here if he was an executive in a Fortune 500 company, right? Well, I wasn't an executive. I was the mailman. And the secretary wasn't mine, but we had a little thing. It was fun." He grins. "Don't ask how I delivered the mail if I didn't really know who I was delivering it to, but I got lucky. I had another female friend that would put stamps on all of the envelopes so I knew if it was going to zone A, B, C, D, E, F, G, H, all the way through M. Each office had the letter on it so I knew which one was which." He grins. "Did that job for twenty years."

"Sounds amazing," I say.

"Well, it's not like I don't know to read and write completely. I never graduated high school, and I figured I got some grandkids who are struggling and I want to show them that granddaddy can do it too."

"That sounds great," I say.

"Yeah." He rubs his forehead. "I always used to say, who needs book smarts if you got street smarts? Because I got plenty of street smarts. But these kids these days, they don't got so much street smarts. Some of my grandkids, they ain't got no common sense, so they're going to need some book smarts. You know what I'm saying?"

I nod slowly. "I think so."

"So what, you're an attorney?"

"Yes, sir."

"Huh. You went to law school then, huh?"

"Yes, sir."

Well, you never know. You don't always need to go to law school to be an attorney."

"Most of us go to law school."

"Not that guy in that show." I stare at him for a couple of seconds, puzzled. "You know, Suits, that one with that Harvey Specter guy."

"Oh, I've heard of it. I've never really watched it. Too much time actually studying the law to watch shows about it."

He says, "You want me to read to you or something?"

"Sure, if that's what you normally do."

"Skye had me reading this book by Charles Dickens. You know him? He wrote that all-of-a-twist book and that Christmas book. What's it called again? Hey, Skye," he says loudly.

"Yes?" she says, turning around with a ghost of a smile at the corner of her lips.

"What's that Christmas book by Charles Dickens that you wanted us to read last Christmas?"

"*A Christmas Carol*," she says, grinning. "With Ebenezer Scrooge."

"Ah, yeah. That was it. Bah humbug," he says, and Skye giggles.

"You see, you remember that."

"I guess I do. Well, there's another one called *A Tale of Two Cities*. Skye says it's good, so I figured maybe I could start with that."

"Sure," I say. "I didn't realize you liked Charles Dickens so much," I say, looking over at Skye.

"I do, but I guess you also have to remember you don't know everything about me."

"I know I don't," I respond. "But maybe I want to."

"Oh, Lord. Are you two flirting right here in front of me? Can I at least read my pages first?" Bobby says and I start laughing.

"Come on. Where's the book?" I lean back and I wait for him to grab the book and start reading. He's not an awful reader at least. There are some words he trips over and I try to be patient as I sound out the words for him and wait for him to repeat them. He reads two pages and then blinks as he looks up at me.

"I'm slow, aren't I? Are you looking at me thinking how does this old man not know how to—"

"I'm impressed," I say. "Not many people would try to learn to read so late in life."

"Where are you going to say old?" he says, chuckling. "Are you calling me an old man?"

"Not a while, sir. You'll be an old man soon enough, though."

"You got kids?"

"No," I say.

"Well, I'm hoping you're not married, seeing as you and my Skye are doing whatever you're doing." I nod at him for a couple of seconds.

"I'm not married, don't worry."

"Good, good. Are you thinking of getting married?" He lowers his voice then. "Are you in love with Skye?" I stare at him for a couple of seconds and frown slightly. "You don't want to answer the question."

"This is just all very new with Skye and myself," I say quickly. I don't want to tell him that we're in a situationship because I don't even really understand what the situationship is or how it's really going to work out long term, considering that I already want to change the rules of the situationship.

"I know you like her," he says. "You can't deny that. I see the way you smile when she talks. I see the way you look at her." He grins. "That's the way I used to look at my old woman. She's been dead ten years now."

"Oh, I'm sorry."

"It's okay. I miss her every day. Can't lie, don't miss the nagging though. Put the toilet seat down, do the dishes every single day, ten times a day. I used to tell her, 'Get off my case, woman.' She would say, 'I'd get off your case if you would do it,' and then we'd bicker back and forth and she'd tell me to sleep on the couch, but I'd always crawl back into the bed and...well, we'd have that makeup sex and it would be all worth it in the end." He grins. "Miss her, I do. Sometimes I think about getting another, but what am I going to do at my age with another woman? I ain't really got much to offer. I mean, I got my kids and my grandkids, but what woman wants to take them on? If I'm being true to myself, I still love my ex-wife. Could I really tell another woman that

I loved her? I've only told one woman my entire life I loved her. What about you?"

"What about me what?" I ask him, wondering if I should be getting back to the task of reading or continuing to have this personal conversation.

"How many women have you told you love them?"

"I've told my mother that I love her, and she's a woman."

"I would think she's a woman," he says. "She gave birth to you, didn't she?"

"Well, yes. She did."

"How many romantic women have you told that you love them?"

"To be quite honest, I have never told any women that I love them," I say softly, not wanting Skye to hear.

"You've never told a woman you love her?" His eyes are narrowed now. "This, I find hard to believe. How old are you, pushing fifty?" I stare at him and he bursts out laughing. "Just joking. I know you're not fifty. I would not let a fifty-year-old man be with my Skye."

"Okay. Yeah. Well, I'm in my thirties."

"So you like her?" he asks again, and I just stare at him for a couple of seconds. I look over to make sure Skye isn't listening to the conversation and lean forward.

"I do like her. I think she's very special and—"

"Don't tell me it's complicated," he says. "It's never as complicated as people like to say it is. You either like her or you don't. You either want her in your life or you don't. You either want a commitment with her or you don't. Let me just say this because I can tell that you respect her and you care about her feelings, right?"

"I do." I nod.

"Don't play around with her. If she's not the one for you, if she's not someone you can seriously see making your wife, let her go. She's got a tender heart. She's a good woman and she deserves a good man." I stare at him for a couple of seconds.

"I'm not making her do anything she doesn't want to do."

"You're a good-looking guy. You're her boss. I can see that she likes you," he says. "Women, sometimes they have hope that things are going to change. I'm not saying that she has hope that things are going to change, but you know what I mean." I nod silently. "So think about it. You like her and you stay with her and you try and see if you can make this thing work, or you like her and you let her go and let her find the right man for her. That's the least you can do. I'm saying this because she's like a granddaughter to me. I love her. She's been coming here for years. She dedicates every Saturday, and sometimes during the week when she's not working, to come in and read with us. She's a good one. If I was fifty years younger, I'd give it a shot." He bursts out laughing. "Though, I don't know that my wife would've liked that."

"I don't know that she would've liked that either," I say, laughing, and he nods.

"Back to the book."

"Let's do it," I say, nodding slowly.

Chapter Twenty-Nine

Skye

Kingston is very quiet when we leave the literacy center and I'm nervous that he didn't enjoy himself. "Hey, how did it go?" I ask as we step out into the street. He stares at me for a couple of seconds, his eyes hovering over my lips before moving back to my eyes.

"It was a really great experience," he says. "Thank you for inviting me."

"Oh, I'm so glad that you enjoyed it. Did you have fun with Bobby?"

"He's a great reader and he has lived a full life," he says. "I was glad to meet him and talk to him. How was your time with Arthur?"

"Great," I say, nodding slowly. "He is amazing. He grew up in South Carolina back in the days of Jim Crow and he went to an all-black school, but then he had to drop out to help his family. Well, he just tells me so much about what it was like in the South in those days, and I feel like I get a history lesson every time. But it's amazing because it's real life. I'm just glad that there are people here who want to tell their stories, are happy to tell their stories. Honestly, one of the reasons he wants to become fully literate is because he wants to write a book." I grin at him. "How cool is that?"

"That sounds pretty amazing," he says, nodding. "You're a pretty special person, aren't you, Skye?"

I blush slightly at his intense gaze. "You're only just realizing that?" I say teasingly, wanting to make the mood a little lighter. "Now, are you ready for lunch?"

"I am more than ready," he says. "I need to feast."

"On me or on food?" I ask.

He growls as he grabs my hand and pulls me toward him. "What if I say both?" He presses his lips down into mine and I feel his fingers in my hair.

I shiver slightly as I kiss him back and reach up and rub the hair at the nape of his neck. He growls some more against my lips and pulls back slightly to stare into my eyes.

"So, what's for lunch?

"Well, there's this cute little sandwich store that's close to here and I thought we could get some subs and take them to Central Park and have a picnic in the park." He raises a single eyebrow. "What, is that too cliché?"

"No, it sounds great. But I do ask one thing."

"Sure. What is it?"

"Can we get a Frisbee?"

"A Frisbee?"

"Yeah. I've always wanted to play Frisbee in the park. Every time I jog through or go there, I see people playing Frisbee and I've never done it."

"We can get a Frisbee," I nod. "Maybe at a bodega or something."

"Sounds good."

We walk toward the sandwich shop and there's a feeling of contentment in my stomach. This is starting to feel like a real date. This is starting to feel like a real relationship, and that makes me a bit uneasy. I look over at Kingston and he's smiling as he walks. He has a content look on his face that I don't normally see in the office. In the office, he's usually serious and full of pent up energy.

"What are you thinking?" he asks when he catches me looking at him.

"I'm thinking that when you're outside of the office you see him so much lighter. When you're in the office, you seem so full of heaviness."

"I think that's because when I'm in the office I'm focused on work, and the cases and the money and..." He shrugs. "Nothing else in life enters my mindset at that time. But when I'm outside of the office..." He pauses and gives me a small smile. "When I'm outside of the office with *you*, I don't even think about work."

"Does that make you mad at me?" I ask. "Are you resentful of the fact that your mind isn't on work 24/7?"

"The opposite," he says. "I like thinking about kissing you and touching you and learning more about you and just being with you."

"And are you going to say being inside of me?" I giggle.

He shakes his head. "You know what I've noticed about you, Skye?"

"No. What's that?"

"When you're uncomfortable or when you think situations are becoming too serious, you try to make a joke or you're self-deprecating, or maybe you try to start an argument with me."

"I don't do that," I say quickly.

He nods slowly. "You do. I get it, it's some form of self-preservation, but you don't have to self-preserve against me."

"I'm not. I'm just being me and we're just having fun,

right? This is just our fun dates, fun nights, fun...I think we can both admit that this is a little bit more than just a fun date or fun night or whatever."

"Well, it's only the second weekend that we've done it, so I think we're in trouble, don't you?" His voice is soft and his eyes look everywhere but at me.

"Define, I think we're in trouble?" I try not to bite my lip. I will not flirt. I will not ask him if he thinks about me when I'm not with him, like I do with him. I will not pull him into my arms and kiss him.

I will not act desperate, like I need him to fall in love with me and make me his forever. Though, I wouldn't exactly cry if he told me he wanted to spend eternity with me.

I'm such a loser.

"I think if we're both enjoying these days, hanging out together, even more than the sex, then it means we enjoy being with each other."

"Not that there's anything wrong with that," I say quickly.

"No, there's nothing wrong with that."

"But then it might complicate the guidelines we set up for this situationship, right? Where we're not supposed to catch feelings, and we're not supposed to see each other as more than a booty call or friends with benefits. I mean, you're my boss with benefits, and my friend with benefits, because I do consider us friends now, but it's nothing more than that," I say quickly.

"Isn't it?"

I stare at him for a couple of seconds before we reach the sandwich shop. "We're here, look. Let's get some subs."

"I recommend the meatball sub, but we're going to continue this conversation later," he says softly.

"Oh? What, at Tiffany's when you get me a diamond ring?" He smiles and doesn't say anything and I can feel my heart racing as we walk into the sandwich shop. I don't know what's going on or why I'm feeling like this or why he's talking like this, but suddenly I feel nervous. Suddenly I feel like we went from zero to 100 and I don't even remember pressing down on the gas. Suddenly my heart is racing and my skin is burning, and as I stare at his face, I know that I love him.

He's handsome and he's funny and he's caring and he's smart and he's the best sex I've ever had in my life, even though I know it can't be anything, that he doesn't want anything. Hell, *I* don't want anything. He'd just be a complication in my life. Even though I know all of this, I still want him to be my favorite mistake. I still want him to be the one that makes my heart pang because there's just something about Kingston Chase that I know I will never forget.

"What do you want?" he asks as we stand at the counter.

"A meatball sub with extra meatballs and provolone," I grin. "And some salt and vinegar chips."

"We'll get two of those," he says to the lady behind the counter as he pulls out his credit card.

"No, what are you doing?" I say quickly. "I planned the date. I—"

"You're not paying for this," he says. "I am."

"But..."

"But nothing," he says. "When I take a woman on a date, when I'm wooing her, I want to show her through words and actions and, sue me, money that I can take care of her."

"But we already said this isn't a date, we—"

"It's a date, Sky," he says softly. "We can call it something else, but let's be real here: this is a date."

"But what if I start catching feelings for you and thinking that we're going to end up like Max and Lila?"

"We'll take it one day at a time and see where it goes," he says. "I'm not scared of feelings," he says, but I can tell from his tone and the way his body stills slightly that he is scared. He's as scared as me. Maybe he does feel something for me? Maybe he...

His phone rings then and he glances down at the screen.

"It's Remington." He frowns. "I'm not sure why he's calling me because I'm pretty sure he had a hot date this morning."

"But you want to answer?"

"I'll take it when we walk to the park, if you don't mind."

"Oh, no. You can take it now."

"If you let me pay for the food, I'll take it." He squeezes my hand. "I really want to focus on..."

"Focus on what?" I ask softly.

"Nothing," he says quickly.

He takes a deep breath and runs his fingers through his dark hair, and he looks at me as if he's as confused by his own emotions as I am.

"This is a cluster, isn't it?" he says, chuckling slightly and shaking his head.

"Depends on if you think a cluster is something good or bad?"

"I don't even know," he says. "But I feel like I'm in a maze and I don't know the way back out again."

"I know what you mean," I admit. "So what do we do?"

"We do what we set out to do," he says.

"And what's that?" I ask him.

"We try and find the right path."

"But..."

"But nothing. We walked into the maze thinking we were on one path, but maybe we need to go on another one to find our way out."

I blink at him. "You're confusing me."

"Trust me," he laughs. "I'm confusing myself."

He pays for the sandwiches and I grab the bag and we head out. He frowns as he sees that Remington's calling him again.

"Sorry, I'm going to answer this. He doesn't normally call me this many times."

"It's okay," I say, and watch as he barks into the phone.

"Hey, Remington. What's up?"

I stare at his throat and his muscular arms and I swallow hard as we stand to the side.

"You what?" He looks shocked. "Are you sure? No?" He takes a deep sigh. "Wow. How are you feeling?"

I wonder what's going on. I cannot tell from the only side of the conversation I can hear. I hope it's nothing bad. I hope no one's died. I hope it's not about the firm. I swallow hard as I watch Kingston talking into the phone. His eyes turn to mine and they're wide and shocked.

"So are you going to take a test? I know that might be hurtful, but you need to know. Yeah. Yep." He nods as he continues speaking to Remi. Then he's silent for a couple of minutes, just nodding his head. "I understand. Of course. I could make a joke right now, but I don't think it's the time or the place, but just know I'm here for you. Okay? Call me later if you need to. Sure." He hangs up.

I stare at him for a couple of seconds and he just shakes his head as he puts his phone back into his back pocket. "What's going on?" I ask, hoping that he'll tell me. "I mean, you don't have to tell me what's going on if it's like, a matter of privacy or..."

"Remington just found out he's a father." He makes a face and wrinkles his nose.

"What?" My eyes widen. "What are you talking about?"

"I guess he has a seven-year-old little girl." Kingston shrugs. "He's going to get a paternity test to make sure, but he's pretty confident that the girl is his."

"What? But I thought he was never married?"

Kingston chuckles lightly, "He's never been married. It sounds like it's a product of a one-night stand and she never told him."

"Oh, whoa," I say, staring. "That's crazy."

"It is. I feel bad for him in a way."

"Because he has a kid?"

"No, because he has a kid and he didn't know about it for seven years." His expression changes and he grabs my hands. "Hey, if you were to get pregnant, you would tell me, right?"

"I'm not going to get pregnant, I'm on birth control and—"

"Let's just say you did. You'd tell me, right?"

I nod slowly. "I'd tell you. I mean, I wouldn't want you to think I was after your money or something."

"But I would never think that of you, Skye. I promise."

"Okay. So shall we go to the park and..."

He shakes his head, "Do you mind if we go back to my place?

"Oh?" I ask him.

"I kind of just want to be with you right now."

He licks his lips and I frown slightly, "But you are with me?"

He leans forward and kisses the side of my neck. I feel his hand running down the side of my body and I melt against him.

"I want to fuck you," he whispers in my ear. "I know that this is not just about us fucking, but from the first moment I saw you this morning, I wanted you in my bed. I wanted to be inside of you. I wanted you naked. I want to fuck you right here and right now, and I don't want to get arrested for fucking you in the park. Because believe you me, that's what would be happening."

I stare at him for a couple of seconds with a small smile and giggle. "So tell me how you really feel," I say, and he frowns slightly.

"You're not mad at me, are you?"

"No," I say as I slip my fingers down the front of his jeans and squeeze. He groans and I can feel his hardness twitch slightly. I laugh as I move my hand.

"You're going to fucking tease me right here and right now. There's an alleyway right over there," he says. "I can have you there in ten seconds, bend you over, lift up that dress, slip your panties on the side and slide into you so hard and fast that no one would even know we were fucking by the time we were done."

"So what? You're saying you're a two-minute man?"

"If I have to be." He grins and licks his lips. "I mean, if you'd rather we go to the park first and play Frisbee and eat these sandwiches, that's fine, because I want to respect you. But I'm not going to lie. I want that dress off of you and I want you in my bed and I want you riding me so hard and so fast that I don't know which way is up and which way is down."

"Okay," I say softly. "Let's do it. Let's go home and fuck."

Chapter Thirty

Kingston

"Oh my God, you are so fucking beautiful." I pull off Skye's dress and stare at her in her white bra and panties. She looks up at me with a gentle smile on her face, then steps forward and undoes my shirt. Her fingers fumble over the buttons, but I don't help her as she undoes each one and then pulls it off of my arms. She runs her fingers across my biceps and down my stomach and plays with my abs, and I think about all the hours in the gym that got me to this point. "You like them," I say as she nods silently and reaches down to unbuckle my jeans.

She licks her lower lip as she slides my zipper down and pulls my jeans off. I step out of them, and now I'm just standing here in my black briefs staring at her.

"Are you sure you don't want to eat your lunch first?" she asks, staring at me before pressing her lips to my chest.

"There's nothing I want to eat other than your pussy right now," I say, picking her up and carrying her to my bed before dropping her down. Her eyes are wild and laughing and she moans as I reach down and pull her panties off and slide them over her ankles. She looks up at me with beguiling eyes, and I lean down and kiss her on the lips. "Take your bra off for me," I say, staring at her.

She sits up slightly, her red hair over her shoulder as she reaches back to undo her bra. She pulls the straps down and throws it to the ground and I stare at her naked breasts before moaning and leaning in and sucking on a nipple.

My right hand reaches down across her soft skin, down to her thighs, in between her legs. My fingers find her sweet spot and rub gently. She moans as she wiggles on the bed and I love how wet she is already.

"No fair," she mumbles up as she looks at my black briefs. "I want you naked too."

"Your wish is my command," I say and quickly jump off the bed and throw my briefs to the ground. She stares at my cock, large and hard, and licks her lips. I want to feel those lips on me, sucking me dry. But right now, all I need is to be inside of her. I run my fingers across her clit some more, and she moans slightly as her legs shift open a little bit. I kiss down to her belly button and then across her mound and between her legs, sniffing in her fragrance. She moans again as my nose gently grazes her clit, and my tongue enters her hard and fast as if it's my cock working its way inside of her. She groans as I grab her ankles and squeeze. Her body shifts a little bit as I continue fucking her with my tongue before quickly pulling out and sucking on her clit. Her entire body shakes as she cums, and I feel the wetness all over my mouth. I lick her and lap her up eagerly before kissing up her body toward her face. She stares at me and plays with my hair.

"You are a bad boy.

"And I don't want be good," I say as I bring her into me. I grab her by the waist and she stares at me slightly confused.

"I was thinking that we could do something a little different today," I say.

"What?" She narrows her eyes at me. "Are you saying that...?"

"No, not anal. We'll work our way there," I say, grabbing her by the hips. "I was thinking doggy style." She grins at me, gets down on all floors, and sticks her ass up in the air. I groan as I rub my fingers across her ass cheeks and then give her a light, little tap. She looks back at me and winks.

"Ooh. Have I been a bad girl?"

"You've been a really bad girl. I slap her ass again and she groans.

"Oh yeah, baby. Mama likes."

"Oh yeah?" She's turning me on and making me harder, so I grab my cock and rub it against her entrance from behind. She moans as her ass sits up in the air higher, and I can't stop myself from sliding deep and hard inside of her.

"Oh, fuck," she moans as I pull out and reach underneath her and start playing with her clit again. "Oh my gosh. What are you doing to me?" she says, screaming as I thrust inside of her again. My right hand starts playing with her breasts and she moans as I slide in and out, going faster and faster. I can feel her pussy lips tightening on my cock and I just love it. I love being inside of her. It's a feeling I will never get enough of. "Oh my gosh. Please, please don't stop, Kingston," she screams as I move faster and faster, grabbing her hips and slamming her ass back into me. I can feel myself cumming, and I know that it's not going to be much longer.

I pause for a second to slow everything down. But then she slams her ass back against me and I know I can't resist. I slam into her a couple more times and feel myself bursting inside of her. She shivers as she cums on my cock again, and

I pull out and grab her and pull her down onto the bed with me, kissing her hard and fast as both of our bodies tremble against each other.

"Oh my gosh," she says. "I was disappointed that we didn't have the picnic, but not anymore." She grins. "This is better than a picnic anytime of the day." She touches my lips and makes a sappy face.

"What is it?" I ask.

"Does this kind of go against the rules though?"

"Does it matter if we go against the rules?"

"We're supposed to have our fun dates and then have sex, but we didn't have the date yet. We went to the literacy organization, but that wasn't a date. I just wanted to see how you would do in an environment like that."

"Oh?" I stroke the side of her face. "How did I do?"

"You did amazing," she says. "Not that there was that much doubt, but..."

"But what?"

"I just wanted to see if you'd make a face or be angry that I was making you volunteer."

"Why would I do that?"

"I don't know. I wanted to see if you cared more about money than helping people."

"I don't," I say. "I like to help people."

"I've noticed you don't really have any pro bono cases at the office. And I mean, sure, you're an attorney, and sure, you fight for your clients, but a lot of the cases that you take, well..." She makes a face. "It seems like you're all about the money."

"I could see why you would think that. And you know what? It has been a while since I've had a pro bono case, and maybe that needs to change." I touch her lower lip. "What, are you trying to make me a better man or something?"

"Or something," she says, giggling. She leans forward and sucks on my lower lip and runs her fingers down my back.

"So Remington Parker is a dad." Her eyes are wide. "I cannot wait to hear what Juniper is going to say."

"Why would she say anything?" I ask.

"Well, she is his assistant, and she knows he's a man whore." She laughs. "She'll probably be like, 'Oh, I bet there are ten other kids going to come out the woodwork.'"

"Yeah, I guess. Why are we talking about Juniper right now when we should be talking about us and which position we want to do next?"

"I'm thinking about giving her a makeover," she says. "I know she really wants to find a man, and well…"

"I think that's a good idea," I say. "She's not a ugly girl, but she's not really doing much with her looks."

"Hey, that's not nice," she says, slapping me in the arm.

"What? I'm just being honest. Men are visual creatures. And well, she's great at her job, but she's not attracting anyone with those dowdy clothes and those glasses that she wears, Skye. Not even a little bit."

"I know, and I think she knows that as well. I think Lila and I are going to give her a makeover. Maybe Marie as well. By the way, is she actually going to be working for Gabe or…"

"To be honest, I'm not really sure what's going on with that." I shake my head. "I'll most likely find out in the meeting next week."

"Cool," she says. "That will be interesting."

"Oh, why do you say that?" She blushes slightly.

"Well, I shouldn't say anything."

"Shouldn't say anything about what?"

"Marie's always had a crush on Gabe."

"She has?" I frown. "But she's like, nineteen."

"Yeah. Well, it's not like Gabe's fifty."

"But he is in his early thirties."

"Yeah, so? She likes an older man. Sue her."

"She's pregnant and about to have a baby."

"I'm not saying that she's going to get with him or anything. I'm just saying that it will be interesting if she starts working for him when she used to have a crush on him."

"I suppose." I shrug. And then kiss her on the cheek. "But let's not talk about them anymore. Let's talk about us."

"What about us do you want to talk about?"

"Well, can we agree to call our Saturday dates, dates and not just fun nights or whatever?"

"Yes," she says.

"And can we agree that the Saturday dates will last the entire weekend if we want them to?"

"Maybe," she says.

"And can we agree that while we're going to be professional in the office," I pause, and she wrinkles her nose.

"Yeah. What about it?"

"That we can still get up to some fun times in the office?"

"What?" Her jaw drops. "What are you talking about?"

"Okay. I'm not going to lie, Skye. Last week I wanted you over my desk so badly, and when I say so badly, it was all I could think about for two hours when I was supposed to be going through case files. And well, is it really going to hurt if we have a little bit of fun in the office?"

"I mean, I thought you didn't want to complicate things, that you wanted to keep things separate."

"I know. It's just sex though, right? As long as we're professional about work, we can fuck wherever we want."

"I think you just want me for my body," she says, shifting slightly.

"No. Why would you say that?"

"I think this is just all about sex for you." She rolls over and on top of me and glances down. She's sitting just above my crotch, and I stare at her naked breast. I reach up and squeeze them slightly and she moans as she pushes her head back and starts grinding back and forth on me. "I think all you want from me is sex." She pouts as she shifts back so that my cock is now between her legs and she's sliding up and down it. I groan as my fingers touch her waist and move her back and forth.

"I think all you want is to be inside of me." She looks down at me. "Is that true? Or is that not true?" I groan as she positions herself right over the tip of my cock. She shifts slightly so that the tip is now inside of her. I know that if I move her forward slightly, she'll be completely on top of my cock. I want to feel her bouncing up and down on me. I want to feel myself inside of her again. "Or maybe it's about us getting along and chatting and also getting to know each other." She bites down on her lower lip. "Or is it just about the sex?"

I stare at her for a couple of seconds and groan. I lift her up off of me and position her next to me on the bed and she starts laughing.

"What did you do that for?"

"It's not just about the sex," I say, frowning. "It should just be about the sex. Gosh, I love fucking you more than I love doing anything else in the world. But I don't want you to think that."

"You don't want me to think what? That all you want is my body?"

I stare at her for a couple of seconds.

"No, because I'm pretty sure I'm into your mind as well."
"You're pretty sure?"
"I mean, I'm very sure."
"So then, you like my mind and you want my body?"
"Yes, Skye. I think there is nothing about you that I don't like," I admit. And she stares at me for a couple of seconds with a shocked expression.

"So, should I start looking for rings then?" She giggles and holds a hand up. "Sorry. Too soon?"

"I'm going to start to think that you're not joking one of these days," I say. "Is this your way of telling me that you are trying to get a ring out of me?"

"No," she says, quickly blushing. "You've already told me you're not looking for a relationship, so you're certainly not going to be looking to get engaged. We've only been hooking up for a couple of weeks now. I don't expect..."

"You don't expect what?"

"I don't expect anything at all from this. I just..."

"I know you're having fun, just like me." I kissed the tip of her nose. "But you never know. Sometimes..."

"Sometimes, what?" she says.

"Sometimes, things change."

"Yeah? Like what?"

"Like sometimes you catch feelings when you least expect."

Chapter Thirty-One

Skye

"Oh my gosh. I cannot believe that you and Kingston have been dating for two months now," Juniper says, staring at me over her cocktail while she shakes her head. "I am in disbelief. How did I not know this?"

"Well, we're not dating, dating," I say, smiling at her. "We've just been hanging out on the weekends, and man, I can't believe it's been two months already either. It's felt like a whirlwind."

"Were you going to tell me?" she asks quietly as she nibbles on a piece of sashimi.

"I'm not really sure what you want me to say?"

"I mean, if I hadn't walked into the office yesterday and seen you dashing away from him and straightening out your shirt, then you may not have felt like you had to tell me."

"It was just something Kingston and I have been keeping to ourselves. And it's not like it's anything special. I don't think it's special to him. Every other Saturday, I plan a date, and the Saturdays I don't plan, he plans, and yeah, we've been spending almost every weekend together, and it's been great. And yeah, maybe we've also been spending a couple of nights together."

"I thought you guys came into the office together a couple of times."

"We try not to, but it's just something that happens, especially if we have early morning sex." I giggle. "Oh my gosh. Do I sound absolutely horrible?"

"No, not at all," Juniper says wistfully. "Good for you. I'd love to have a love affair with someone."

"Oh, yeah?" I ask her. "Anyone in particular?"

"No," she shakes her head. "I mean, I'd just like to be seen, you know?" She shrugs. "It's weird that I work in a law firm where there are a lot of hot attorneys and none of them notice me, not even my own boss.

"But I mean, that's maybe because he's preoccupied by the fact that he now has a daughter."

"I know," she says. "Can you believe it? I think that he's going to have her with him for the first time in a couple of weeks."

"Oh, really? What's going on there?"

"So..." She lowers her voice and looks around. "Just in case," she says, grinning.

"I get it."

"They did DNA tests, and it turns out he is the dad."

"Wow."

"And I guess she wants child support, and he wants visitation, and I guess they're working on it now, but I think that his first visitation is coming up soon. I don't know what he's going to do, because he's a ladies' man through and through, and I don't know what ladies' man knows how to deal with kids," she shrugs, "but anyway..."

"Yeah. I cannot see Remington Parka as a father. This is going to be crazy."

"Yeah, but my point being, even he doesn't notice me, and I work for him, and he notices every other woman in the world."

"True, but maybe it's good that he didn't notice you. You wouldn't want to complicate your life, right?"

"Yeah, but it would be nice to be noticed by someone."

"I know I've brought this up before, and Lila has as well, but would you be open to a makeover?" I ask her, not wanting to offend her.

"Yeah," she says slowly. "I really would. It's been me and my dad for a really long time, and he doesn't really know anything about clothes or makeup or hair, and I guess I just never really learned, but I don't want to be single for the rest of my life. I don't want to be a spinster, and I certainly don't want to be invisible in every room. So if you could even make it so a guy on the side of the street working on a construction site whistles at me, that would be cool."

"Oh, I can do more than that. I can't do this weekend because I have plans."

"With Kingston?"

"Yeah, with Kingston," I say, smiling, "But what about the following weekend?"

"Okay. Are you sure?"

"Yeah, it'll be fine. I'll just tell Kingston I can't meet up that weekend.

"You'd do that for me?"

"Yes," I reach over and squeeze her hands. "You're one of my best friends now, Juniper, and if you want a man, we're going to make sure you get you a man. I mean, I think you can get a man looking like you do, but if you want to wow everyone in the office, I can get you there. Trust me. You just have to listen to what I say."

"Girl, I'm more than willing to. You're so naturally gorgeous. If I looked even half as good as you," she grins.

"I think you're going to look better," I say.

My phone beeps and I look down at it. It's Kingston.

"What's going on?" she asks.

"He wants to know what I'm up to."

"Ooh, but it's Thursday night."

"I know. He probably wants me to come over. I bet he's horny."

She laughs. "So is sex with him good?"

"Um," I grin. "Let's just say good is an understatement. On a scale of one to ten, he's a thirty."

"A thirty? Whoa. I wouldn't mind a thirty in my life."

"Yeah? We'll get you a fifty."

"I just want to have sex," she says.

"What?" I blink at her. "You're not a virgin."

She looks me up and down and makes a face. "Come on now. Does it look like I've been getting plenty of sex?"

"I mean..." I pause. "I don't know."

"Well, let's just say I haven't. I've wanted to save myself for the right guy, a man that's going to sweep me off of my feet, but obviously that hasn't happened, because I don't even put myself out there anyway, but I'm ready now. If I'm going to write the romantic book of the year, I have to be able to write some good sex scenes, and I'm not going to be able to write some good sex scenes if I've never even had sex."

"We will definitely make sure that you get laid by the hottest dude on the market. He's going to be flipping you back and forth."

"I hope so." She leans back and sips on her cocktail. "So you're going to go over and see Kingston tonight?"

"Yeah, I'm thinking about it, but..." I lick my lips nervously.

"What is it?" she asks.

"So a couple of weeks ago, actually, maybe over a month ago, I applied to be on a TV show and I just got an in-person audition."

"Oh, no way. What show?"

"Love is Blind."

"Oh my gosh. I love that show. I was just watching the UK version. It was so good."

"Yeah, I'm going to be on the US version if I get cast, but I would need to have two months off of work and it's just kind weird and complicated to bring it up now"

"Why? Oh, you mean because of Kingston? Is he your boyfriend then?"

"No. If he was my boyfriend, I would not even consider going on the show. It's just...we aren't boyfriend and girlfriend. We're boss and employee with benefits, but only a little bit more."

"So you are dating?"

"Technically, yes, but officially, no." I sigh. "Kingston is not looking for a relationship and he doesn't want anyone in the office to know. I don't know why at this point, because he's always all over me half the time."

"I know. I mean, I caught you guys. I don't know what I caught you guys doing, but it was obvious you'd been doing something."

I grin at her. "Let's just say that he was having some fun with my fun bags." I wink at her and she giggles.

"Okay. I'm not sure I want to know exactly what he was doing."

I stare at her. "Probably not."

"Oh my gosh. You're not going to leave me hanging. I do want to know, Skye. You have to tell me."

"I'm embarrassed," I say, blushing.

"Come on. Tell me."

"Fine. Let's just say that he was titty-fucking me." I giggle and drink some more of my cocktail. "I don't know why I just said that. I'm embarrassed. Do not judge me."

"I'm not judging you. But that makes sense why you rushed to button back up your shirt, and it was wrinkly and not buttoned correctly, and why your bra was on his desk still."

I blush. "I know. At least you didn't see anything of his, right?

"If you're asking if I saw his manhood, no. Remember, he pushed his chair under the desk?"

"I remember. We were so embarrassed. I promised him that you most likely didn't understand what you'd seen, because you're not a woman of the world like that. But obviously, you kind of knew what was going on."

"I knew that your bra was off and your top had been off at some point. I don't know what else was happening." She laughs. "You're totally having an office romance affair and it's great."

"I'm really enjoying being with him. We go on these dates, and yeah, the sex is great, and I just love the feel of him and the touch of him, but I just like being with him as well." I sigh. "But I don't want to ask him if he's feeling anything more for me or if anything's going anywhere, because well, he hasn't brought it up."

"Oh," she says. "I understand. Are you going to tell him about the show?"

"I don't know." I sigh. "I have to decide by tomorrow

evening though, because they want to know if I'm going to accept the audition or not." I bite down on my lower lip. "Maybe I will tell him tonight."

"Yeah. I mean, if you really think that you want to go on the show."

"I do. Why not? I'm kind of like you."

"What? You're a virgin?"

"No, I'm not a virgin, Juniper." I laugh at the idea. "I just told you my boss was titty-banging me."

"Well, it wasn't inside you, inside you." She giggles. "Maybe he was doing that because you're not letting him inside of you all the way."

"Oh, he's been inside of me." I wink at her. "All the way."

"No way," she says, and then laughs. "I don't know why I said that. I already could tell that you guys were banging, banging."

"Yeah. He got a thirty for a reason."

"I bet he did."

"Honestly," I lower my voice and lean forward, "We've done some other stuff as well, and let's just say that this man knows how to work his fingers, his tongue, his cock, his thumb."

"His thumb," she says and looks at me in confusion.

"Let's just say that if a guy offers to thumb your ass, don't say no."

"What?" Her eyes widen.

"I'm not talking about this anymore. We're at a restaurant and we're drinking and I don't want to gross you out, but let's just say that Kingston Chase has got some moves." My phone pings again. "Hey, do you mind if I take this real quick? I'll be right back."

"Not at all," she says. "In fact, Remi sent me a couple of

text messages that I should probably answer, so I'll just do that while you take your call."

"Sounds good. I'll be right back." I get up and leave the table and head outside and call Kingston. He answers on the second ring.

"Where are you?" he says.

"I am having drinks with Juniper, remember?"

"Oh. Yeah, yeah. I was wondering what was going on."

"Okay. What's up?"

"I wanted to know if you wanted to come over tonight."

"I don't know. I mean, we'll see each other on Saturday."

"Yeah. Well, I was kind of thinking we could see each other tonight as well. You know, get our fun times on a little earlier this week?"

"Kingston."

"Obviously, if you are not interested in that, it's fine. I can call someone else. I just—"

"Excuse me?"

"I'm just saying. I'm just joking," he says, though, for a few moments, I don't actually think he's joking.

"I heard back from *Love is Blind*," I blurt out, and I'm not sure why.

"*Love is Blind*. What's that?"

"The show I told you about, the dating show?"

"What dating show?"

"The dating show I told you I was applying to be on, because—"

"Oh, okay. So what about them?"

"I have an audition for the next step," I mumble.

"Oh," he says.

"And I have to let them know by tomorrow evening."

"Okay, so what are you saying?"

"I'm saying I'm wondering what you think I should say." I feel awkward and weird and uncomfortable as I stand here. If he tells me not to move forward, I'll know that I mean something to him, that this is more than just a friends with benefits, let's-see-how-it-goes situation. I'll know that he's falling for me, like I've been falling for him.

"Is this something that you really want?"

"What do you mean?"

"What do you think I mean? Is this something that you really want?"

"I want a boyfriend. I want a commitment. I want to find the love of my life, yeah," I say, honestly.

"Then I guess you should do it."

"Okay. I guess I will let them know. If I get on the show, will you allow me to take the time off, or will I have to reach out to HR?"

"If you get on the show, we can figure something out," he says. "It depends on how long you'll be away."

"Okay, then. Fine. I will check when I have the audition." My heart feels sad that he doesn't care enough to tell me not to do it.

"Okay, then. So are you going to come over tonight?"

"You still want me to come over tonight?"

"I bought some anal beads and a butt plug for you."

I let out a sigh. "Really?"

"What? You liked the anal play that we did before, and I figured this was—"

"Sometimes you just don't have a clue, do you, Kingston?"

"So you're saying you didn't like the anal play?"

"That's not what I'm saying. I just told you that I'm applying to be on a dating TV show, and that I have an audition coming up and you're telling me that you want to fuck me up the ass."

"You didn't say you disliked it when I fucked you in any of the positions we have fucked in before or when I ate your ass out or—"

"You know what? I think I'm just going to go home tonight."

"We don't have to do fucking anal. I just thought it would be something new for you to try. Shit. When you go on that dating show, you can tell them you could teach them new tricks."

"Really?"

"What? I'm just saying, seeing as this is something you really want to do, and—"

"Who said this is something I really want to do? I was just mentioning—"

"I literally just asked you to come over tonight, and you start telling me about how you have an audition for a reality dating TV show. Did I ask you about that? No. I just wanted to see you. I missed you. I wanted to be with you tonight. I wanted to touch you, and yet you just wanted to tell me about how you want to go out and fuck other men."

"That is literally not how the conversation went, Kingston. I was just..." I pause. "You know what? Forget it. Look, I've got to go back inside. Juniper is waiting for me. I'll speak to you later, okay?"

"So are you coming over tonight or not?"

"I'm not coming over tonight, Kingston. Bye."

I hang up and power my phone off. I'm infuriated, absolutely infuriated. I head back inside the restaurant, take a seat, and wait for Juniper to come back from wherever she has gone. "Hey, sorry about that." She smiles. "Just went to the restroom."

"No worries." I signal to the waiter. "Two more, please," I say loudly, and he nods.

"Hey..." She frowns. "Is everything okay?"

"I'm an idiot. Kingston is an idiot. I'm done. I'm absolutely fucking done. It's over."

"What's over?"

"Whatever the situation with him and me was, it's no longer going to happen."

"So you're not going over tonight or—"

"No, I'm not going over tonight. All he wanted to do was fuck me up the ass. Do I look like the sort of person that wants to be fucked up the ass every fucking night?" I go off and take a deep breath. "Sorry. I didn't mean to just start going crazy on you."

"It's okay, but I thought you said you enjoyed it..." Her voice drifts off.

"It was fine. It felt different, and it's been nice experimenting with him, but I don't expect the man that I've allowed to fuck me in the ass to tell me to go on a dating reality show, and then, after he hears about the dating reality show, tell me about the other shitty ass things he wants to do." I wrinkle my nose. "Quite literally."

She giggles. "Do I want to know why that's literally?"

"No," I say, chuckling, and take a deep breath. "You know what, one piece of advice, Juniper?"

"Yeah?"

"One. Never, ever mess around with your boss."

"Oh. Trust me when I say that's not even going to be a problem." She laughs. "Remington Parka has never looked at me. I don't even know that he knows that I'm a woman. He would never want me."

"I'm just saying that if, at such a time, he does look at you and he does proposition, and you are even tempted for a second, just say no. It is not worth it. I don't even want to go to work tomorrow, but I have to because I need the money."

She stares at me, "But I thought you had—"

"I quit my job on the weekends because I was spending all my time with fricking Kingston, and I can hardly be going on dates with Kingston and working bachelor parties at the same time, can I?"

"No," she says, shaking her head.

"And he keeps me so busy during the week that I haven't had time to get another job in the evenings." I sigh. "He's monopolized all my time, and for what? Just so that he can fuck me when he wants me?"

"But you liked spending time with him, right?"

"I did. I guess I'm just annoyed and frustrated." I can feel tears running down my face. "I'm hurt. I feel stupid, because I shouldn't be hurt. I feel stupid, because he told me in the very beginning that this wasn't going to be anything. I just didn't think he would so casually tell me to accept the offer to go on a dating show. He didn't even hesitate. He didn't even say that he wouldn't be comfortable with it. He basically was like, 'Good luck. I hope you meet the man of your dreams.' Like, stab me in the heart, why don't you?"

"You like him?" she asks.

I stare at her for a couple of seconds.

"You like him, like him. You love him."

I shrug and look away, because the truth of the matter is that I'd realized, for a while, that I'd been in love with him, but I'd ignored it because I knew my feelings meant nothing and could go nowhere. Maybe a part of me had hoped, in the back of my mind, that he was developing feelings for me as well. But no man that was developing feelings for me would tell me to go on a dating show. "I'm just a fucking idiot," I say. "I guess I fucked up again."

"Hey. Don't be so down on yourself, Skye. It's not your fault that you fell for him."

"He warned me, before we even started this arrangement, 'Don't fall for me. Don't get any plans in your head that we're going to end up like Lila and Max, because it's never going to happen,' and I got so upset. I even went off on him, and look where we are. I fell for him. I am an idiot. How can a man tell me, 'Don't fall for me,' and then I fall for him?"

"Because you just don't know what's going to happen in life, girl."

"I guess you're right. You just don't know." I shake my head. "I feel like a bit of a fool."

"You shouldn't. So what are you going to do now?" she asks.

"What am I going to do now? I guess I'm going to go into work tomorrow morning and be the best actress I can fucking be. I'm going to pretend I don't care that he doesn't care. I'm going to pretend I'm excited for this audition, and I'm going to tell him that our fun dates and our fun nights are over. So if you want that makeover this weekend, it's on," I say. "I don't even have to wait until next weekend."

"Wait. Are you sure? I don't—"

"I'm sure. I can't continue like this. I was an idiot, Juniper. I fell in love with my boss. I fell in love with the one man that told me, 'Do not fall in love with me. You will never have a long-term relationship with me.' I don't know how I could have been so stupid, and now I have to be the best actress of my life and pray that I do get onto *Love is Blind*, and pray that I find someone that I can love and to be with, at least fifty percent as much as I love to be with Kingston, because he's special."

"I'm sorry," she says. "Maybe he..."

"Maybe he, nothing," I say. "It doesn't matter to me. I was the dumb one. I know it was me, and I just have to move on with my life. I'm not going to let him know what he's done to me. I'm not going to let him know that I'm in love with him. I'm not going to let him know that I wish that he and I could have a happily ever after."

Chapter Thirty-Two

Kingston

"I cannot believe she fucking canceled our date." I mumbled to myself. "I spent freaking $300 on theater tickets and she canceled our date." I'm pissed off, and angry, and all I can think about is the fact that Skye has ended things with me. I call her number and listen to it go to voicemail.

"Hey, Skye, it's me. 'Me' being your boss, Kingston Chase, also known as your weekend lover. I'm not really sure what's going on, but can you call me back, please?" I hang up the phone and head to the bedroom again. I lie down on the bed and close my eyes. I have no idea what I'm going to do. The last two months have flown by and I feel like I was living a life I'd seen in movies. Skye was everything I could have ever hoped for in a lover and a friend, and every weekend was more magical than the next. The lines had even become blurred at work. We'd fucked in my office, we'd fucked in the HR room, we'd fucked in the elevator, we'd fucked in the restroom, and I hadn't cared if anyone had found out, I hadn't cared if we were about to be caught. It took everything I had to keep my hands off of her. My phone rings and I blink when I don't recognize the number.

"Hello, Kingston Chase?"

"Hi, this is Pool Draft calling from Geronimo Productions."

"Okay. How can I help you?"

"Are you the employer of Skye Redding?"

"Yes, I am. How can I help you?"

"Oh, hi. Yeah, so I'm calling from Geronimo Productions. We've got Skye on a short list of candidates to be in our upcoming production of a reality dating TV show. However, we would need for her to have a minimum of two to three months off of work. We like to call to ensure that this isn't going to be a problem with the employer. These relationships don't always work out, and we don't want people to lose their jobs and have nothing by the time filming has ended."

"What? Didn't she just have the audition today?"

"She did have her second audition today. When she applied, she sent in a little video saying why she wanted to be on the show. Today's was just to ensure that she was going to be a fit. We definitely think we would like to move forward with her. I'm sure you know she's very bubbly, she's very pretty, and any man would be lucky to have her. I do think that the producers are going to offer her a position on this show, which would start filming in a couple of weeks in Croatia, so I just—"

"In Croatia?" I blink. "What?"

"Yeah, Skye actually seemed really excited about that fact. Turns out she's always wanted to travel to Europe."

"Yeah." I say as I remember how much travel matters to Skye. "So you're saying she's on the show?"

"Yeah. We definitely want to offer her a position on the show. I'm just following up to ensure that that's not going to be an issue with you, her employer."

"I mean, if that's what she wants."

"Great. Between you and me, there are a couple of guys that I think she will match with perfectly. We looked at the information they filled out and we think they're very compatible. One man in particular is also into travel, and I think if they hit it off, we..." He pauses. "Well, I shouldn't say too much. I just get excited when I feel like we have some really strong candidates for the show."

"Yeah, I'm sure you do. Well, was there anything else you wanted to ask?"

"No, but it was great speaking to you. I'm so glad that Skye has an employer that's understanding about her desire to find love."

"Yeah. She's very lucky." I hang up and I can feel the anger seeping through my bones. Is this fucking for real? "So she can find love?" I mutter under my breath. "When she has a man who loves her right here." As soon as the words are out of my mouth, I freeze. "Fuck." I press my hands to my temples and massage my forehead. "I'm in love with her. I'm in love with Skye Redding. I should have known it. I should have known it from the first moment I let her sleep over. I should have known it from all the times she made jokes about me buying her a wedding ring and me not completely freaking out. I should have known it from the time she dragged me to a rom-com movie and I didn't immediately leave. And then the time she begged me to take her to a concert from some female singer that wailed on and on about love. Should have known from the time we went to the nightclub and spent hours dancing the night away before slipping back to my place and making love all night.

Fuck." I mutter under my breath. "I love her. I want her and there's absolutely nothing I can do to stop what has already been set in motion."

I told her before we even started this charade that I wasn't looking for love, that she and I were not going to be like Max and Lila. I told her that this was just fun, and she'd gone and she'd applied to a dating TV show, and now she was going to be on it and they had a perfect man for her. I've lost her. I take a deep breath and call her again. I'm about to throw my phone against the wall because I think it's going to hit voicemail again, but she answers.

"What is it?" she snaps.

"No need to talk to me like that," I say, my heart pounding.

"You have been calling me all night. I'm not going into the office to do any work. I'm not."

"I was hoping that we could hang out."

"I don't want to hang out. Like I told you earlier today, what we had is done. I'm not going into a situation where I'm looking for my husband while fucking my boss. That's not a conversation I want to have on the show. 'Oh, who was the last guy you were seeing?' 'Oh, I was seeing my boss. We were hooking up every weekend.' 'When did you stop hooking up?' 'Oh, the week before I got here.' I'm not going to do that."

"Okay. Maybe I just want to hang out. Maybe it's not about sex."

"It's always about sex with you. It's only ever been about sex."

"That's not fair, Skye. We've done a lot more together than just have sex."

"Yeah, sure, but ultimately it's been a precursor to sex, right?"

"Are you telling me you didn't enjoy the sex?"

"I love the fucking sex, but I need more now, okay? And I no longer want to have sex with you. I am kind of done with your penis I need a new penis."

"Really?" I'm pissed now. "You're fucking done with my penis?"

"Yeah. I thought you'd be happy to hear that."

"Why the fuck would I be happy to hear that?"

"Because you want me to find another penis to enjoy, right?"

"Excuse me?"

"You're the one that was like, 'Go ahead and apply to the show,' and—"

"I did that because you're the one that told me that it was important for you to—"

"Important for me to what?" she cuts me off.

"Can I see you please? This is a conversation we should have in person."

"I just don't even want to talk about this right now. I am processing a lot and—"

"Can I see you tomorrow? I got us tickets to—"

"I have plans tomorrow." She cuts me off again and I can feel my blood boiling.

"How can you have plans tomorrow? It's Saturday. Our day." Did my voice break? Shit. Why do I feel so disappointed? I do not want to admit that I've been looking forward to Saturday all week.

"Yeah, well, I have plans with someone else tomorrow and I can't break them."

"But we literally had plans for tomorrow up until today." Out comes the attorney in me. I need to make sure I don't grill her.

"Actually, I canceled all plans yesterday. I only told you today."

I press my lips together to stop from cursing in aggravation. How and why did this get so complicated?

"So who are your plans with?" I ask casually, like I'm not ready to go off. I feel like a petulant child thats just been told Christmas has been canceled. I'm far more devastated than I should be. Maybe I'm slightly heartbroken. Or just disappointed. My heart is definitely not involved.

I do not love spending my Saturdays with Skye more than I've loved any other free time.

I do not love making her laugh.

Or making her glare at me.

Or watching the way she plays with her eye.

Or reapplies her lipgloss hourly.

Or the way she checks me out when she thinks I'm not looking.

Or the way she kisses me when we're together.

I do not love any of it.

"It's none of your business, Kingston."

"What's going on here? Is it another guy? You're going on a date already?" I sound accusatory. My attitude would not fly in a court of law. I feel hot, like a dagger has been pushed into my chest. My collar feels tight and I clench and unclench my fists.

"It's with Juniper, okay? I'm taking Juniper to get some new clothes and a makeover and—"

"I see." I lick my lips, feeling lighter again. I shouldn't be so happy to hear she's not going on another date with a man. "Can I see you afterwards?" Do I sound pathetic? I feel like a school boy asking a girl to Homecoming.

I am so sprung.

Fuck!

She lets out a deep sigh.

"You'll see me on Monday morning in the office."

"Please. It's important."

"What's so important that it can't wait till Monday?"

"Really? You want me to do this on the phone?"

"Yeah, do it on the phone."

"I don't want you to."

"You don't want me to what?"

I stare at my reflection in the mirror, and for a few seconds, I don't recognize myself. For a few seconds, I don't even know what I want. I don't know if I'm reacting to the news of her being on the dating show, if I'm reacting to the realization that I'm in love with her, or if I'm reacting to the fact that I'm confused as fuck.

"Nothing. I'll see you on Monday."

"Okay, bye." She hangs up and I throw the phone to the floor then march to the kitchen and grab a beer.

I chug it within a minute and grab another one before I head to the couch and turn on the TV. I find my fingers clicking on the Netflix sign and then searching for *Love is Blind*.

"Let me at least see what show you're going to be on," I mumble to myself as I sit back to watch the first episode.

I need to get my shit together before I lose it.

I don't want Skye to be on this show. I don't want Skye to date someone else. I don't want Skye to be with someone else. I don't want Skye to find love with anyone else because I want Skye to love me, because I love her, and I need her, and I want her, and I can't wait until Monday morning to tell her.

I jump up and hurry back to my bedroom and pick up my phone to scroll through the numbers on the HR website. I have a call to make and a favor to ask and I can only hope that it will be granted. I can only hope that I have a chance to make things right. I can only hope that Skye loves me as well and that this isn't all in vain because I fucked up. I fucked up real bad and now I need to get my act together because I need her to know that I love her, and I want her, and I will wait the rest of my life for her.

Chapter Thirty-Three

Skye

I stand outside the Macy's and wait for Juniper to show up. I look at my watch and frown. She's already five minutes late. My phone vibrates and I look down and see that Juniper is calling me.

"Hey, is everything okay?" I ask her as I answer.

"Yes. Don't be mad at me."

"What are you talking about? You're not going to be super, duper late, are you? I can go and grab a bite or something if—"

"No, I'm not going to make it."

"What do you mean you're not going to make it? Juniper, you've been wanting this, right?"

"I do want it, but I just don't think it's the right time. I—"

"Juniper. It's going to be okay. I promise. I know it seems like it's going to be a big change, but—"

"No, it's not that. It's not going to be the right time for me today because..." She sighs. "I'm sorry. I know I should have probably asked first, but he begged me not to."

"What are you talking about? Who begged you not to?"

"It was..." She sighs again. "Oh my gosh. I hope I didn't mess up. I'm really sorry, but..."

"What's going on? You're confusing me."

"Kingston called me last night and..."

"What?"

"He asked me if I could tell him where I was meeting you today because he really wanted to see you and he really wanted to tell you something. And he begged me to let him see you today instead of me and said he'll set it up with you so we can rearrange the makeover for next week. I'm so sorry. I—"

"I cannot believe he did that. What the..."

I pause as I realize that I feel a presence next to me. I look up and see Kingston's blue eyes staring down at me. He has a solemn look on his face.

"Hey, Juniper, I'm not mad at you. Kingston just arrived. I'll talk to you later, okay?"

"Okay. Good luck."

"Thanks, girl," I say, and hang up.

"How dare you?" I immediately say, pushing my finger into Kingston's chest. "How dare you cancel my plans because..."

"Because what?" he says, giving me a kiss on the cheek.

"What are you doing?"

"Saying hello. You look pretty," he says, looking me up and down. "Really beautiful."

"Um, okay. That doesn't excuse the fact that you went and changed my plans when I didn't say it was okay. You asked me yesterday if I would see you and change my plans and I said no, and you went behind my back and—"

"Because I've been a fool, Skye."

"Sorry. What?"

"I've been a fool," he says slowly.

"Okay, and this is new to you?"

He chuckles slightly. "Are you saying you consider me a fool?"

"I'm saying that you might not be as smart as you think."

"Really?"

"Yes, really." I glare at him.

"You may be right. I want to take you somewhere."

"Where are you taking me?"

"Somewhere special."

"Um, I don't really know what that means and I don't really think that I want to go anywhere with you right now. If I'm not going to be giving Juniper a makeover, I think I'm just going to go home and watch TV and—"

"And nothing," he says. "Please, just give me five minutes."

"I don't want to give you anything," I say, my heart pounding.

It's hard for me to look at him without feeling love and excitement and joy. I just want to kiss him, to touch him, but I know I need to stop. I know I cannot allow these feelings to grow anymore.

"Please, Skye, just five minutes."

"Why should I give you five minutes?"

"Because I love you," he says. "And I am hoping you love me too. I'm hoping you're going to forgive me for being an idiot. I'm hoping that you're going to forgive me for saying I think it's okay for you to go on that dating show because hell no I'm not okay with it."

"What?" My heart stops.

"I love you, Skye," he says loudly, and a woman to the right looks at us.

"He said he loves you. You need a hearing aid or something?"

"No. Thank you." I look over at him. "Are you for real? Is this because you're jealous now that I'm going to meet someone new or..."

"Skye, we spent the last two months dating and sleeping together and being together and working together and I've loved every moment of it. I love spending time with you. I love being with you. I love touching you. I love you sleeping over. I love your little snores."

"I don't snore. I mean, loudly."

He grins. "And I love your little jokes about the engagement ring. So much so that I want to get you a ring."

My jaw drops.

"What?"

"Not an engagement ring," he says quickly. "A promise ring. A promise that I am ready to be committed. A promise that I want you to be my girlfriend. A promise that I want this to be official. I want everyone in the office to know. I want everyone in the world to know that I love you. I want to make this something real. I want to make this something special. I want you to know that I was a fool when I said to you we were never going to end up like Max and Lila. I was a fool when I told you not to get your hopes up. And you know what?"

"What?" I say.

"I think I was saying it because I wanted a reaction. I think I was saying it because I wanted to see what you would do or think or feel. I wanted to know if you felt that spark that I felt from the very beginning."

"You felt a spark from the very beginning?"

"From the first time I laid eyes on you." He grins. "Why do you think I hired you?"

"Because of my brilliant resumé."

He bursts out laughing then. "Your resumé was not all that."

"But you said that Max made a huge mistake by hiring Lila and you wouldn't do such a thing."

"I say a lot of things." He grins. "Doesn't mean they're always true."

"So you love me?"

"I do," he says. "And what about you?"

"What about me?" I ask him, teasingly.

"How do you feel about me?"

"I love you, you goof. Of course I love you." I wrap my arms around his neck. "I have loved you for ages now and I just love being with you and touching you and kissing you and I felt like a fool for falling for the man that told me to never fall for him."

"I guess we were both fools, but I'm glad you're a fool too." He grins. "Makes me feel better about myself."

"It should make you feel better about yourself. So, were you serious about the ring or was that a joke?"

He bursts out laughing. "I'm serious, and guess what?"

"What?"

"I make $50,000 a month."

"Whoa. You make a lot of money."

"So I figure if the engagement ring I get you is $150,000..."

"Yeah?"

"Then the promise ring I get you could be up to $75,000."

"You are not going to buy me a ring for $75,000. Hell no. You're out of your mind."

"I might be a little bit out of my mind, but I remember the very first thing you said to me was you needed to know my salary so you knew how much you could spend on a ring. You don't have to spend seventy-five grand on a ring, but if you want to..." He grins. "I'd be more than happy to spend that. In fact, I have some appointments at some jewelry stores."

"No way."

"Yep. I was hoping that you would say yes to coming to look at some with me."

"I mean, I won't say no." I grin. "But you're not spending that much money."

"And I have one other surprise."

"What is it?"

"We're going on a trip tomorrow."

"Excuse me?"

"I wanted to make it a super surprise, but I know you. You're going to want to pack. So we're going to do some shopping today."

"We're going to do shopping because we're going where?"

"See if you can guess."

"New Jersey?"

"Really? You think I'm so romantic that I'm going to take you to New Jersey?"

I giggle girlishly. "Okay. Texas?"

"Do you want to go to Texas?"

"No," I say, laughing. "Where are you taking me?"

"We're going to go to Paris," he says. "And we're going to get chocolate croissants."

"Oh my gosh. You're joking."

"Nope. I've hired a private plane."

"I'm going on a private plane? That must have cost loads of money."

"You know what, Skye? I've spent my entire working career trying to make as much money as possible. Taking cases, doing things that I don't necessarily personally agree with for the money, and I don't even spend it. I want to spend it now. I want to spoil you. I want it to have been worth it."

"Um, I don't know what to say to that, but I'm going to say no to a trip to Paris. What is it? An overnight trip?"

"No," he says, shaking his head. "We're going to spend three days in Paris and then go to London, then Amsterdam, then come back. It will be about ten days total. It would've been longer, but I have a case coming up that I have to prepare for."

"But ten days? I—"

"You don't want to go," he says. "I mean, that's fine. I shouldn't have overstepped. I shouldn't have—"

"No, I want to go, but Juniper's makeover. If I don't do it today, I was going to do it next weekend."

"Then can you do it the weekend after that?" he asks hopefully. "I mean, if you'd rather just get back, we can cut out Amsterdam and go another time."

"But I *really* want to go to Amsterdam. I want to see Anne Frank's house."

"Okay. I'll speak to Juniper and see if she's okay with waiting the two weeks."

"I cannot believe this. Who knew you were so romantic and so sweet?"

"Not me," he says as he picks me up and spins me around. "But I guess you just bring it out in me, Skye Redding."

"I'm glad I do, Kingston Chase."

I press my lips to his and his tongue slips into my mouth as he holds me close to him.

"I love you so much, Skye. I can't believe I almost lost you."

"I know, because you were being so goofy."

"Um, so you're going to email or call the producers of that show and tell them that you're not taking the position?"

"Sorry, what?" I blink. "What are you talking about?"

"Um, one of the producers of the show said that you are going to be selected and asked if you would get the time off."

"Huh?" I stare at him. "Are you sure?"

"Yeah. They wanted to confirm that I was okay with you taking a couple of months off so you could go to Croatia."

"What? What are you talking about Croatia? They were going to be filming in North Carolina from what I know."

"North Carolina?" He furrows his brow. "But I got a call yesterday and..." He frowns. "Huh. Hold on a second."

He grabs his phone and it rings. "Hello? This is Gabe."

"Gabe?"

"Uh, yeah."

"This is Kingston."

"Hey, what's up?"

"Why did you call me from this number yesterday saying that you were a producer on a dating show?"

He groans. "Oh. It wasn't me. It was Marie and Lila." He chuckles. "I can't believe you fell for that shit. I didn't think I had that good of a voice."

"What do you mean that good of a voice?"

"I thought for sure you would've been able to tell it was me. I thought that's why you hung up."

"No, I had no clue it was you. What is going on?"

"Uh, I guess you got to speak to your girl about that. Lila and Marie just said they wanted me to make this call and pretend I was the producer. I didn't really ask questions."

"Fine." Kingston starts laughing and hangs up. "Do you know anything about this?" he asks.

"I mean, I did tell Lila that I was really upset that you

told me to go on to the show and that you seemed to have no issue with it and that you were going to give me the time off. And she was like, 'He sounds like an idiot. He has no idea what he's saying.' And that was it. She didn't tell me that she was going to have someone call and pretend to be a producer. I am so mad. I can't believe she did that."

"I'm not." He grins. "I think I know why she did it."

"Oh?" I ask.

"They did it because I was being a fool. They did it because it didn't even cross my mind what it actually meant for you to be on a show like that. They did it because it spurred me into action, knowing that I didn't want to lose you. I've known that I love you for a while and I was okay with the status quo. I was okay with what we had because I didn't feel threatened. But what we had wasn't enough. What we had was surface level and I want to step it up a notch. I want you to know that I claim you, that I want you, that I need you. You are my everything."

"I love you," I say softly as I kiss him on the lips.

"Not as much as I love you. Though I do have a question." He grins.

"What?"

"Are you going to submit an application to the newspaper that I am the best boss of the year now, or...?"

I burst out laughing and shake my head. "You may be the best boyfriend, but you're definitely still not the best boss." I giggle. "Yeah, that's not going to happen."

"I think you have that wrong that I'm not the best boss, don't you?"

"I promise, you'd definitely win the not the boss of the year award."

"Okay," he says. "But what about the boss of your heart?"

"Oh, you'll definitely win the boss of my heart award

because I love you more than anything and I'm so glad that we're on this journey together, figuring out our lives and love and just where we want to go from here. You know I wouldn't want to do life with anyone else other than you, right? And you know I want you to move in with me."

"But Elisabetta," I say, frowning.

"You barely see her. Isn't she having a full-blown love affair with that old guy?"

"Yeah." I nod. "But I don't know that it's going well. I mean, she does seem happy enough."

"See?" he says. "She's not going to miss you and I miss you every night that you're not by my side."

"You really want me to move in with you?"

"More than anything. I want you to live with me forever because I will love you forever, and when it's time, we'll become engaged and then married and have kids and—"

"Whoa, what? Have kids? You want to have kids?"

"With you Skye, I want to do everything. I want to travel the world and explore and I want to be the subject of your book. Shit, you can even call it *My Lover Kingston Chase* if you want."

"I am not going to call my book *My Lover Kingston Chase*."

"Fine. You can just call it *Kingston*."

I giggle. "You're a goof, you know that?"

"I know, but only when I'm with you. I love you."

"I love you more. I love you to the moon and back. I love you to the bedroom and back," I say, grinning.

"Then let's go, honey."

"After we go shopping," I say.

"Fine." He groans. "But let's do it quickly because there's nothing I want more than to have you by my side forever."

"Um, what's that got to do with your bedroom?"

"Nothing, but I just thought it sounded sweet."

"You are sweet," I say, kissing him.

He grabs my hand and squeezes it. "I cannot wait to spend the rest of my life with you."

"It's a good thing you don't have to wait then, because we will be exploring and traveling forever," I say. "And nothing means more to me than going on this journey with you."

Thank you for reading Not The Boss of The Year. I hope you enjoyed the book.

You can read a BONUS CHAPTER here!

The next book in the series is Juniper and Remington's, I Won't Be in on Monday. You can get it here.

Printed in Great Britain
by Amazon